Dreamsicles®

FOURTH EDITION

Secondary Market Price Guide
& Collector Handbook

EDITORIAL

Managing Editor: Jeff Mahony
Associate Editors: Melissa A. Bennett, Jan Cronan, Gia C. Manalio, Mike Micciulla, Paula Stuckart
Assistant Editors: Heather N. Carreiro, Jennifer Renk, Joan C. Wheal
Editorial Assistants: Timothy R. Affleck, Beth Hackett, Christina M. Sette, Steven Shinkaruk

WEB (CollectorsQuest.com)

Web Reporter: Samantha Bouffard
Web Graphic Designer: Ryan Falis

PRODUCTION

Production Manager: Scott Sierakowski

ART

Creative Director: Joe T. Nguyen
Assistant Art Director: Lance Doyle
Senior Graphic Designers: Marla B. Gladstone, Susannah C. Judd, David S. Maloney, Carole Mattia-Slater, David Ten Eyck
Graphic Designers: Jennifer J. Bennett, Sean-Ryan Dudley, Kimberly Eastman, Melani Gonzalez, Caryn Johnson, Jaime Josephiac, Jim MacLeod, Jeremy Maendel, Chery-Ann Poudrier

R&D

Product Development Manager: Paul Rasid
R&D Specialist: Priscilla Berthiaume

ISBN 1-585-981-40-0

306 Industrial Park Road
Middletown, CT 06457

CollectorsQuest.com

Table Of Contents

Foreword By Kristin Haynes

Hi Friends,

I'm excited to announce the 10th Anniversary of the Dreamsicles® collection. Wow, I can hardly believe it's been ten years! It seems like just yesterday that Cast Art launched the line. We were so overwhelmed by the large initial orders that came in from the stores and we've been so busy ever since that the time has just flown by. The Collector's Value Guide™ is a wonderful way to look back on the past and take a trip down memory lane.

The Dreamsicles Club and *The ClubHouse* magazine have been great ways to keep in touch will all you collectors through the years, as well as keep you informed of our upcoming pieces and events. Thanks for your thoughts and all of the pictures you have sent to the club. Keep them coming, you have great ideas and stories to share!

As always, I am grateful for your support and loyalty to my work. I have lots of fun new ideas to create for the next ten years and promise to keep the happy little faces coming.

Angel Hugs,

Introducing The Collector's Value Guide™

Welcome to the 2001 edition of the Collector's Value Guide™ to Dreamsicles! Kristin Haynes' cherubs have been charming collectors for an entire decade. Whether you've been a fan since the beginning, or have just discovered the wonder and awe of these angelic figurines, this guide is your complete source for all of your Dreamsicles information.

With the Collector's Value Guide™ guiding your way, prepare to learn about everything Dreamsicles has to offer in 2001. From new releases to recent retirements, the Collector's Value Guide™ makes keeping track of your collection simple and enjoyable. Here you will find detailed information and color photos for every Dreamsicles piece, as well as updated secondary market values to help determine the value of your collection. Hours of fun are in store for you as you learn more about your Dreamsicles!

Look Inside To Find:

- A fascinating interview with Dreamsicles creator Kristin Haynes
- A list of recently retired and suspended Dreamsicles pieces
- Great craft and display ideas
- The Top 5 most valuable Dreamsicles figurines
- A spotlight on Kristin's other collectible line, "Love, Kristin."
- And much, much more!

The Dreamsicles® Story

A Decade Of Dreamsicles

It hardly seems like it's been 10 years since Kristin Haynes' adorable cherubs were first produced by Cast Art Industries. Incredible, but it's true! What originally started out as a modest line of 29 figurines has now multiplied to over 1,000 pieces in all! From wreath-wearing cherubs to warm-hearted animals, the Dreamsicles line continues to produce comforting, cherished figurines each year that are loved by collectors the world over.

Cherub Appeal

The secret behind the enduring popularity of Dreamsicles might reside in their angelic appearance. Hasn't everybody wished that they could have a tiny angel on their shoulder in times both good and bad? Kristin Haynes' creations bring these angelic hopes and dreams to life. Often wearing handcrafted wreaths made from dried flowers and ribbon, each Dreamsicles cherub seems to have a distinct appearance and personality of its own.

While the Dreamsicles line might have started out as a collection of giftware items, its fans just couldn't seem to get enough of them and soon, Dreamsicles made the transition to a full-fledged collectible phenomenon. Dreamsicles grew in popularity thanks to repeat purchases from gift buyers who discovered that they couldn't own just one. People began buying Dreamsicles for themselves, as well as for others.

Touched By An Angel, And A Bunny, And A Cow, And A Pig . . .

Who were the "Original 29" Dreamsicles cherubs that Cast Art introduced in 1991? Actually, they weren't all cherubs. Only six of the figurines were cherubs. There were also four musicians, seven bunnies and 12 other animals. These pieces are identifiable by a four-digit product code starting with the number "5." And while all of the "Original 29" were popular, it was indeed the cherubs that took the collectible world by storm.

One decision that helped elevate the Dreamsicles line to the status of "collectibles" was the introduction of limited edition pieces, starting with three which were introduced in 1992. With pieces limited in availability, collectors began scouring the secondary market to find the pieces they might have missed.

A collectible line just isn't complete without a club to bring collectors together. In 1993, Cast Art introduced the Dreamsicles Club for the thousands of fans who had been clamoring for the creation of such an organization. Today there are close to 100,000 members in the Club – an impressive number for a group that is less than a decade old. Club members are eligible to receive the yearly Symbol of Membership piece, in addition to other Members Only figurines that are not available to the general public.

Alphabet Soup

Dreamsicles began receiving proper names rather than descriptions in 1993. That same year, the numerical classification system was streamlined to assist both collectors and retailers. This system consisted of a two-letter prefix that started with the letter "D," as well as a three-digit product number. This information could be found on the underside of the pieces or on the attached plaques on limited edition figurines. More changes came about in 1997 in the numbering system. All Dreamsicles items were given a five-digit numerical code that started with the number "1." Dreamsicles Day figurines, which had previously been marked by the prefix "DD," had their prefix changed to "E."

New Additions To The Family

Traditional angels joined the cherubs in the Heavenly Classics line in 1995. Combining elegance with the fanciful, Heavenly Classics consists of 27 pieces, all of which have since been suspended or retired. The following year, the cherubs were paired with children in the Dreamsicles Kids collection. Within two years, the line quickly grew to over 50 pieces. Another line that continues to prove popular are the "holiday cherubs." Many of these cherubs are similar to the regular cherubs, except for their wreaths, which feature berries and poinsettia leaves.

Then in 1999, the Golden Halo Collection was created. Each Golden Halo figurine was specially selected by Kristin Haynes to be adapted from one of her classic cherub designs. Each Golden Halo cherub is distinguishable by the golden accents in its wreath and wings. In 1999, the first totally new Golden Halo sculpture was offered to Dreamsicles Club members. Named "Golden Memories," proceeds from this cherub helped benefit the American Cancer Society.

Partially inspired by Kristin's trip to Alaska, the Northern Lights collection brought a welcome and chilly blast of excitement into the Dreamsicles family in 1999. These figurines are easily recognizable due to their cool, blue hue. From Santas to snow angels, the Northern Lights collection features many whimsical designs.

Is There Anything Else?

Although figurines remain the most popular Dreamsicles collectibles, there are other products available that can liven up any room of the house. Bells, bookends, candle holders, hinged boxes and miniature clocks are just some of the items Cast Art has introduced since 1991.

Plush collectors also caught Dreamsicles excitement in 1999 with the release of Angel Hugs. There are now over 50 of these cuddly cherubs and animals available.

Dreamsicles For A New Millennium

Even after a decade of providing smiles for collectors both young and old, the Dreamsicles show no signs of aging. Each year seems to bring even more new fans, as well as new cherubs, into the wonderful world of Dreamsicles. For example, whether celebrating the addition of a new arrival into the world, or sending a grown child off to college, the two "Class of 2000" and six "Baby 2000" figurines are a perfect choice to commemorate these special moments. For hundreds of thousands of collectors, the appeal of Dreamsicles is truly timeless!

Cast Art Biography

Founded in December 1990, Cast Art Industries, Inc. was the brainchild of Scott Sherman, Frank Colapinto and Gary Barsellotti. The young company achieved phenomenal success just months after opening their doors with the release of Kristin Haynes' angelic creations and has since gone on to become a leader in both the collectible and giftware markets. In addition to Dreamsicles, there are several other popular product lines that are produced by this Corona, California, company.

Another one of Cast Art's flagship collectible lines, Ivy & Innocence, made its debut in 1997 as a series of cottages that hearken back to a simpler time. The Slapstix collection, on the other hand, is a line in which clowning around is not only allowed – it's encouraged! And these are just two of Cast Art's hot collectible lines. To see a complete list of their collectibles and to find out more about releases and retirements, you can check out the Cast Art official web site at *www.castart.com.*

In addition to their many collectible products, Cast Art also manufacturers several lines of gifts, any of which are sure to delight savvy shoppers and their lucky recipients. The Chicken Soup For The Soul gift collection is based on the inspirational book series of the same name. The books' lessons are brought to life through a mother hen character that is found on figurines, magnets, stationery and plush. Cast Art recently announced that they would be merging with Papel Giftware, another leading manufacturer – a union which is sure to provide fans of the company with many new and exciting lines of products.

Kristin Haynes Biography

Kristin Haynes, the personality behind the cherubic expressions of the Dreamsicles collection, has been a creative talent since growing up in Utah. Her mother, watercolorist Abbie Whitney, provided Kristin and her three siblings with all the supplies and encouragement needed to ensure that their artistic dreams would be realized. Kristin found she enjoyed the three-dimensional possibilities that clay offered and soon sculpture became her primary means of expression.

While studying sculpture as a fine arts major at the University of Utah, she met her future husband, Scott Haynes. Together, they settled in California in 1978 where they welcomed their first child, Harmony, into the world. Kristin's creativity led to the creation of her first company, Dicky Ducksprings. This unique name came from a humorous incident in Kristin's childhood, when her father's repeated falls into a spring as a boy earned him the nickname "Dick the Duck." When Kristin traveled to the spring on vacation as a child, it became known as the "Dicky Duck Springs" to her family.

Kristin's earliest sculptures were of animals and the now-familiar blue-eyed cherubs. Kristin's wares became a recognized sight at arts and crafts fairs throughout Southern California. Although she had planned to ease up on her strenuous sculpting schedule after the birth of her sons Dustin and Patrick, the popularity of her designs continued to grow.

Kristin knew she needed a partner to help her produce her figurines in the mass quantities needed to satisfy the demand for them. Although she met with some early rejection, a new giftware company was willing to take a chance on her. That company was Cast Art Industries of Corona, California. Cast Art president Scott Sherman changed the name of Kristin's line from "Kristin's Creations" to "Dreamsicles," and soon the first 29 Dreamsicles made their national debut.

Cast Art Industries of Corona,California

The popularity Dreamsicles had experienced as a local California creation was miniscule compared to the immediate national attention the figurines received. The line was named "Best Selling New Category" by Gift Creations Concepts (GCC) in 1991 and they soon became the number-one product in gift stores across the country.

Kristin's ideas come from careful observation of her surroundings. The universal appeal of her cherubs is partially due to the meticulous detail Kristin works into every tiny pose and facial expression. And when her children were babies, they often helped to inspire her tiny cherubs. In fact, a family trip to Alaska helped lead to the creation of the Northern Lights line in 1999.

In 1998, Kristin and her family moved from their Idaho farmhouse to rural Washington. Kristin can still find inspiration for new figurines by looking out the window of her new home and at the wonders of nature all around.

Kristin's role as one of the premier artists in the world of collectibles led to the addition of a new line titled "Love, Kristin" that was released by Cast Art in 1999. This "Heartland Collection" consists of folk-art-style children engaged in such activities as fishing, picnicking and gardening.

A Conversation With Kristin

Recently, CheckerBee Publishing had the opportunity to interview Dreamsicles artist Kristin Haynes. Come join us as she talks about her new home, her family and new developments in the Dreamsicles line.

CheckerBee Publishing: You recently moved to a new home in the mountains outside of Spokane, Washington. Is your piece "Castle in the Sky" at all based on this move? Also, can you tell us about your new home?

Kristin Haynes: Well, it's not exactly a castle. It's more of a cabin. We moved into the home temporarily because we were going to build a new house. It's a neat place for my kids to get to know other kids. The new house is a little bit more remote. It's a cedar and shingle house that blends into the forest. One side in the front overlooks the mountain range and in the back there's a big wetlands that's a refuge for ducks and geese. It's a charming setting. You've got different environments from every angle. So, as far as a castle goes, it's not as majestic but it seems like a castle to me.

CheckerBee: You have a number of pieces dedicated to "Mom." As a mother of three, what would be your ideal Mother's Day present?

Kristin: I think Dreamsicles are a great Mother's Day gift, but, for obvious reasons, my kids wouldn't give them to me. I like teddy bears, so my daughter has given me those from time to time.

CheckerBee: In 2001, you add to your Spanish *Love Notes* and *Our Daily Blessings* collections. What inspired these collections and do you plan to create pieces for these collections in any other languages in the future?

Kristin: It depends on what kinds of requests we get from collectors. There are a large number of Spanish-speaking Dreamsicles collectors, especially throughout California, so it seemed like a relevant thing to do. We'll probably expand on the concept of translating existing English pieces into Spanish at some point in the future.

CheckerBee: So that was an idea that came from collectors?

Kristin: It really did. Many different ideas come from feedback from both Cast Art sales representatives and collectors.

CheckerBee: Recently, you created a series of four very lifelike, elegant angels, beautifully done with long flowing hair and gowns. Can you tell us about these pieces? How long did it take you to do such detailed sculpting?

Kristin: With those particular pieces, I collaborated with other artists. We did a whole series called Heavenly Classics that consisted of more elegant, larger angels. What I would do is create the little cherubs while other artists created the big ones. I collaborate occasionally on Dreamsicles figurines, but more so with the artwork that is licensed and then put on fabric and such. There are two artists, Tim and Arline Fabrizio, who draw the pictures, so it's a neat teamwork arrangement. We interact quite a bit and it's fun. Also, there are two or three other sculptors that work at Cast Art who helped with the angels.

CheckerBee: Can you tell us about a time when you felt particularly "touched by an angel?"

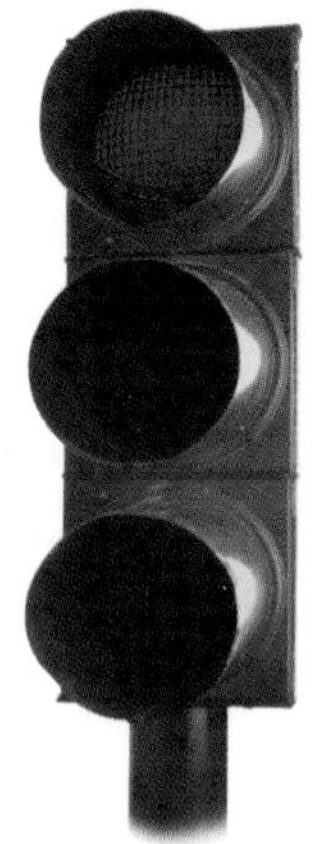

Kristin: Daily! There are reminders of angels all the time. I remember once we were in New York and my youngest son was probably six. When you don't live in a big city like that, you're not tuned in to its dangers. We were crossing the street and I didn't realize that the cars start going before the light turns green. You think that even if the light turns green, the cars are going to wait for you to get across the street. Well, when they see it's going to turn green they never stop. There was a truck coming and my son was right behind me and we had his hand, but people on the curb could see that this truck was not going to stop. My daughter jumped out and grabbed him as well, but it was just a split second before the truck went barreling by and we made it onto the curb. I think things like that make you feel like somebody's there to grab you out of harm's way. There are also times times when I've created a piece that particularly comforted somebody and they relay that to me. I just feel blessed that I'm able to make these cherubs and that they're touching other people.

CheckerBee: How did it feel to be asked to sculpt "A Collector's Delight" for the 2000 International Collectibles Exposition?

Kristin: We've done a couple of them now, and it really is a thrill to be able to do that, specifically because they chose us out of all the other companies. It's neat because people really want to collect those pieces. Even if they don't collect Dreamsicles, they buy those figurines because they're rare and you can only get them at those shows. I meet many people who say, "This is the first one that I've ever bought, but they're wonderful and

I definitely need to buy some more." So you feel, in all regards, like it's a thrill to be able to make them. It's a good feeling.

CheckerBee: The *Band of Angels* mini-figurines are adorable. A lot of artists have said that music has a powerful impact on their work. Do you feel this way? Do you or does any one in your family play a musical instrument?

Kristin: My husband is a composer and a musician and my daughter graduated with a degree in vocal performance. I'd like to say that music has inspired me, but I laugh when I listen to my daughter because I am *so* not musical. Obviously, she inherited her ability from her father, because I am clueless when it comes to the intricacies of music. I can relate to what music does for people and how it inspires them. I can also relate to the artistic outpouring that comes when somebody can play an instrument, but I don't necessarily surround myself, or even work with, music going. I don't mind when it is, but I don't specifically put Beethoven on or anything.

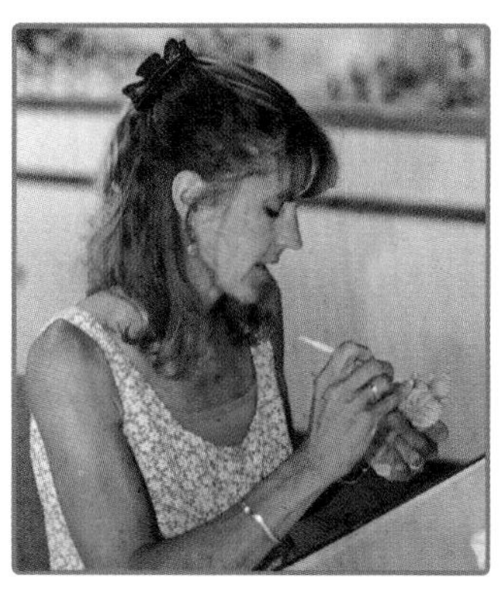

CheckerBee: What is your favorite part of your job as the Dreamsicles artist?

Kristin: Well, it has to be sculpting the pieces and seeing how they turn out. I really enjoy just sitting down and sculpting a new piece, especially if I have an idea that I really want to see conveyed the way I can see it in my mind. That's what's fun, when it comes out how I wanted it to.

CheckerBee: Do you have any special memories of important events that have occurred in your life during the past year?

Kristin: Building the house has really been a special time. People always tell you that it's a nightmare to build them, but it really has been a fun experience. We picked out the block in February, when there was still snow on the ground. The spot was located in the dense forest and we had to clear the whole thing. Watching every phase of it come to life was really fascinating. We've remodeled other houses and that's fun, but you're still working around what's already there. Actually getting to do it from the ground up was really terrific.

Also, all three of my kids graduated this year. My daughter graduated from college, my middle son from high school and my younger son graduated from middle school. My daughter put so much time in, she was determined to hit that goal. For my middle son to graduate and be gone has left a hollow spot, but we're thrilled that he is happy and doing well. Our 14-year-old keeps us hopping. Those were some big events.

CheckerBee: How do you foresee the Dreamsicles line growing in the next year?

Kristin: We don't have any new lines like we did with Northern Lights in 1999. I think I'll just be adding to those already established lines, including redoing some of the pieces that have been popular. There will be some fun new ideas and maybe a few more additions that are more along the lines of home decor, in terms of being functional. Things are gravitating that way in the giftware industry, where you buy something that you can actually use.

CheckerBee: Is there anything else you would like to say to your fans?

Kristin: Thanks! I've had some really moving letters recently. I had some that really hit home because they were about teenage kids that were killed in car accidents and a Dreamsicles figurine was given to comfort the letter writer. With my kids being that age, you're just so nervous about them getting in cars. When they're younger, you can hover over them and protect them to a certain extent. When they get behind the wheel, they're beyond you. You can't see what they're doing and you just hope that they're using their judgement because their lives are still ahead of them. It really hit home this year because of those letters. I just wanted to convey some warm feelings to the fans that have had to go through these things and I'm glad that Dreamsicles could help them.

I actually had something else hit home the other day when I talked to my grandmother who is moving into an assisted living home. She has always been my #1 fan. Many grandparents are Dreamsicles fans because the cherubs remind them of their grandchildren or when their own children were young. My grandmother decided that, out of everything she has, she's taking her whole Dreamsicles collection with her to her new home. It brought tears to my eyes to know that they'll be there with her. I appreciate all the people who continually convey their thoughts to me. I'm always saying thanks.

For a calendar of Kristin Haynes' personal appearances and signing schedule, check our web site at:

What's New?

Want a sneak peek at what's "in store" for 2001? The following section is a look at the newest additions to the Dreamsicles line, all of which should be hitting stores in the coming months. Be sure to plan your shopping now! You certainly wouldn't want to miss any of these cherubic cuties!

Dreamsicles® Day Figurine

Ten Treasured Years . . . Ten stars – which symbolize ten years of Dreamsicles – burst out of this special treasure chest.

Limited Editions

Smooth Sailing (10th Anniversary Limited Edition) . . . You won't want to miss this special piece commemorating the 10th anniversary of Dreamsicles!

Cherubs

Always . . . Two bright-eyed cherubs sitting on a cloud affirm their eternal love for each other by holding a large heart between them proclaiming "Always."

As Big As Me . . . Just try wrapping your arms around such a large, stuffed bunny! This little cherub loves to cuddle with its big-eared pal.

Be My Love? . . . The armful of candy and flowers this cherub holds should erase any doubt regarding the answer to its question. Who wouldn't love to be the recipient of such thoughtful gifts?

Bee Mine . . . Somebody special will be buzzing with the news that this cutie only has eyes for them. What a perfect Valentine's Day gift for a special loved one!

Born To Love . . . As this cherub cuddles its precious rag doll, it makes it clear that even the tiniest little angels have love in their hearts that they are eager to share.

The Bunny Trail . . . This cherub pulling a bunny toy is eager to discover what surprises await along the bunny trail. If there are chocolate eggs to be found, this little angel will be especially excited.

Comfort & Joy . . . Like a warm security blanket, mothers can supply both comfort and joy to a little cherub. Even older cherubs appreciate an occasional comforting word from Mom (although they won't always admit it). Show Mom you care with this precious figurine.

Dear To My Heart . . . An armful of hearts is an enduring symbol of love that will show someone special that they are dear to your heart. This cherub has plenty of extra hearts for you, too!

Egg Hunt . . . Is there any other animal that you would rather have sniffing out hidden eggs than a rabbit? The basket full of Easter eggs is proof that this bunny "nose" where the best treats can be found.

Filled With Love . . . A bouncing bundle of joy takes flight under the watchful eye of its guardian angel. Aerial acrobatics might come naturally to angels, but it's the baby's first flight! The balloon the baby is holding is filled with love, so this flight should be smooth sailing.

First Kiss . . . The tenderness of a first kiss is perfectly captured by this figurine. One shy cherub is depicted holding a rose in its hand as it awaits a peck on the cheek from its less bashful admirer.

Gentle Friends . . . After a busy day of hopping around the meadow, nibbling carrots and scampering with its animal friends, a sleepy bunny rabbit rests peacefully in the tender and gentle arms of a loving cherub.

Great Big Hugs . . . A jumbo teddy bear makes a "beary" thoughtful Valentine's Day gift, especially with a large heart patch on its chest. This tiny cherub seems determined to carry this large symbol of love to someone special – the card at the base says "For My Valentine!"

Grown With Love . . . The three potted plants in this cherub's wheelbarrow spell out the letters M-O-M. A little water, a little plant food and a lot of mom's love are the key to how this garden grows.

Handful Of Love . . . This little angel's hands are overflowing with plenty of pink hearts that it plans to give away in celebration of Valentine's Day. Don't worry – it hasn't forgotten to save one for you!

Hearts & Roses . . . Two lovebirds rest cheek-to-cheek atop their romantic perch of hearts. And they're not alone, a little cherub with a watchful eye rests on a cloud beneath them.

Honey Mine . . . Give this adorable celestial cherub to someone you think is as sweet as honey – we're sure they'll love to "bee" your valentine. Just be sure to keep the bees away!

I Feel Pretty . . . Two tufted birds make the perfect touch to the large, flowery hat that this cherub is trying on. This dressy darling knows that it's as pretty as a picture.

I Had A Dream . . . This cherub is resting on a cloud of love. In case you couldn't tell from the roses and the hearts, the heart-shaped pillow lets everyone know that this little cherub is "Dreaming of You."

Little Ducky . . . A web-footed friend receives a warm hug from a cherub perched on a beautifully decorated Easter egg. You'll "quack up" over these two humorous Easter buddies who would love to find a place in your holiday display.

Love Birds . . . These two "tweet-hearts" share time together in a cozy cage held securely by a delightful Dreamsicles cherub. Listen carefully and you'll hear the beautiful music these lovebirds make together!

Love Is In Bloom . . . Even though a bountiful bouquet of roses will eventually wither away, this cherub knows that if properly cared for and nurtured, love blooms all year round.

Love You Bunches . . . If you treat her with love, kindness and respect, Mom will love you bunches in return. Of course, giving Mom flowers (or a Dreamsicles cherub) on Mother's Day never hurts, either.

Message To Grandma . . . Let Grandma know just how much you love her and appreciate all that she does for you with this wreath-wearing bundle of joy holding an "I Love Grandma" sign.

Message To Mom . . . Send Mom a message of love with this delightful Dreamsicles cherub. Although she knows that you love her, it's always nice to hear it again from time to time. This figurine is sure to find a special place in her heart and on her shelf.

Message To You . . . Surprise someone special to you with this little cherub. The note says "I Love You," as if the delightful hearts at the base could imply anything else.

Mom's Special Rainbow . . . There isn't a raindrop in sight as a colorful rainbow pokes out from the clouds, ready to brighten up an already spectacular day. The smiling cherub and its birdy companion make this piece even more special.

Moms Make Days Bright . . . A large sunflower and a mother's love are all it takes to put a smile on this cherub's face. This colorful springtime figurine will brighten up any home and will make a perfect Mother's Day present that is sure to put a smile on Mom's face.

Mother's Little Angels . . . These four mischievous cherubs might be a handful at times, but they never get into any real trouble. All in all, they're still angels at heart – just like your little ones!

My Grandma . . . Three cheers for Grandma! Let Grandma know the large influence she has had on your life with this miniature cherub who holds a heart-shaped sign which simply reads, "Grandma."

My Love . . . For those who have trouble saying those three little words, this cherub will let everyone who sees this figurine know that "I Love You."

Number One Mom . . . This cherub isn't shy about letting everyone know who holds the #1 spot in its heart. This little superstar is proud to announce that mom is "numero uno." If you feel the same, let everyone know it with this adorable figurine.

On The Right Track . . . A toy choo-choo train serves as the perfect mode of transportation for a traveling teddy bear, as well as the perfect medium for displaying its message. Teddy won't be gone long – he can only go as far as the cherub pulls him.

She's The Best . . . This charming cherub is a stylish dresser in its pastel T-shirt. It doesn't need to say a single word to convey its message of love for mom.

Special Mom . . . All mothers are special, but you can let your mom know that she holds an extra-special place in your heart by giving her this wonderful miniature cherub.

Special You . . . This cherub may be small in size, but it has no problem telling the whole world that "You're Special." Why don't you do the same for someone special to you?

Springtime Friends . . . Bunnies, bunnies everywhere! Three romping rabbits frolic around their loving new pal. Get this figurine before it's "hare" today and gone tomorrow.

Stop And Smell The Roses . . . A heart-adorned vase full of beautiful red and pink roses is pleasant to look at, and even more pleasing to smell. Heaven surely must have sent this heavenly scent.

Sweet Heart . . . Who says only flowers or chocolates should be given on Valentine's Day? As this cherub awaits its true love, a large cake on its lap is sure to satisfy any sweet tooth. Let's hope its loved one doesn't think it's too pretty to eat!

Sweeter When Shared . . . These two cherubs have discovered that a giant lollipop tastes twice as sweet when it is shared with someone you love.

Teddy Love . . . These two teddy bears make the perfect companions for a smiling cherub. The warm, fuzzy teddies are the lucky recipients of a great, big bearhug.

Thoughts Of You . . . A reclining cherub thinks nothing but happy thoughts (about you, of course) as it daydreams inside a large, frilly heart. This piece is the perfect way to show someone in your life that they are on your mind . . . and in your heart.

Timeless Story . . . The timeless tale of "The Easter Story" is read by a cherub sitting atop a beautiful Easter egg, as a stuffed bunny sits on the grass nearby. This figurine would make the perfect surprise in someone's Easter basket!

Valentine Wishes . . . This cherub is playing Cupid as it makes the rounds among the Dreamsicles with its basket full of special Valentine cards. It even has one picked out especially for you!

We'll Stick Together . . . Three is never a crowd when these three cherubs get together. They believe the more, the merrier – and we'd have to agree!

Angel Hugs™

Be Mine . . . This angelic plush cherub wants you and nobody else. Show it some love and kindness by taking it home with you and it will be yours forever.

Best Friends . . . Best friends never run out of love for one another, so why not give your best friend a "Best Friends" Angel Hugs plush cherub? Surely you won't want your best friend to miss out on this little cutie.

Hug Me . . . It's no secret what this plush cherub wants – hugs, hugs and more hugs! Its soft cuddly body is perfect for giving and receiving hugs from people both big and small.

I Love Grandma . . . If you ever enjoyed cuddling on your grandma's lap when you were little, you can return the favor now that you're all grown up by giving Granny this cuddly cutie.

I Love Mom . . . Even if you've grown up and left home, this cherub will remind Mom that she is never far from your thoughts and warm wishes. After all, there's nothing better than a mother's love – except the love of her children for her.

I Love You . . . Give this plush cherub to that special someone that you love with all your heart. If you do, they will surely love you back even more in return.

Roses For Mom . . . This generous cherub has a bouquet of roses to give to Mom. This plush angel with lots of hugs makes the perfect Mother's Day gift. It even has the word "Mom" embroidered in a heart on its foot.

Clocks

Pocket Watch Clock . . . This clock is too beautiful to stay hidden in your pocket. A timely cherub stands proudly next to this elegant, heart-shaped timepiece which will surely enhance any room in your home.

Frames & Photo Holders

First Kiss Frame . . . Relive your first kiss over and over again with this intricately detailed, arch-shaped frame. Standing against a pillar, one cherub prepares to sneak a kiss past its blushing mate.

From The Heart Frame . . . Show someone that you love them with a heart-shaped frame in the style of an old-fashioned valentine. This elegant frame is decorated with flowers, hearts, stars and two cherubs.

Mom's Little Angel Photo Holder . . . The darling cherub holding its stuffed bunny is ready to look after your own little angel (or angels). You can proudly display three precious pictures with this adorable photo holder.

Special Friends . . . This unique photo holder featuring two charming cherubs is perfect for displaying pictures of your best friend. And if you have more than one special friend, don't worry – there are holders for three photos!

Boxes

First Kiss Hinged Box . . . Store away precious memories and mementos in this handy box topped by two cherubs and decorated with a flowered ribbon. The lid removes so you can tuck special mementos and trinkets away for safekeeping.

Musicals/Waterglobes

Basket Of Love . . . With a handful of roses, two cherubs embrace in their bountiful rose-filled basket of love, accompanied by the tune "Love Me Tender."

Cupid's Touch . . . The adorable little cherub in this miniature waterglobe has been playing Cupid. And this cherub knows that no one can resist "Cupid's Touch" – especially you!

First Kiss . . . A tiny cherub puckers up, ready to bestow a first kiss on its companion. It's sure to be the first of many for this lovestruck couple who are serenaded by the tune "Endless Love."

Gentle Heart . . . The base of this miniature waterglobe is decorated with flowers, hearts and ribbon and a shy cherub who sits inside the globe can't wait to give you its "Gentle Heart."

Love Note . . . This miniature waterglobe which features a cherub with a fistful of roses and a heart that reads "Love" is the perfect present for the love of your life.

Moonlight Romance . . . The two cherubs featured in this special waterglobe are in the mood for romance as they rendezvous on a crescent moon to the music of "Through The Eyes Of Love." One cherub brought a bunch of flowers for the occasion, delighting his sweetheart.

A Special Gift . . . A large pink bow is wrapped around one lucky cherub who sits atop a "special gift." What could it be? Only the cherub who bestowed it knows for sure. The "Theme From Love Story" adds a romantic touch to this waterglobe.

Won't You Be Mine? . . . "Won't You Be Mine?" asks a bouquet-carrying cherub to his delighted companion. You won't have to guess as to the answer to that question . . . this beautiful waterglobe plays the tune "I Will Always Love You."

News From The Dreamsicles® Club

Are you one of the thousands of members that has already enrolled in the Dreamsicles Club? If not, you don't know what you're missing! Since its creation in 1993, the Dreamsicles Club has become the best source for exclusive figurines and Dreamsicles news and is ideal for collectors who just can't get enough of Kristin Haynes' cherubs.

Members receive all sorts of goodies that no Dreamsicles fan will want to live without. These benefits include a subscription to the quarterly newsletter, *The ClubHouse,* a Symbol of Membership piece, a plush Angel Hugs figure and a chance to obtain special Members Only figurines that can't be found in stores. Also included with membership is a copy of the 2001 Collector's Value Guide™ to Dreamsicles published by CheckerBee Publishing. This full-color guide serves as a perfect complement to *The ClubHouse* newsletter.

Helping to celebrate a decade of Dreamsicles, the Symbol of Membership figurine for 2001 is "Dreamsicles Rule." This regal figurine carries a staff topped by the letters "DC" and wears a sash that proudly proclaims "Dreamsicles Rule." Instead of a crown, the little angel wears its traditional handcrafted wreath atop its head. This Symbol of Membership piece indicates that Dreamsicles will rule the collectible world for many decades to come. The little cherub is fit for a king, but doesn't cost a princely sum to add to your collection.

The Dreamsicles Club has included plush Angel Hugs with membership in the past, but this year, lucky members will receive an Angel Hugs key chain with their enrollment. Now you can have your own special angel looking after you wherever you go! The key chain is also perfect for attaching to a purse, backpack or anywhere else you might want to find a little heavenly guidance.

Over the course of the year, members are given the opportunity to add exclusive Members Only figurines to their collections. Collectors can expect information on exciting new pieces during the coming year.

Club members also have their own virtual clubhouse found at *www.dreamsiclesclub.com* to visit for all the latest Dreamsicles news, as well as special Member's Only information. Your personalized Membership Card allows you to access all that the web site has to offer. From the web site, you can also send a personally inscribed Dreamsicles Club eCard to special friends and collectors.

"Dreamsicles Dollars" were introduced by the Dreamsicles Club in 1999. These "dollars" might not be legal tender, but they are redeemable toward Dreamsicles collectibles from your authorized local retailer. These gift certificates are awarded to individuals by the Dreamsicles Club for contributions such as signing up new members or renewing memberships for additional years.

A one-year membership into the club is still only $27.50. The entire package, a $50 value, arrives in a beautiful collectors' box. You can enroll by signing up on-line.

www.dreamsiclesclub.com

or

by contacting the Dreamsicles Club directly at 1120 California Avenue, Corona, CA 91719-3324.

Recently Retired & Suspended Dreamsicles®

This section lists each of the pieces which were retired or suspended in 2000. In each category, you will find a listing of the piece, as well as the year it was introduced and its stock number.

Retired

Special Dreamsicles® Pieces

- ❑ Above And Beyond (1998, CD112)
- ❑ First Blush (1997, CD109)
- ❑ Ship Of Dreams (1999, CD117)
- ❑ Summertime Serenade (1998, CD111)
- ❑ Tic-Tac-Toe Family Board Game (1999, CD116)

Northern Lights™

- ❑ Sleddin' (1999, 60007)

Suspended

Cherubs

- ❑ Best Friends (1996, DC342)
- ❑ Bless This Child (1999, 10734)
- ❑ Dios Es Amor (2000, 11261)
- ❑ Daisy (1998, 10551)
- ❑ Rose (1998, 10550)
- ❑ Sunflower (1999, 10782)
- ❑ Dreamy Thoughts (1999, 10877)

Cherubs, cont.

- ❑ Early Riser (1999, 10873)
- ❑ Easter Artist (1998, 10325)
- ❑ El Senor Es Mi Pastor (2000, 11258)
- ❑ En Todo Da Gracias (2000, 11256)
- ❑ The Frog Prince (1999, 10765)
- ❑ Get Well Wishes (1998, 10320)
- ❑ Happy Thoughts (1999, 10871)
- ❑ Heads Up (2000, 11226)
- ❑ Hey Diddle, Diddle (2000, 11096)
- ❑ Hickory, Dickory, Dock (2000, 11099)
- ❑ High Tea (1999, DC021)

Cherubs, cont.

- ❑ Humpty Dumpty (1998, 10372)
- ❑ I Love Mommy (1995, DC226)
- ❑ It's Your Birthday (1995, DC304)
- ❑ Jack And Jill (2000, 11097)
- ❑ Jack Be Nimble (2000, 11100)
- ❑ Kindergarten Cherub (1999, 10724)
- ❑ Kiss, Kiss (1995, DC213)
- ❑ Little Bo Peep (1998, 10375)
- ❑ Little Cupid (1995, DC212)
- ❑ Little Giggles (2000, 11225)
- ❑ Little Leaguer (1998, 10366)
- ❑ Loves Me, Loves Me Not (1999, 10644)
- ❑ Mary Contrary (1999, 10766)
- ❑ Mary Had A Little Lamb (2000, 11101)
- ❑ Mini Ark – Elephant (1999, 10889)

Cherubs, cont.

- ❑ Mini Ark – Giraffe (1999, 10890)
- ❑ Mini Ark – Peacock (1999, 10887)
- ❑ Modesty (1999, 10870)
- ❑ Mother-To-Be (1997, 10155)
- ❑ Ocean's Call (1996, DC317)
- ❑ On Bended Knee (1994, DC196)
- ❑ Pensando En Ti (2000, 11245)
- ❑ Pues Dios Asi Amo Al Mundo (2000, 11257)
- ❑ Pumpkin Patch Cherub (1993, DC206)
- ❑ Sisters (1997, DC427)
- ❑ Thanksgiving Cherubs (1994, DC207)
- ❑ Think It Over (1999, 10874)
- ❑ The Wedding March (1997, 10121)
- ❑ Un Angel Te Cuida (2000, 11246)
- ❑ You're My Shining Star (1999, 10712)
- ❑ Young Love (1995, DC214)

Golden Halo Collection

- ❑ The Flying Lesson – Golden Halo (1999, 10935)
- ❑ Golden A Child's Prayer (1999, 10798)
- ❑ Golden Bundle Of Joy (1999, 10795)
- ❑ Golden Little Dream (1999, 10797)

Golden Halo Collection, cont.

- ❑ Golden Make A Wish (1999, 10663)
- ❑ Golden Thinking Of You (1999, 10932)
- ❑ Golden Wildflower (1999, 10662)

Holiday Cherubs

- ❑ Christmas Devotion (1999, 10852)
- ❑ Cute And Cuddly (2000, 11341)
- ❑ Fuzzy Wuzzy (2000, 11342)
- ❑ Lighting The Tree (2000, 11433)
- ❑ My Big Buddy (2000, 11343)

Northern Lights™

- ❑ Sweet Treat (2000, 60123)

Northern Lights™ Musicals & Waterglobes

- ❑ Love Hearts (2000, 60033)
- ❑ Rainbow Dreams (2000, 60035)

Northern Lights™ Ornaments

- ❑ Flocked Northern Lights Ornament Assortment (2000, 11376)

Animals & Other Figurines

- ❑ Ghostly Assortment (1999, 10973)
- ❑ Halloween Ride (1994, DA659)

Animals & Other Figurines, cont.

- ❑ Halloween Surprise (1999, 10928)
- ❑ Scarecrow & Friends (1993, DA653)

Boxes

- ❑ Cherub In Manger Box (1998, 10456)
- ❑ Flower Cart Box (1998, 10353)
- ❑ Guardian Angel Box (1997, 10037)
- ❑ Morning Glory Birdhouse Box (1999, 10769)
- ❑ Sunflower Birdhouse Box (1999, 10772)
- ❑ Tiny Dancer Box (1997, 10036)

Cake Toppers

- ❑ Cake Topper (1999, 10757)

Candle & Votive Holders

- ❑ Bride & Groom Candlestick (1999, 10759)
- ❑ Two Log Night (1998, 10119)

Clocks

- ❑ Wedding Clock (1998, 10529)

Desk Accessories

- ❑ Cherub Business Card Holder (2000, 11136)
- ❑ Letter Opener (1999, 10903)
- ❑ Note Pad Caddy (1999, 10902)

Frames

- ❑ Cherub Rainbow Frame (1998, 10347)
- ❑ Heart Picture Frame (1997, 10225)
- ❑ Wedding Bells Frame (1999, 10760)

Musicals & Waterglobes

- ❑ Christmas Chorus (2000, 11274)
- ❑ Lullaby And Goodnight (1999, 10613)

Ornaments

- ❑ Flocked Cherub Ornament Assortment (2000, 11378)
- ❑ Flocked Christmas Ornament Assortment (2000, 11377)

Plates

- ❑ 25th Anniversary Plate (1999, 10762)

Potpourri Holders

- ❑ Fresh As Spring (2000, 11006)

Wreaths

- ❑ Christmas Wreath (2000, 11316)

The Top Five

This section showcases the five most valuable pieces in the Dreamsicles collection based on their current value on the secondary market.

The Flying Lesson (LE-10,000)

Cherub Figurine, DC251
Issued: 1993 • Retired: 1993
Market Value: $1,200

Bundles Of Love

Heavenly Classics Figurine, HC370
Issued: 1996 • Suspended: 1996
Market Value: $1,000

Cherub (LE-10,000)

Cherub Figurine, DC112/5112
Issued: 1992 • Retired: 1993
Market Value: $450

Santa In Dreamsicle Land

Limited Edition, DX247
Issued: 1992 • Retired: 1993
Market Value: $320

By The Silvery Moon (LE-10,000)

Limited Edition, DC253
Issued: 1994 • Retired: 1994
Market Value: $318

How To Use Your Collector's Value Guide™

1. Locate your piece in the Value Guide. The Value Guide begins with a chronological listing of Special Dreamsicles pieces including Dreamsicles Club figurines, Dreamsicles Day figurines and Limited Editions. Next, you will find alphabetical listings of Dreamsicles in the following categories: Cherubs, Holiday Cherubs, Animals & Other Figurines, Dreamsicles Kids, Heavenly Classics and Northern Lights. The Value Guide section concludes with "Other Dreamsicles Collectibles," including ornaments, musicals, waterglobes and more. Indexes can be found in the back of the book to help you locate your pieces.

2. Find the market value of your Dreamsicles piece. Pieces for which a secondary market price is not established will be listed as "N/E." The market value for any piece which is still current is the 2001 retail price, which you can write on the line provided.

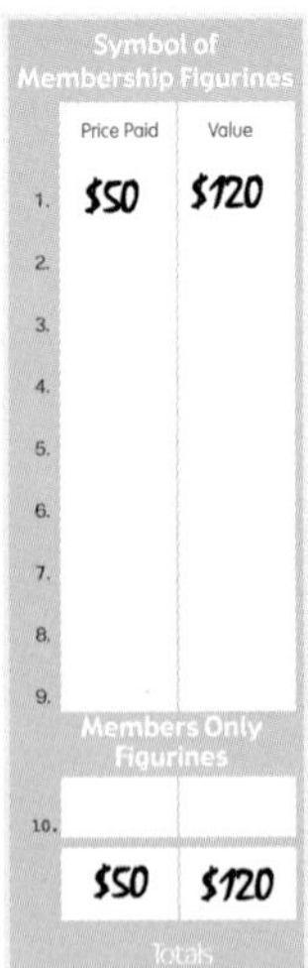

3. Record the original price you paid and the current value of the piece in the corresponding boxes to the side of the page.

4. Calculate the total value for each page by adding together all of the boxes in each column. Be sure to use a pencil so that you can change the totals as your collection grows!

5. Transfer the totals from each page to the "Total Value of My Collection" worksheets beginning on page 191.

6. Add the totals together to determine the overall value of your collection!

Original 29	Color Change	American Cancer Society
One Of The "Original 29" Dreamsicles	Piece Underwent Color Change In 1997	Piece Benefitting The American Cancer Society

Special Dreamsicles ®Pieces

This section features Dreamsicles Club pieces, Dreamsicles Day pieces, as well as Limited Editions. In each section you will find the pieces listed according to the year they were released.

1

A Star Is Born
CD001 • 4″
Issued: 1993 • Retired: 1993
Market Value: $120

2

Join The Fun
CD002 • 3″
Issued: 1994 • Retired: 1994
Market Value: $64

3

Three Cheers
CD003 • 4 1/2″
Issued: 1995 • Retired: 1995
Market Value: $60

4

Star Shower
CD004 • 4 1/8″
Issued: 1996 • Retired: 1996
Market Value: $50

5

Free Spirit
CD005 • 4″
Issued: 1997 • Retired: 1997
Market Value: $45

6

Let's Get Together
CD006 • 3 3/4″
Issued: 1998 • Retired: 1998
Market Value: $40

7

Share The Magic
CD007 • 3 3/4″
Issued: 1999 • Retired: 1999
Market Value: N/E

8

Get On Board
CD008 • 4 1/2″
Issued: 2000 • Retired: 2000
Market Value: N/E

9
New

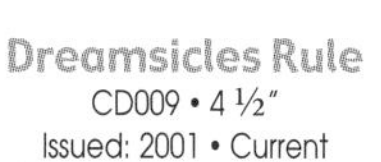

Dreamsicles Rule
CD009 • 4 1/2″
Issued: 2001 • Current
Market Value: $____

10

Daydream Believer
CD100 • 4 5/8″
Issued: 1994 • Retired: 1994
Market Value: $97

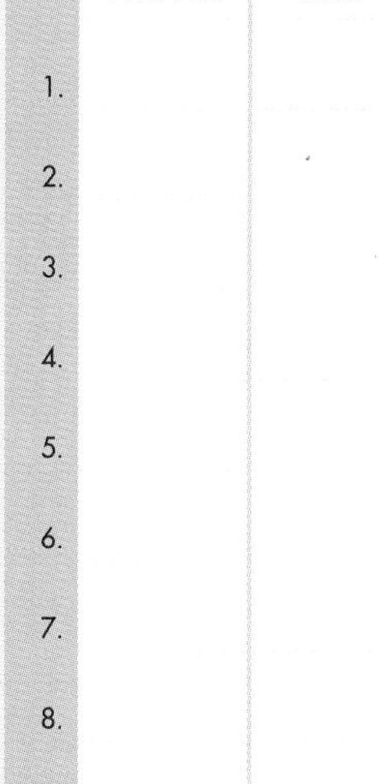

Symbol of Membership Figurines

	Price Paid	Value
1.		
2.		
3.		
4.		
5.		
6.		
7.		
8.		
9.		

Members Only Pieces

	Price Paid	Value
10.		
Totals		

1

Makin' A List
CD101 • 5 ⅜″
Issued: 1994 • Retired: 1996
Market Value: $85

2

Town Crier
CD102 • 4 ½″
Issued: 1995 • Retired: 1995
Market Value: $52

3

Snowbound
CD103 • 4″
Issued: 1995 • Retired: 1996
Market Value: $46

4

Heavenly Flowers
CD104 • 3″
Issued: 1996 • Retired: 1997
Market Value: $40

5

Bee-Friended
CD105 • 4 ¼″
Issued: 1996 • Retired: 1998
Market Value: N/E

6

Peaceable Kingdom
CD106 • 2 ¼″
Issued: 1997 • Retired: 1998
Market Value: N/E

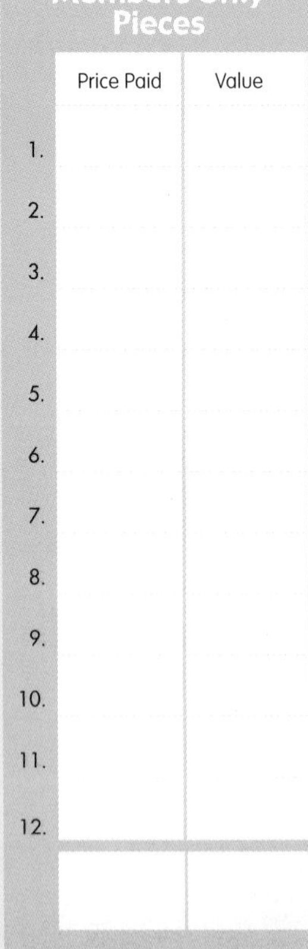

Members Only Pieces

	Price Paid	Value
1.		
2.		
3.		
4.		
5.		
6.		
7.		
8.		
9.		
10.		
11.		
12.		
Totals		

7

First Blush (LE-12,500)
CD109 • 8 ½″
Issued: 1997 • Retired: 2000
Market Value: N/E

8

Sweet Tooth
CD110 • 3 ½″
Issued: 1997 • Retired: 1998
Market Value: N/E

9

Summertime Serenade
CD111 • 3 ½″
Issued: 1998 • Retired: 2000
Market Value: N/E

10

Above And Beyond
5th Anniversary Figurine
CD112 • 7″
Issued: 1998 • Retired: 2000
Market Value: N/E

11

Golden Memories
CD113 • 5 ½″
Issued: 1999 • Current
Market Value: $____

12

Dreamsicles Dollars (Uncut Sheets of $1)
CD114 • 12 ⅝″ x 5 ¾″
Issued: 1999 • Current
Market Value: $____

1

Dreamsicles Dollars (Uncut Sheets of $5)
CD115 • 12 ⅝" x 5 ¾"
Issued: 1999 • Current
Market Value: $____

2

Tic-Tac-Toe Family Board Game
CD116 • 5 ¾" (square)
Issued: 1999 • Retired: 2000
Market Value: N/E

3

Ship Of Dreams
CD117 • 9"
Issued: 1999 • Retired: 2000
Market Value: N/E

4

Dreamsicles 2000 Calendar
CD118 • 12" (square)
Issued: 2000 • Current
Market Value: $____

5

Drummin' Up Fun
CD119 • 3 ¼"
Issued: 2000 • Current
Market Value: $____

6

The Heart Cart
CD120 • 3 ½"
Issued: 2000 • Current
Market Value: $____

7

Footloose Caboose
CD121 • 3"
Issued: 2000 • Current
Market Value: $____

8

Threads Of Love
CD128 • 4 ½"
Issued: 2000 • Current
Market Value: $____

9
New

Dreamsicles 2001 Calendar
N/A • 12" (square)
Issued: 2001 • Current
Market Value: $____

10

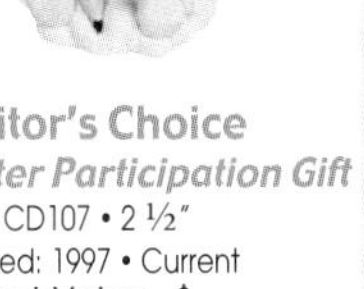

Editor's Choice
Newsletter Participation Gift
CD107 • 2 ½"
Issued: 1997 • Current
Market Value: $____

11

Golden Halo
"Good Samaritan" Award
CD108 • 2 ½"
Issued: 1997 • Current
Market Value: $____

12

Snowflake
Membership Gift, Plush
08008 • 8 ½"
Issued: 1999 • Retired: 1999
Market Value: N/E

Members Only Pieces

	Price Paid	Value
1.		
2.		
3.		
4.		
5.		
6.		
7.		
8.		
9.		

Special Club Pieces

	Price Paid	Value
10.		
11.		
12.		
Totals		

Special Dreamsicles® Pieces

1

Hugged By An Angel
Membership Gift, Plush
08055 • 8″
Issued: 2000 • Current
Market Value: $____

2

New

Angel Hugs Key Chain
Membership Gift, Plush
08056 • 3″
Issued: 2001 • Current
Market Value: $____

3

1995 Dreamsicles Day Event Figurine
DC075 • 3 ½″
Issued: 1995 • Retired: 1995
Market Value: $60

4

Glad Tidings
DD100 • 4 ⅛″
Issued: 1996 • Retired: 1996
Market Value: $53

5

Time To Retire
DD103 • 4 ⅛″
Issued: 1996 • Retired: 1997
Market Value: $38

6

The Golden Rule
E9701 (DD104) • 4 ⅜″
Issued: 1997 • Retired: 1997
Market Value: $45

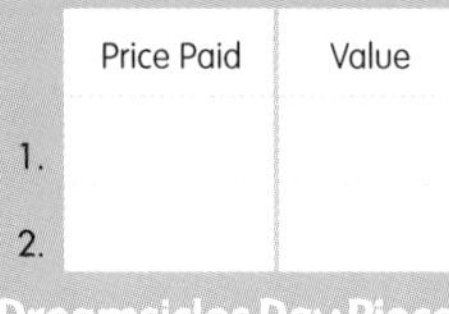

Special Club Pieces

	Price Paid	Value
1.		
2.		

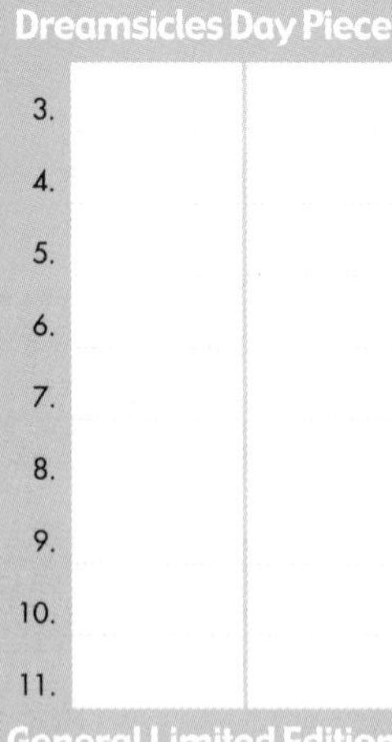

Dreamsicles Day Pieces

	Price Paid	Value
3.		
4.		
5.		
6.		
7.		
8.		
9.		
10.		
11.		

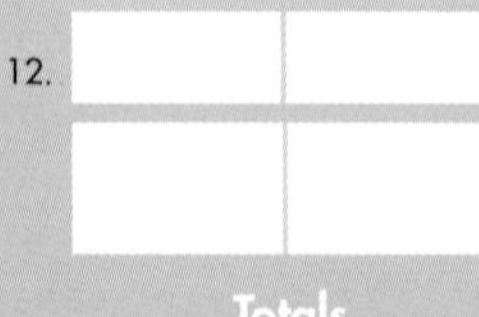

General Limited Editions

	Price Paid	Value
12.		
Totals		

7

A Day Of Fun
E9801 • 4″
Issued: 1998 • Retired: 1998
Market Value: $32

8

Yours Truly
E9901 • 3 ⅝″
Issued: 1999 • Retired: 1999
Market Value: $30

9

I Love Dreamsicles
Plush
08057 • 8″
Issued: 2000 • Current
Market Value: $____

10

With All My Heart
E0001 • 4″
Issued: 2000 • Retired: 2000
Market Value: N/E

11

New

10 Treasured Years
E0002 • 4″
Issued: 2001 • Current
Market Value: $____

12

Cherub (LE-10,000)
DC111 (5111) • 10″
Issued: 1992 • Retired: 1992
Market Value: $125

1

Cherub (LE-10,000)
DC112 (5112) • 10"
Issued: 1992 • Retired: 1993
Market Value: $450

2

The Flying Lesson (LE-10,000)
DC251 • 13" (wide)
Issued: 1993 • Retired: 1993
Market Value: $1,200

3

Teeter Tots (LE-10,000)
DC252 • 6"
Issued: 1993 • Retired: 1993
Market Value: $225

4

By The Silvery Moon (LE-10,000)
DC253 • 8 ½"
Issued: 1994 • Retired: 1994
Market Value: $318

5

The Recital (LE-10,000)
DC254 • 9 ½" (wide)
Issued: 1994 • Retired: 1994
Market Value: $250

6

Picture Perfect (LE-10,000)
DC255 • 7"
Issued: 1995 • Retired: 1995
Market Value: $150

7

The Dedication (LE-10,000)
HC351 (DC351) • 7 ½"
Issued: 1995 • Retired: 1995
Market Value: $195

8

A Child Is Born (LE-10,000)
DC256 • 9 ½" (wide)
Issued: 1996 • Retired: 1996
Market Value: $130

9

Heaven's Gate (LE-15,000)
Five Years Of Dreamsicles
DC257 • 8 ¾"
Issued: 1996 • Retired: 1996
Market Value: $180

10

Happy Landings (LE-5,000)
10156 • 7 ½"
Issued: 1997 • Retired: 1997
Market Value: $310

11

Sleigh Bells Ring (LE-2,500)
10187 • 7"
Issued: 1997 • Retired: 1997
Market Value: $118

General Limited Editions

	Price Paid	Value
1.		
2.		
3.		
4.		
5.		
6.		
7.		
8.		
9.		
10.		
11.		
Totals		

1

Cutie Pie (LE-12,500)
10241 • 8"
Issued: 1997 • Current
Market Value: $____

2

Handmade With Love (LE-10,000)
10324 • 5"
Issued: 1998 • Retired: 1998
Market Value: $135

3
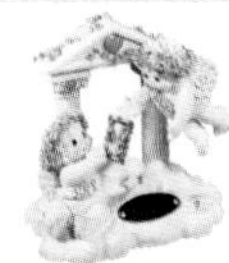

Passage Of Time - Millennium Edition (LE-1999)
10671 • 5 ½"
Issued: 1999 • Susp.: 1999
Market Value: $80

4

Stairway To Heaven (LE-10,000)
10672 • 7 ¾"
Issued: 1999 • Retired: 1999
Market Value: $100

5

Castle In The Sky (LE-10,000)
11400 • 8 ½"
Issued: 2000 • Current
Market Value: $____

6

Live, Love, Laugh (LE- 10,000)
11061 • 4 ¾"
Issued: 2000 • Current
Market Value: $____

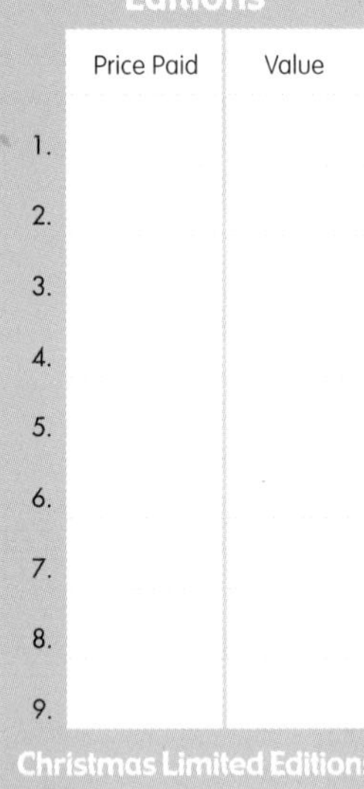

General Limited Editions

	Price Paid	Value
1.		
2.		
3.		
4.		
5.		
6.		
7.		
8.		
9.		
Christmas Limited Editions		
10.		
11.		
12.		
Totals		

7
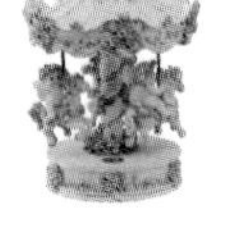

Magical Merry Go Round (LE-7,500)
♪ *Carousel Waltz*
11481 • 11 ½"
Issued: 2000 • Current
Market Value: $____

8

Passage Of Time - Second Edition (LE-2000)
11386 • 5 ½"
Issued: 2000 • Retired: 2000
Market Value: $____

9
New

Smooth Sailing
10th Anniversary Limited Edition
11590 • N/A
Issued: 2001 • Current
Market Value: $____

10

Santa In Dreamsicle Land
DX247 • 10"
Issued: 1992 • Retired: 1993
Market Value: $320

11

The Finishing Touches
DX248 • 9"
Issued: 1993 • Retired: 1994
Market Value: $200

12

Holiday On Ice
DX249 • 8 ½"
Issued: 1994 • Retired: 1995
Market Value: $165

1

Santa's Kingdom
DX250 • 8 ½″ (wide)
Issued: 1995 • Retired: 1996
Market Value: $125

2

Homeward Bound
DX251 • 9″
Issued: 1996 • Retired: 1997
Market Value: $125

3

Time To Dash
10184 • 6 ¾″
Issued: 1997 • Retired: 1998
Market Value: N/E

4

All Aboard!
10364 • 7″
Issued: 1998 • Retired: 1998
Market Value: $102

5

Christmas Eve (LE-5,000)
10420 • 7 ¾″
Issued: 1998 • Retired: 1998
Market Value: $100

6

'Tis Better To Give (LE-5,000)
10421 • 6″
Issued: 1998 • Retired: 1998
Market Value: $73

7

Dash Away!
10791 • 8 ¼″
Issued: 1999 • Retired: 1999
Market Value: $90

8

A Christmas Carol (LE-5,000)
10844 • 6 ¾″
Issued: 1999 • Susp.: 1999
Market Value: $60

9

A Magical Beginning (LE-10,000)
11138 • 6″
Issued: 2000 • Current
Market Value: $____

10

'Tis The Season (Ninth Edition)
11270 • 8″
Issued: 2000 • Current
Market Value: $____

Christmas Limited Editions

	Price Paid	Value
1.		
2.		
3.		
4.		
5.		
6.		
7.		
8.		
9.		
10.		
Totals		

Cherubs

Now celebrating its 10th year, the Dreamsicles line expands in 2001 with the introduction of 45 new pieces. These charming cherubs are crowned with their trademark pastel wreath.

1

1001 Baby Names
10358 • 5 ½"
Issued: 1998 • Susp.: 1999
Market Value: N/E

2

A Is For Apple
Lil' Wonders
11175 • 2 ¾"
Issued: 2000 • Current
Market Value: $____

3

All Better Now
DC246 • 2 ¾"
Issued: 1995 • Susp.: 1997
Market Value: $22

4

Photo Unavailable

All Grown Up
Cracker Barrel Exclusive
11388 • N/A
Issued: 2000 • Current
Market Value: $____

5

All My Lovin'
DC313 • 3 ¼"
Issued: 1996 • Susp.: 1999
Market Value: N/E

6

All Star
10165 • 4"
Issued: 1997 • Current
Market Value: $____

7
New

Always
11514 • 4"
Issued: 2001 • Current
Market Value: $____

8

Amaos Los Unos A Los Otros
Bendiciones
11259 • 3"
Issued: 2000 • Current
Market Value: $____

9

America
11429 • 3 ⅞"
Issued: 2000 • Current
Market Value: $____

10

Among Friends (June)
The Calendar Collection
DC185 • 3 ¾"
Issued: 1994 • Retired: 1995
Market Value: $55

Cherubs

	Price Paid	Value
1.		
2.		
3.		
4.		
5.		
6.		
7.		
8.		
9.		
10.		
Totals		

1

Anchors Aweigh
10526 • 2 ⅞"
Issued: 1998 • Current
Market Value: $____

2

Photo Unavailable

Angel Games
Concepts Direct Exclusive
10980 • 3 ¾"
Issued: 1999 • Current
Market Value: $____

3

Angel Of Peace
11093 • 7"
Issued: 2000 • Current
Market Value: $____

4

Angel Talk
11182 • 2 ¾"
Issued: 2000 • Current
Market Value: $____

5

An Angel's Watching Over You
Love Notes
10684 • 2 ⅞"
Issued: 1999 • Current
Market Value: $____

6

Apple Of My Eye
11439 • 3 ¼"
Issued: 2000 • Current
Market Value: $____

7
New

As Big As Me
11555 • 4 ⅛"
Issued: 2001 • Current
Market Value: $____

8

Autumn Leaves (October)
The Calendar Collection
DC189 • 5"
Issued: 1994 • Retired: 1995
Market Value: $55

9

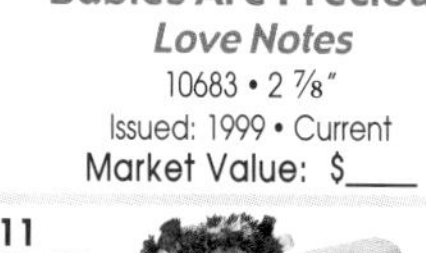

Babies Are Precious
Love Notes
10683 • 2 ⅞"
Issued: 1999 • Current
Market Value: $____

10

Baby And Me
DC054 • 3"
Issued: 1994 • Susp.: 1997
Market Value: $18

11

Baby Boom (blue)
10045 • 3 ½"
Issued: 1997 • Current
Market Value: $____

12

Baby Boom (pink)
10139 • 3 ½"
Issued: 1997 • Current
Market Value: $____

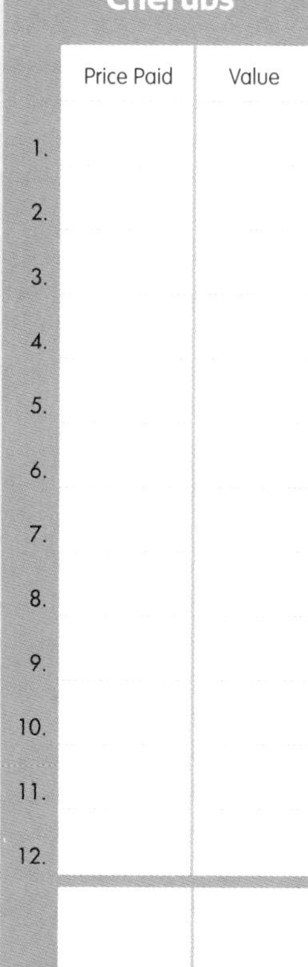

Cherubs

	Price Paid	Value
1.		
2.		
3.		
4.		
5.		
6.		
7.		
8.		
9.		
10.		
11.		
12.		
Totals		

1

Baby Doll
11180 • 2 ¾″
Issued: 2000 • Current
Market Value: $____

2

Baby Kisses
DC080 • 2 ½″
Issued: 1995 • Susp.: 1999
Market Value: $13

3

Baby Love
DC147 • 2 ½″
Issued: 1992 • Retired: 1995
Market Value: $22

4

Baby Of The Century
11025 • 3 ¼″
Issued: 2000 • Current
Market Value: $____

5

Baby Steps
DC415 • 3 ⅝″
Issued: 1996 • Susp.: 1997
Market Value: $24

6

Back Packin'
DC346 • 4 ¼″
Issued: 1996 • Current
Market Value: $____

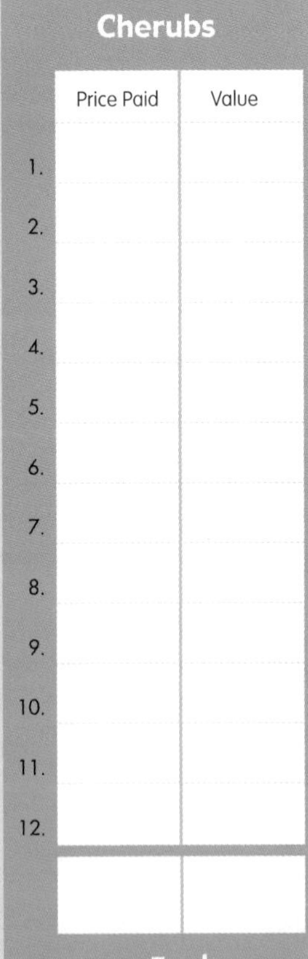

Cherubs

	Price Paid	Value
1.		
2.		
3.		
4.		
5.		
6.		
7.		
8.		
9.		
10.		
11.		
12.		
Totals		

7

Baked With Love
10262 • 4″
Issued: 1998 • Current
Market Value: $____

8

Balance Beam
10714 • 3 ¼″
Issued: 1999 • Current
Market Value: $____

9

The Baptism
10321 • 2 ¾″
Issued: 1998 • Susp.: 1999
Market Value: N/E

10

Bar Mitzvah Boy
DC408 • 4″
Issued: 1995 • Susp.: 1997
Market Value: $19

11

Barrel Of Fun
Cracker Barrel Exclusive
10940 • 3 ⅜″
Issued: 1999 • Current
Market Value: $____

12

Baseball
All Stars
11073 • 2 ¾″
Issued: 2000 • Current
Market Value: $____

1

Bashful
10031 • 4″
Issued: 1997 • Susp.: 1999
Market Value: N/E

2

Basketball
All Stars
11075 • 2 ½″
Issued: 2000 • Current
Market Value: $____

3

Be Good To Yourself
11129 • 3″
Issued: 2000 • Current
Market Value: $____

4
New

Be My Love?
11491 • 5″
Issued: 2001 • Current
Market Value: $____

5

Be My Valentine
10642 • 4″
Issued: 1999 • Current
Market Value: $____

6

Be Thankful
11442 • 3 ⅛″
Issued: 2000 • Current
Market Value: $____

7

Beach Baby
11418 • 3 ⅜″
Issued: 2000 • Current
Market Value: $____

8

Bedtime Prayer
DC703 • 3″
Issued: 1995 • Current
Market Value: $____

9
New

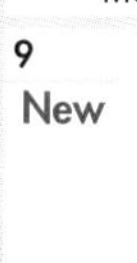

Bee Mine
11508 • 2 ⅜″
Issued: 2001 • Current
Market Value: $____

10

Bee My Honey
Early Release – Spring 1998
10510 • 4″
Issued: 1998 • Current
Market Value: $____

11

Believe In Angels
10879 • 4 ½″
Issued: 1999 • Current
Market Value: $____

12

Berry Cute
DC109 • 3 ⅞″
Issued: 1996 • Susp.: 1999
Market Value: N/E

Cherubs

	Price Paid	Value
1.		
2.		
3.		
4.		
5.		
6.		
7.		
8.		
9.		
10.		
11.		
12.		
Totals		

1

Best Buddies
DC159 • 3 ¾″
Issued: 1995 • Retired: 1998
Market Value: $24

2

Best Friends
DC342 • 6″
Issued: 1996 • Susp.: 2000
Market Value: N/E

3

Best Friends
11432 • 3 ⅞″
Issued: 2000 • Current
Market Value: $____

4

Best Pals
DC103 (5103) • 4 ¾″
Issued: 1991 • Retired: 1994
Market Value: $45

5

Best Pals
Love Notes
10678 • 2 ¾″
Issued: 1999 • Current
Market Value: $____

6

Bible Lesson
11417 • 4 ⅛″
Issued: 2000 • Current
Market Value: $____

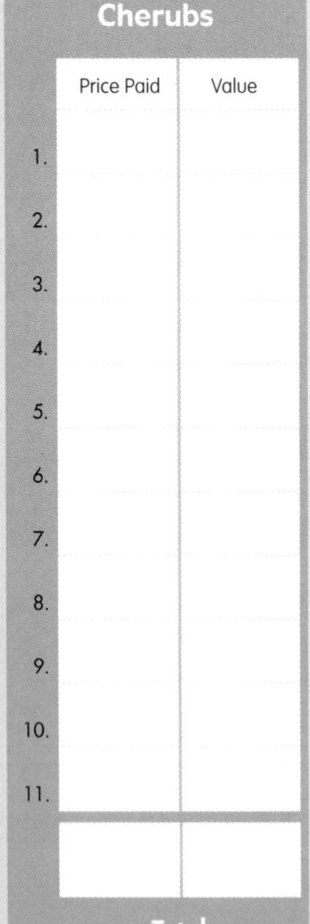

Cherubs

	Price Paid	Value
1.		
2.		
3.		
4.		
5.		
6.		
7.		
8.		
9.		
10.		
11.		
Totals		

7

Bird In Hand
10129 • 3 ½″
Issued: 1997 • Current
Market Value: $____

8

Birdie And Me
DC056 • 2 ½″
Issued: 1994 • Susp.: 1997
Market Value: $18

9

Birthday Delight
11119 • 4″
Issued: 2000 • Current
Market Value: $____

10

Birthday Fun
10323 • 3 ¾″
Issued: 1998 • Current
Market Value: $____

11

Birthday Party
DC171 • 4 ½″
Issued: 1994 • Susp.: 1995
Market Value: $32

1

Birthday Wishes
10166 • 3 ¼"
Issued: 1997 • Susp.: 1999
Market Value: N/E

2

A Bit Of T.L.C.
11421 • 4"
Issued: 2000 • Current
Market Value: $____

3

Bless This Child
10734 • 4 ⅞"
Issued: 1999 • Susp.: 2000
Market Value: N/E

4

Bless This Meal
10064 • 2 ¾"
Issued: 1997 • Current
Market Value: $____

5

Bless Us All
DC089 • 2 ⅝"
Issued: 1995 • Susp.: 1999
Market Value: N/E

6

Blocks Of Love
10264 • 3 ¾"
Issued: 1998 • Current
Market Value: $____

7

Blossom Time
11174 • 2 ¾"
Issued: 2000 • Current
Market Value: $____

8

Blow Me A Kiss
11171 • 2 ¾"
Issued: 2000 • Current
Market Value: $____

9

Blowing Bubbles
Parade Of Gifts Exclusive
10115 • 3 ⅝"
Issued: 1997 • Current
Market Value: $____

10

Blue Logo Sculpture
DC002 • 6 ½" (wide)
Issued: 1992 • Retired: 1994
Market Value: $55

11

Bluebird Of Happiness
11177 • 2 ¾"
Issued: 2000 • Current
Market Value: $____

12

Bluebird On My Shoulder
DC115 • 6"
Issued: 1992 • Retired: 1995
Market Value: $48

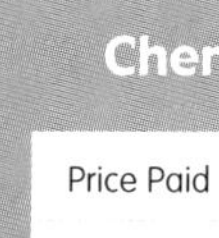

Cherubs

	Price Paid	Value
1.		
2.		
3.		
4.		
5.		
6.		
7.		
8.		
9.		
10.		
11.		
12.		
Totals		

1

Born Again
11192 • 3 ½″
Issued: 2000 • Current
Market Value: $____

2

Born This Day
DC230 • 4″
Issued: 1994 • Retired: 1998
Market Value: $33

3
New

Born To Love
11503 • 2 ½″
Issued: 2001 • Current
Market Value: $____

4

Born To Shop
11128 • 5″
Issued: 2000 • Current
Market Value: $____

5

Bottle Baby
11428 • 4 ¾″
Issued: 2000 • Current
Market Value: $____

6

Bountiful Blessings
11091 • 7 ½″
Issued: 2000 • Current
Market Value: $____

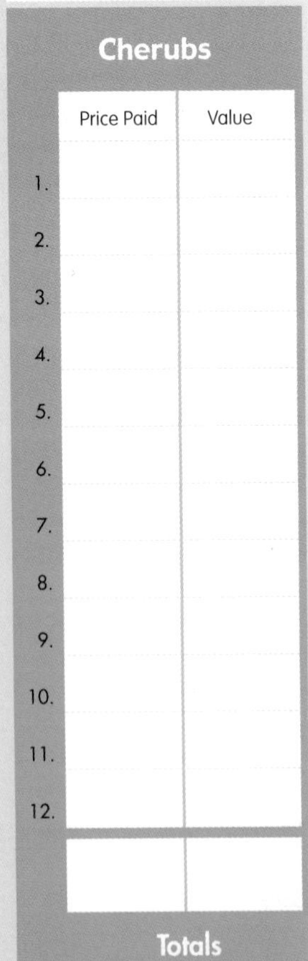

Cherubs

	Price Paid	Value
1.		
2.		
3.		
4.		
5.		
6.		
7.		
8.		
9.		
10.		
11.		
12.		
Totals		

7

Boxful Of Stars
DC224 • 3 ¾″
Issued: 1994 • Susp.: 1995
Market Value: $30

8

A Brand New Start
11030 • 5″
Issued: 2000 • Current
Market Value: $____

9

Bright Eyes
DC108 (5108) • 3 ½″
Issued: 1991 • Retired: 1998
Market Value: $17

10

Brotherhood
DC307 • 4 ½″
Issued: 1995 • Retired: 1998
Market Value: $25

11

Brown Baggin'
DC716 • 3″
Issued: 1996 • Susp.: 1997
Market Value: $23

12

Bubble Bath
DC416 • 5″
Issued: 1996 • Retired: 1998
Market Value: $37

1

Bucket Of Fun
11420 • 3 5/8″
Issued: 2000 • Current
Market Value: $____

2

Bundle Of Joy
DC142 • 2 1/2″
Issued: 1992 • Retired: 1995
Market Value: $20

3

Bunny And Me
DC055 • 2 5/8″
Issued: 1994 • Susp.: 1997
Market Value: $16

4

Bunny Be Mine
10741 • 4″
Issued: 1999 • Current
Market Value: $____

5

Bunny Love
GCC Exclusive
10062 • 3 1/2″
Issued: 1997 • Current
Market Value: $____

6

Bunny Mine
10068 • 3 3/8″
Issued: 1997 • Current
Market Value: $____

7

Bunny Pal
10342 • 2 1/2″
Issued: 1998 • Current
Market Value: $____

8

Bunny Power
10067 • 4″
Issued: 1997 • Current
Market Value: $____

9
New

The Bunny Trail
11552 • 4 3/8″
Issued: 2001 • Current
Market Value: $____

10
Color Change

Burning Love
DC220 • 5″
Issued: 1995 • Susp.: 1997
Market Value: $23

11

Butterfly Kisses
11202 • 2″
Issued: 2000 • Current
Market Value: $____

12

By The Rules
10520 • 2 3/4″
Issued: 1998 • Current
Market Value: $____

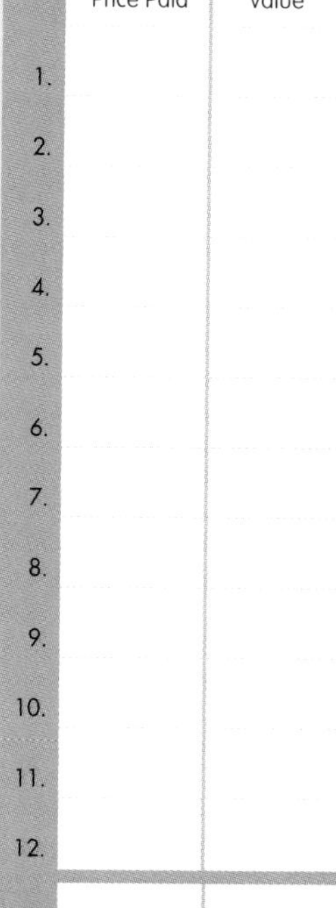

Cherubs

	Price Paid	Value
1.		
2.		
3.		
4.		
5.		
6.		
7.		
8.		
9.		
10.		
11.		
12.		
Totals		

1

Candy Kisses
10995 • 5″
Issued: 2000 • Current
Market Value: $____

2

Caroler #1
DC216 • 6 ½″
Issued: 1992 • Retired: 1995
Market Value: $40

3

Caroler #2
DC217 • 6 ½″
Issued: 1992 • Retired: 1995
Market Value: $40

4

Caroler #3
DC218 • 6 ½″
Issued: 1992 • Retired: 1995
Market Value: $40

5

Carousel
DC174 • 7″
Issued: 1994 • Susp.: 1996
Market Value: $57

6

Carousel Elephant
11474 • 4″
Issued: 2000 • Current
Market Value: $____

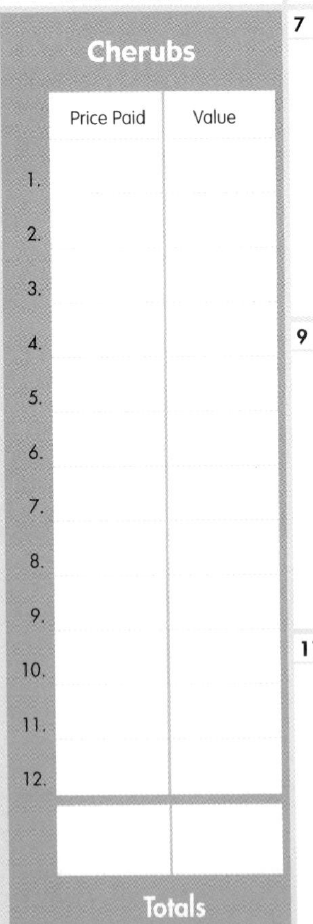

Cherubs

	Price Paid	Value
1.		
2.		
3.		
4.		
5.		
6.		
7.		
8.		
9.		
10.		
11.		
12.		
Totals		

7

Carousel Lion
11473 • 4″
Issued: 2000 • Current
Market Value: $____

8

Carousel Tiger
11475 • 3 ¾″
Issued: 2000 • Current
Market Value: $____

9

Catch A Falling Star
DC166 • 4 ½″
Issued: 1993 • Retired: 1997
Market Value: $23

10

Celebrate!
11027 • 3 ¼″
Issued: 2000 • Current
Market Value: $____

11

Celebrate The Day!
11118 • 4 ½″
Issued: 2000 • Current
Market Value: $____

12

Charity
10171 • 2 ⅜″
Issued: 1997 • Susp.: 1999
Market Value: N/E

1

Charm And Grace
11132 • 4 ½″
Issued: 2000 • Current
Market Value: $____

2

Chatter Box
10039 • 3 ½″
Issued: 1997 • Current
Market Value: $____

3

Cherry, Cherry Pie
10695 • 3 ¼″
Issued: 2000 • Current
Market Value: $____

4

Cherry On Top
10697 • 3″
Issued: 2000 • Current
Market Value: $____

5

Cherub And Child
DC100 (5100) • 5 ½″
Issued: 1991 • Retired: 1995
Market Value: $75

6

Cherub For All Seasons (set/4)
DC114 (5114) • 8″
Issued: 1992 • Retired: 1995
Market Value: $88

7

A Child's Prayer
DC145 • 2 ½″
Issued: 1992 • Retired: 1995
Market Value: $22

8

A Child's Prayer
DC405 • 4″
Issued: 1995 • Susp.: 1999
Market Value: N/E

9

The Christening
DC300 • 4 ¾″
Issued: 1995 • Susp.: 1997
Market Value: $32

10

Circus Parade
10583 • 4 ⅞″
Issued: 1998 • Susp.: 1999
Market Value: N/E

11

Class Of 2000
11149 • 4″
Issued: 2000 • Current
Market Value: $____

12

Class Of 2000
11150 • 4″
Issued: 2000 • Current
Market Value: $____

Cherubs

	Price Paid	Value
1.		
2.		
3.		
4.		
5.		
6.		
7.		
8.		
9.		
10.		
11.		
12.		
Totals		

1

Close To You
11125 • 5 ¾″
Issued: 2000 • Current
Market Value: $____

2

A Collector's Delight (LE-2000)
I.C.E. Exclusive
SP003 • N/A
Issued: 2000 • Retired: 2000
Market Value: $____

3

Come To Papa
DC088 • 2 ¼″
Issued: 1995 • Susp.: 1999
Market Value: N/E

4
New

Comfort & Joy
11578 • 3 ¼″
Issued: 2001 • Current
Market Value: $____

5

Computer
All Stars
11084 • 2 ¾″
Issued: 2000 • Current
Market Value: $____

6

Corona Centennial
N/A • 3″
Issued: 1996 • Retired: 1996
Market Value: $225

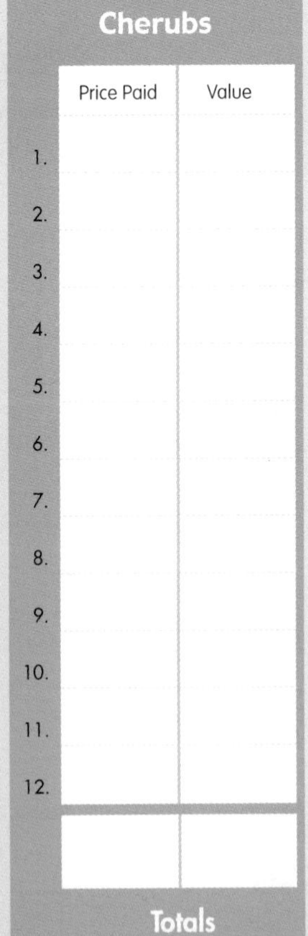

Cherubs

	Price Paid	Value
1.		
2.		
3.		
4.		
5.		
6.		
7.		
8.		
9.		
10.		
11.		
12.		
Totals		

7

Costume Party
10205 • 3 ¾″
Issued: 1997 • Susp.: 1998
Market Value: $23

8

Counting Sheep
DC417 • 5″
Issued: 1996 • Susp.: 1999
Market Value: N/E

9

Cow Pal
10335 • 2 ½″
Issued: 1998 • Current
Market Value: $____

10

Creo En Ti
Notas De Amor
11243 • 3 ⅓″
Issued: 2000 • Current
Market Value: $____

11
Color Change

Crossing Guardian
DC422 • 5″
Issued: 1996 • Retired: 1998
Market Value: $42

12

Cuddle Blanket
DC153 • 2″
Issued: 1994 • Retired: 1995
Market Value: $21

1

Cuddle Up
DC324 • 2 1/4"
Issued: 1996 • Current
Market Value: $____

2

Cupid's Arrow
DC199 • 5 1/4"
Issued: 1994 • Susp.: 1997
Market Value: $25

3

Cupid's Bow
DC202 (5133) • 7 1/2"
Issued: 1992 • Susp.: 1993
Market Value: $118

4

Cut-Out Cutie
Parade Of Gifts Exclusive
10097 • 4"
Issued: 1997 • Current
Market Value: $____

5

Cycle Cutie
11414 • 4 7/8"
Issued: 2000 • Current
Market Value: $____

6

Daddy's Little Angel
10523 • 3 1/4"
Issued: 1998 • Current
Market Value: $____

7

Daffodil Days
DC343 • 3 1/2"
Issued: 1996 • Retired: 1998
Market Value: $36

8

Daisy
Dreamsicles Garden
10551 • 3 1/2"
Issued: 1998 • Current
Market Value: $____

9

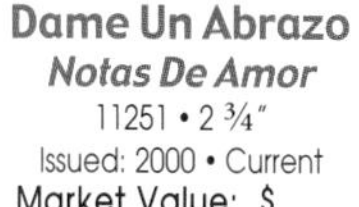

Dame Un Abrazo
Notas De Amor
11251 • 2 3/4"
Issued: 2000 • Current
Market Value: $____

10

Daydreamin'
10332 • 6 1/2"
Issued: 1998 • Retired: 1999
Market Value: N/E

11

Dear Diary
10162 • 2 1/4"
Issued: 1997 • Current
Market Value: $____

12
New

Dear To My Heart
11512 • 2 1/2"
Issued: 2001 • Current
Market Value: $____

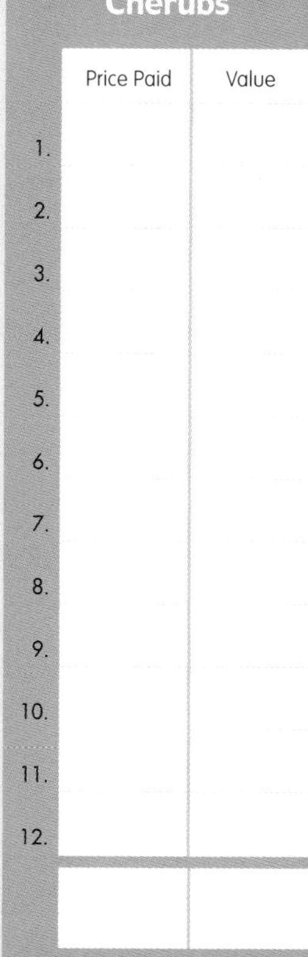

Cherubs

	Price Paid	Value
1.		
2.		
3.		
4.		
5.		
6.		
7.		
8.		
9.		
10.		
11.		
12.		

Totals

1

Declaration Of Love
10635 • 3 ⅜"
Issued: 1999 • Current
Market Value: $____

2

Devotion (blue)
10528 • 3"
Issued: 1998 • Current
Market Value: $____

3

Devotion (pink)
10628 • 3"
Issued: 1998 • Susp.: 2000
Market Value: N/E

4

Dios Es Amor
Bendiciones
11261 • 3 ⅜"
Issued: 2000 • Susp.: 2000
Market Value: N/E

5

Doctor
All Stars
11080 • 2 ¾"
Issued: 2000 • Current
Market Value: $____

6

Doggie Pal
10340 • 2 ¼"
Issued: 1998 • Current
Market Value: $____

Cherubs

	Price Paid	Value
1.		
2.		
3.		
4.		
5.		
6.		
7.		
8.		
9.		
10.		
11.		
12.		
Totals		

7

Don't Rock The Boat
DC404 • 5 ½"
Issued: 1995 • Susp.: 1997
Market Value: $32

8

Double Dip
DC349 • 5"
Issued: 1996 • Susp.: 1999
Market Value: N/E

9

Dream A Little Dream
DC144 • 2 ½"
Issued: 1992 • Retired: 1995
Market Value: $20

10

Dream, Dream, Dream
Early Release – Fall 1997
10247 • 2 ⅞"
Issued: TBA • Current
Market Value: $____

11

Dream On
10365 • 4 ¾"
Issued: 1998 • Susp.: 1999
Market Value: N/E

12

Dream Time
11408 • 6 ½"
Issued: 2000 • Current
Market Value: $____

1

Dream Weaver
10159 • 3 5/8"
Issued: 1997 • Retired: 1999
Market Value: $13

2

Dreamin' Of You
10030 • 3 1/8"
Issued: 1997 • Retired: 1999
Market Value: N/E

3

Dreamsicles Ark Assortment (set/7)
10564 • Various
Issued: 1998 • Current
Market Value: $____

4

Dreamsicles Logo
11060 • 5"
Issued: 2000 • Current
Market Value: $____

5

Dreamy Thoughts
10877 • 10"
Issued: 1999 • Susp.: 2000
Market Value: N/E

6

Dreidel, Dreidel
DC302 • 2 5/8"
Issued: 1995 • Susp.: 1997
Market Value: $23

7

Dressed Like Mommy
Noah's Exclusive
11380 • N/A
Issued: 2000 • Current
Market Value: $____

8

Drum
Band Of Angels
11196 • 2 3/4"
Issued: 2000 • Current
Market Value: $____

9

Duckie Pal
10341 • 2 3/8"
Issued: 1998 • Current
Market Value: $____

10

Eager To Please
DC154 • 2"
Issued: 1994 • Retired: 1995
Market Value: $20

11

Early Riser
10873 • 4 1/2"
Issued: 1999 • Susp.: 2000
Market Value: N/E

12

Easter Artist
10325 • 3 3/4"
Issued: 1998 • Susp.: 2000
Market Value: N/E

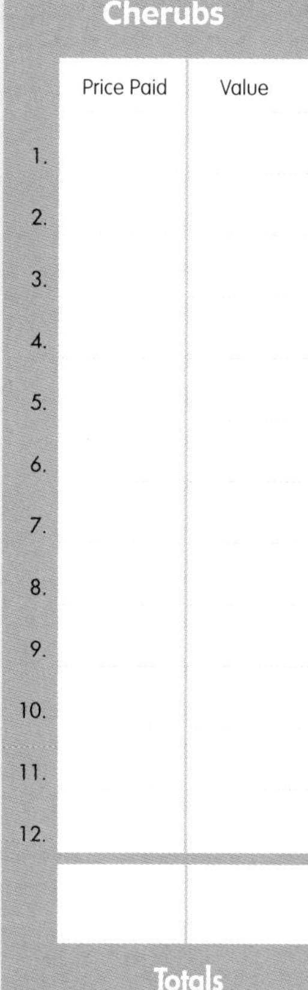

Cherubs

	Price Paid	Value
1.		
2.		
3.		
4.		
5.		
6.		
7.		
8.		
9.		
10.		
11.		
12.		
Totals		

1

Easter Basket
10322 • 3″
Issued: 1998 • Current
Market Value: $____

2

Easter Colors
10738 • 3 5/8″
Issued: 1999 • Current
Market Value: $____

3

Easter Delivery
10739 • 3 1/2″
Issued: 1999 • Current
Market Value: $____

4

Easter Eggspress
10790 • 5 1/8″
Issued: 1999 • Current
Market Value: $____

5

Easter Morning
DC312 • 2 7/8″
Issued: 1996 • Susp.: 1998
Market Value: $22

6

The Easter Story
10737 • 3 1/2″
Issued: 1999 • Current
Market Value: $____

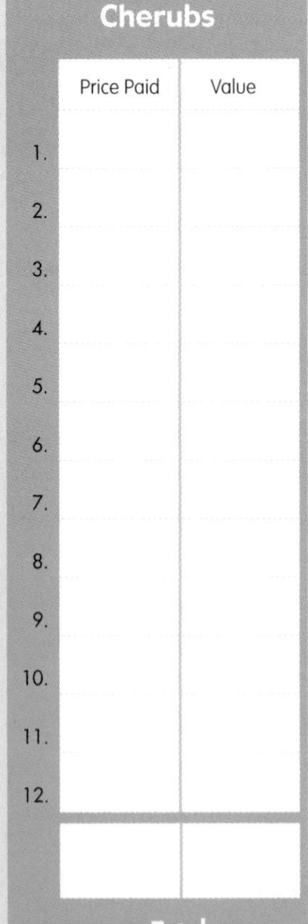

Cherubs

	Price Paid	Value
1.		
2.		
3.		
4.		
5.		
6.		
7.		
8.		
9.		
10.		
11.		
12.		
Totals		

7

The Easter Trail
10740 • 3 7/8″
Issued: 1999 • Current
Market Value: $____

8

Easy Rider
DC414 • 3 3/4″
Issued: 1996 • Susp.: 1997
Market Value: $22

9
New

Egg Hunt
11557 • 4″
Issued: 2001 • Current
Market Value: $____

10

Eggstra Special
10063 • 3 5/8″
Issued: 1997 • Current
Market Value: $____

11

El Senor Es Mi Pastor
Bendiciones
11258 • 3 1/4″
Issued: 2000 • Susp.: 2000
Market Value: N/E

12

Elephant Pal
Dreamsicles Pals
10344 • 2 3/8″
Issued: 1998 • Current
Market Value: $____

1

Embrace The New Day
11407 • 4 ⅝"
Issued: 2000 • Current
Market Value: $____

2

En Todo Da Gracias
Bendiciones
11256 • 3 ⅜"
Issued: 2000 • Susp.: 2000
Market Value: N/E

3

Eres Mi Rayito Del Sol
Notas De Amor
11250 • 2 ¾"
Issued: 2000 • Current
Market Value: $____

4

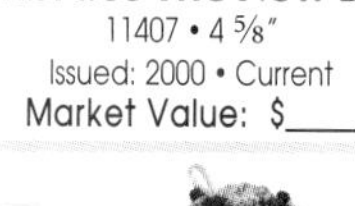

Es Mas Apreciado Dar Que Recibar
Bendiciones
11255 • 2 ⅝"
Issued: 2000 • Current
Market Value: $____

5

Faith (blue)
10627 • 3"
Issued: 1998 • Current
Market Value: $____

6

Faith (pink)
10527 • 3"
Issued: 1998 • Current
Market Value: $____

7

Fall Friends
11438 • 3 ⅜"
Issued: 2000 • Current
Market Value: $____

8

Fast Friends
10729 • 3 ¾"
Issued: 1999 • Current
Market Value: $____

9

Feet First
DC320 • 3 ¼"
Issued: 1996 • Susp.: 1997
Market Value: $19

10

Felicity
10174 • 2 ½"
Issued: 1997 • Susp.: 1999
Market Value: N/E

11

A Few Good Men
10717 • 3 ¼"
Issued: 1999 • Current
Market Value: $____

12
New

Filled With Love
11579 • 5 ¾"
Issued: 2001 • Current
Market Value: $____

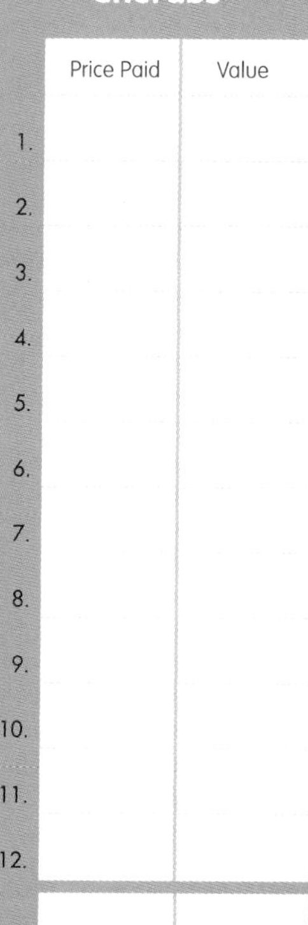

Cherubs

	Price Paid	Value
1.		
2.		
3.		
4.		
5.		
6.		
7.		
8.		
9.		
10.		
11.		
12.		
Totals		

1

Finger Food
DC083 • 2 ¼″
Issued: 1995 • Susp.: 1999
Market Value: N/E

2

Fire Drill
10521 • 3″
Issued: 1998 • Current
Market Value: $____

3

Firefighter
All Stars
11085 • 2 ¾″
Issued: 2000 • Current
Market Value: $____

4

First Born
10130 • 4 ⅜″
Issued: 1997 • Current
Market Value: $____

5

First Communion
DC301 • 3 ¾″
Issued: 1995 • Susp.: 1997
Market Value: $30

6
New

First Kiss
11528 • 3 ¾″
Issued: 2001 • Current
Market Value: $____

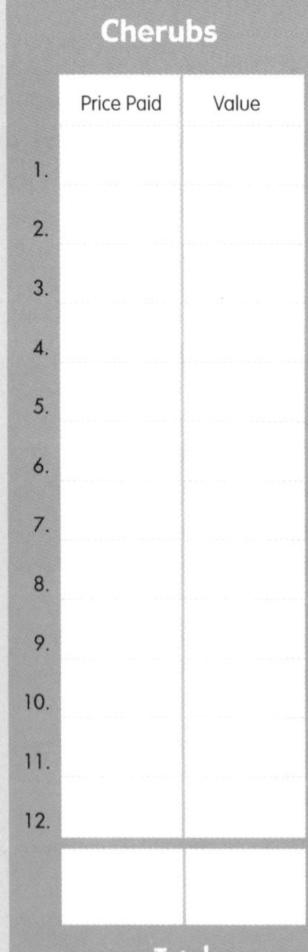

Cherubs

	Price Paid	Value
1.		
2.		
3.		
4.		
5.		
6.		
7.		
8.		
9.		
10.		
11.		
12.		
Totals		

7

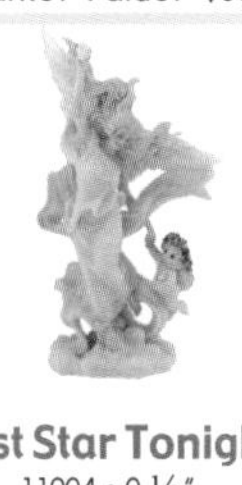

First Star Tonight
11094 • 9 ½″
Issued: 2000 • Current
Market Value: $____

8

First Steps
10990 • 4 ½″
Issued: 2000 • Current
Market Value: $____

9

Flower Power
Early Release – Summer 1999
10792 • 3 ½″
Issued: 2000 • Current
Market Value: $____

10

Flute
Band Of Angels
11197 • 2 ¾″
Issued: 2000 • Current
Market Value: $____

11

Follow Me
10050 • 4 ¼″
Issued: 1997 • Retired: 1998
Market Value: $33

12

For God So Loved The World
Our Daily Blessings
10690 • 3 ¼″
Issued: 1999 • Current
Market Value: $____

1

Original 29

Forever Friends
DC102 (5102) • 4 ½"
Issued: 1991 • Retired: 1994
Market Value: $52

2

Forever Friends
Expressions
10276 • 3 ¾"
Issued: 1998 • Current
Market Value: $____

3

Forever Friends
Love Notes
11208 • 2 ¾"
Issued: 2000 • Current
Market Value: $____

4

Original 29

Forever Yours
DC110 (5110) • 10"
Issued: 1991 • Retired: 1995
Market Value: $86

5

Forget Me Not
DC325 • 2 ¼"
Issued: 1996 • Current
Market Value: $____

6

Forty Winks
DC233 • 3 ½"
Issued: 1995 • Susp.: 1997
Market Value: $27

7

Fountain Treat
Early Release – Fall 1997
10244 • 5"
Issued: TBA • Current
Market Value: $____

8

Free Bird
DC234 • 3 ¾"
Issued: 1995 • Susp.: 1997
Market Value: $20

9

A Friend Loveth At All Times
Our Daily Blessings
10688 • 2 ¾"
Issued: 1999 • Current
Market Value: $____

10

Photo Unavailable

Friends Are Forever
Harris Communications Exclusive
10864 • N/A
Issued: 2000 • Current
Market Value: $____

11

Friendship Cherubs (set/2)
DC175 • 2"
Issued: 1994 • Retired: 1999
Market Value: $17

12

The Frog Prince
10765 • 4 ⅜"
Issued: 1999 • Susp.: 2000
Market Value: N/E

	Price Paid	Value
1.		
2.		
3.		
4.		
5.		
6.		
7.		
8.		
9.		
10.		
11.		
12.		
Totals		

1

From The Garden
11052 • 14"
Issued: 2000 • Current
Market Value: $____

2

From The Heart
10116 • 2 ½"
Issued: 1997 • Current
Market Value: $____

3

Garden Stroll
11054 • 13 ½"
Issued: 2000 • Current
Market Value: $____

4

Gecko Guava
10005 • 3 ⅝"
Issued: 1996 • Susp.: 1997
Market Value: $18

5
New

Gentle Friends
11551 • 5 ½"
Issued: 2001 • Current
Market Value: $____

6

Get Better Soon
DC245 • 3"
Issued: 1995 • Susp.: 1997
Market Value: $20

7

Get Moovin'
11453 • 3 ¾"
Issued: 2000 • Current
Market Value: $____

8

Get Well Soon
DC244 • 4"
Issued: 1995 • Retired: 1997
Market Value: $21

9

Get Well Wishes
10320 • 2 ⅞"
Issued: 1998 • Susp.: 2000
Market Value: N/E

10

Giddy Up
11416 • 5 ⅜"
Issued: 2000 • Current
Market Value: $____

11

Give Us This Day Our Daily Bread
Our Daily Blessings
11068 • 3 ½"
Issued: 2000 • Current
Market Value: $____

12

Go For The Gold
DC315 • 3 ⅞"
Issued: 1996 • Susp.: 1998
Market Value: $22

Cherubs

	Price Paid	Value
1.		
2.		
3.		
4.		
5.		
6.		
7.		
8.		
9.		
10.		
11.		
12.		
Totals		

1

God Bless America
DC706 • 3 ½"
Issued: 1995 • Susp.: 1997
Market Value: $20

2

God Is Love
Our Daily Blessings
10689 • 3 ⅜"
Issued: 1999 • Current
Market Value: $____

3

God's Word
10157 • 3 ⅜"
Issued: 1997 • Current
Market Value: $____

4

Golf
All Stars
11074 • 3"
Issued: 2000 • Current
Market Value: $____

5

A.

B.

A.

B.

The Good Book
DC361 • 3 ⅜"
Issued: 1997 • Current
Market Value: **A.** Gray Bible – $____ **B.** Tan Bible – N/E

6

Good Shepherd
DC104 • 4"
Issued: 1994 • Susp.: 1996
Market Value: $35

7

Goodness Me
10160 • 2 ⅞"
Issued: 1997 • Retired: 1999
Market Value: N/E

8

Got Hugs?
Love Notes
11205 • 3"
Issued: 2000 • Current
Market Value: $____

9

Gracias
Notas De Amor
11248 • 3"
Issued: 2000 • Current
Market Value: $____

10

Color Change

The Graduate
DC135 • 5"
Issued: 1994 • Current
Market Value: $____

11

Graduation Day
DC219 • 4 ¼"
Issued: 1995 • Current
Market Value: $____

Cherubs

	Price Paid	Value
1.		
2.		
3.		
4.		
5.		
6.		
7.		
8.		
9.		
10.		
11.		
Totals		

1

Grand Old Flag
DC232 • 3″
Issued: 1995 • Susp.: 1997
Market Value: $20

2

Grandma I Love You
Expressions
10273 • 3 ¾″
Issued: 1998 • Current
Market Value: $____

3

Grandma's Attic
Cracker Barrel Exclusive
11387 • N/A
Issued: 2000 • Current
Market Value: $____

4

Grandma's Or Bust
DC227 • 4″
Issued: 1995 • Susp.: 1999
Market Value: N/E

5

Granny's Cookies
DC228 • 2 ½″
Issued: 1995 • Susp.: 1999
Market Value: $15

6
New

Great Big Hugs
11497 • 3 ¾″
Issued: 2001 • Current
Market Value: $____

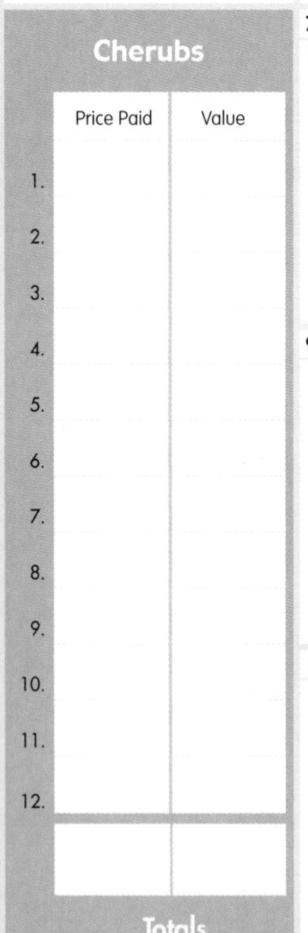

Cherubs

	Price Paid	Value
1.		
2.		
3.		
4.		
5.		
6.		
7.		
8.		
9.		
10.		
11.		
12.		
Totals		

7
New

Grown With Love
11572 • 4 ¼″
Issued: 2001 • Current
Market Value: $____

8

Guitar
Band Of Angels
11195 • 2 ¾″
Issued: 2000 • Current
Market Value: $____

9

Haley
DC321 • 4″
Issued: 1996 • Susp.: 1997
Market Value: $26

10

Hand In Hand
DC431 • 3 ½″
Issued: 1997 • Current
Market Value: $____

11

Handful Of Hearts
DC204 • 3 ½″
Issued: 1993 • Current
Market Value: $____

12
New

Handful Of Love
11513 • 2 ½″
Issued: 2001 • Current
Market Value: $____

1

Hang Loose
10004 • 3 ⅝″
Issued: 1996 • Susp.: 1997
Market Value: $27

2

Happy Birthday Cherub
DC133 • 4″
Issued: 1994 • Susp.: 1995
Market Value: $28

3

The Happy Couple
10219 • 6 ¼″
Issued: 1997 • Current
Market Value: $____

4

Happy Feet
DC164 • 3″
Issued: 1995 • Susp.: 1999
Market Value: N/E

5

Happy First Birthday
10701 • 2 ⅜″
Issued: 1999 • Susp.: 1999
Market Value: N/E

6

Happy Graduate
DC705 • 4 ¼″
Issued: 1995 • Current
Market Value: $____

7

Happy Heart
DC211 • 2 ⅞″
Issued: 1995 • Current
Market Value: $____

8

Happy Home
10733 • 3 ⅞″
Issued: 1999 • Current
Market Value: $____

9

Happy Second Birthday
10702 • 3″
Issued: 1999 • Susp.: 1999
Market Value: N/E

10

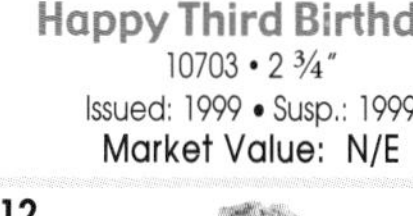

Happy Third Birthday
10703 • 2 ¾″
Issued: 1999 • Susp.: 1999
Market Value: N/E

11

Happy Thoughts
10871 • 2 ¾″
Issued: 1999 • Susp.: 2000
Market Value: N/E

12

Harvest Helper
11055 • 15″
Issued: 2000 • Current
Market Value: $____

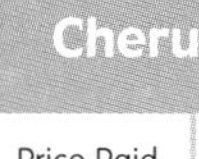

Cherubs

	Price Paid	Value
1.		
2.		
3.		
4.		
5.		
6.		
7.		
8.		
9.		
10.		
11.		
12.		
Totals		

1

Have A Heart
DC198 • 3 ¼"
Issued: 1994 • Susp.: 1997
Market Value: $24

2

Hawaiian Love Song
10003 • 5"
Issued: 1996 • Susp.: 1997
Market Value: $33

3

Hear No Evil
10040 • 5 ½"
Issued: 1997 • Current
Market Value: $____

4

Hear No Evil, See No Evil, Speak No Evil (set/3)
10098 • Various
Issued: 1997 • Current
Market Value: $____

5

Heart Hugs
Lil' Wonders
11173 • 2 ¾"
Issued: 2000 • Current
Market Value: $____

6

Heart On A String
10261 • 2 ½"
Issued: 1998 • Current
Market Value: $____

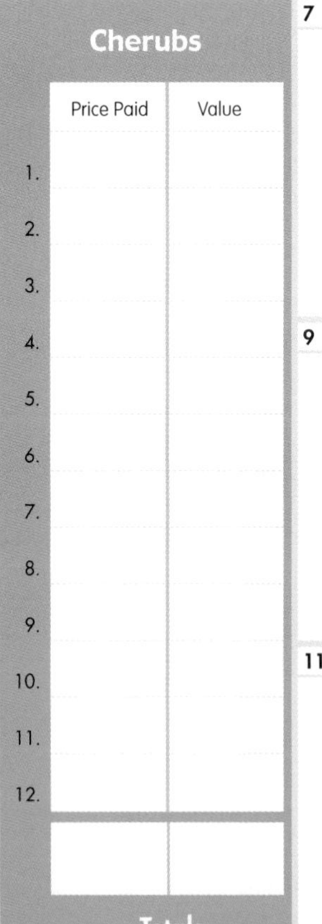

Cherubs

	Price Paid	Value
1.		
2.		
3.		
4.		
5.		
6.		
7.		
8.		
9.		
10.		
11.		
12.		
Totals		

7

Heart Throb
DC193 • 2 ¾"
Issued: 1995 • Current
Market Value: $____

8

Heart's Desire
DC090 • 2 ½"
Issued: 1995 • Susp.: 1999
Market Value: N/E

9

Hearts And Flowers
DC433 • 3 ½"
Issued: 1997 • Susp.: 1999
Market Value: N/E

10
New

Hearts & Roses
11496 • 3 ⅞"
Issued: 2001 • Current
Market Value: $____

11

Heartstrings
DC197 • 2 ½"
Issued: 1994 • Current
Market Value: $____

12

Heaven Will Provide
11005 • 4"
Issued: 2000 • Current
Market Value: $____

1

Heavenly Dreamer
DC106 (5106) • 5 ½″
Issued: 1991 • Retired: 1996
Market Value: $32

2

Heavenly Harmony
Concepts Direct Exclusive
11406 • N/A
Issued: 2000 • Current
Market Value: $____

3

Hello Dolly
DC702 • 3 ½″
Issued: 1995 • Susp.: 1997
Market Value: $21

4

Help Is Close By
Early Release – Fall 1999
10975 • 3 ½″
Issued: TBA • Current
Market Value: $____

5

Helping Hands
Early Release – Spring 1998
10506 • 3 ½″
Issued: TBA • Current
Market Value: $____

6

Here's A Hug
Love Notes
10681 • 3″
Issued: 1999 • Current
Market Value: $____

7

Here's Looking At You
DC172 • 4″
Issued: 1994 • Retired: 1995
Market Value: $42

8

Here's My Hand
10248 • 4 ¼″
Issued: 1997 • Retired: 1999
Market Value: N/E

9

Here's My Heart
10260 • 2 ½″
Issued: 1998 • Current
Market Value: $____

10

Hey Diddle Diddle
10373 • 5″
Issued: 1998 • Susp.: 1999
Market Value: N/E

11

Hey Diddle, Diddle
Nursery Rhymes Storybooks
11096 • 3 ¼″
Issued: 2000 • Susp.: 2000
Market Value: N/E

12

Hickory, Dickory, Dock
Nursery Rhymes Storybooks
11099 • 3 ¼″
Issued: 2000 • Susp.: 2000
Market Value: N/E

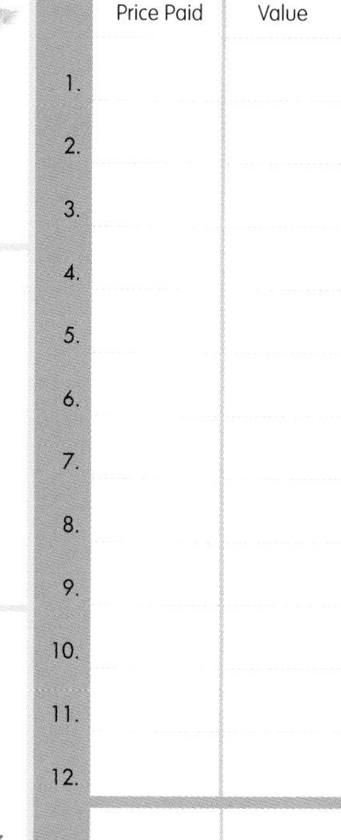

Cherubs

	Price Paid	Value
1.		
2.		
3.		
4.		
5.		
6.		
7.		
8.		
9.		
10.		
11.		
12.		
Totals		

1

High Tea
DC021 • 2″
Issued: 1999 • Susp.: 2000
Market Value: N/E

2

Hold Tight
Cracker Barrel Exclusive
DC018 • 3 5/8″
Issued: 1996 • Current
Market Value: $____

3

Holiday Magic (December)
The Calendar Collection
DC191 • 5″
Issued: 1994 • Retired: 1995
Market Value: $58

4

Holy Smoke
11401 • 7 1/4″ (wide)
Issued: 2000 • Current
Market Value: $____

5

Home Sweet Home
10381 • 3 3/4″
Issued: 1998 • Current
Market Value: $____

6
New

Honey Mine
Thinking Of You
11507 • 2″
Issued: 2001 • Current
Market Value: $____

7

Hope Has Arrived
10512 • 4 1/2″
Issued: 1998 • Current
Market Value: $____

8

Horn Of Plenty
11443 • 3 3/8″
Issued: 2000 • Current
Market Value: $____

9

Housewarming
10525 • 3 1/4″
Issued: 1998 • Susp.: 1999
Market Value: N/E

10

How Do I Love Thee?
10986 • 3″
Issued: 2000 • Current
Market Value: $____

11

Hugabye Baby
DC701 • 3″
Issued: 1995 • Retired: 1997
Market Value: $19

Cherubs

	Price Paid	Value
1.		
2.		
3.		
4.		
5.		
6.		
7.		
8.		
9.		
10.		
11.		
Totals		

1

Huge Hugs
10181 • 4 ½″
Issued: 1997 • Susp.: 1999
Market Value: N/E

2

Hugs 'N Kisses
Abbey Press Exclusive
10786 • 3″
Issued: 2000 • Current
Market Value: $____

3

Humility
10173 • 2 ⅝″
Issued: 1997 • Susp.: 1999
Market Value: N/E

4

Humpty Dumpty
10372 • 4 ¼″
Issued: 1998 • Susp.: 2000
Market Value: N/E

5

Humpty Dumpty
Nursery Rhymes Storybooks
11098 • 3 ¼″
Issued: 2000 • Current
Market Value: $____

6

Hunny Bunny
11455 • 2 ⅞″
Issued: 2000 • Current
Market Value: $____

7

Hushaby Baby
DC303 • 3 ¾″
Issued: 1995 • Susp.: 1996
Market Value: $22

8

I.C.E. Figurine (LE-2,300)
I.C.E. Exclusive
SP001 • 6″
Issued: 1994 • Retired: 1995
Market Value: $175

9

I Believe In You
Love Notes
10673 • 2 ¾″
Issued: 1999 • Current
Market Value: $____

10

I Can Read
DC151 • 2″
Issued: 1994 • Retired: 1995
Market Value: $21

11
New

I Feel Pretty
11570 • 8 ¼″
Issued: 2001 • Current
Market Value: $____

12
New

I Had A Dream
11498 • 2 ⅞″
Issued: 2001 • Current
Market Value: $____

Cherubs

	Price Paid	Value
1.		
2.		
3.		
4.		
5.		
6.		
7.		
8.		
9.		
10.		
11.		
12.		
Totals		

1

I Love Grandma
10710 • 3″
Issued: 1999 • Current
Market Value: $____

2

I Love Mommy
DC226 • 2 ¾″
Issued: 1995 • Susp.: 2000
Market Value: N/E

3

I Love Surprises
11120 • 2 ¾″
Issued: 2000 • Current
Market Value: $____

4

I Love You
DC225 • 4 ½″
Issued: 1995 • Susp.: 1999
Market Value: N/E

5

I Love You
Expressions
10271 • 3 ¾″
Issued: 1998 • Current
Market Value: $____

6

I Love You Mom
10706 • 3 ¼″
Issued: 1999 • Current
Market Value: $____

Cherubs

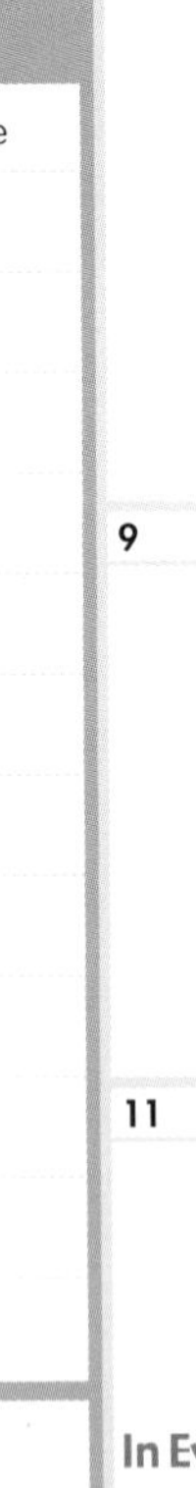

	Price Paid	Value
1.		
2.		
3.		
4.		
5.		
6.		
7.		
8.		
9.		
10.		
11.		
12.		
Totals		

7

I Miss You
Love Notes
10677 • 2 ¾″
Issued: 1999 • Current
Market Value: $____

8

I Thee Wed
11117 • 4 ½″
Issued: 2000 • Current
Market Value: $____

9

I Thought Of You
Lil' Wonders
11179 • 2 ¾″
Issued: 2000 • Current
Market Value: $____

10

Ice Dancing
Early Release – Fall 1997
10256 • 4″
Issued: 1998 • Retired: 1999
Market Value: N/E

11

In Everything Give Thanks
Our Daily Blessings
10691 • 3 ⅜″
Issued: 1999 • Current
Market Value: $____

12

In Full Bloom
10713 • 5″
Issued: 1999 • Current
Market Value: $____

1

In My Prayers
Lil' Wonders
11176 • 2 ¾"
Issued: 2000 • Current
Market Value: $____

2

Inline Skater
All Stars
11078 • 2 ¾"
Issued: 2000 • Current
Market Value: $____

3

Integrity
10175 • 2 ⅛"
Issued: 1997 • Susp.: 1999
Market Value: N/E

4

Color Change

Intervention
DC425 • 3 ¾"
Issued: 1996 • Susp.: 1998
Market Value: $20

5

Irish Eyes
DC322 • 2 ⅞"
Issued: 1996 • Susp.: 1999
Market Value: N/E

6

It Is More Blessed To Give
Our Daily Blessings
10692 • 3 ⅝"
Issued: 1999 • Current
Market Value: $____

7

It's A Boy!
Baby 2000
11029 • 3 ¾"
Issued: 2000 • Current
Market Value: $____

8

It's A Girl!
Baby 2000
11028 • 3 ¾"
Issued: 2000 • Current
Market Value: $____

9

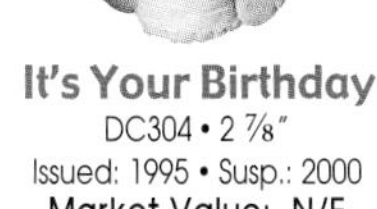

It's Your Birthday
DC304 • 2 ⅞"
Issued: 1995 • Susp.: 2000
Market Value: N/E

10

It's Your Day
10220 • 5"
Issued: 1997 • Retired: 1998
Market Value: $26

11

Jack And Jill
Nursery Rhymes Storybooks
11097 • 3 ¼"
Issued: 2000 • Susp.: 2000
Market Value: N/E

12

Jack And The Beanstalk
10376 • 4"
Issued: 1998 • Susp.: 1999
Market Value: N/E

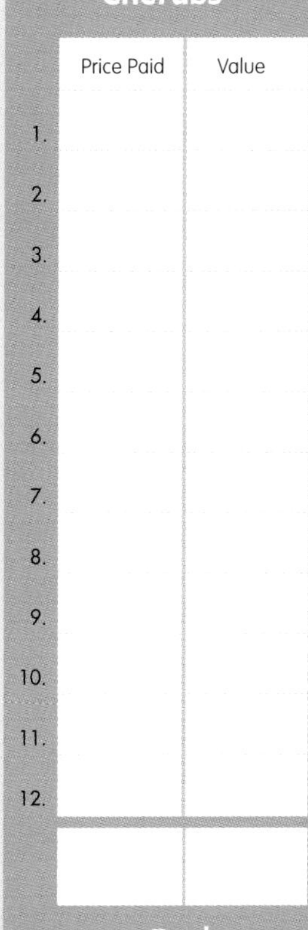

Cherubs

	Price Paid	Value
1.		
2.		
3.		
4.		
5.		
6.		
7.		
8.		
9.		
10.		
11.		
12.		
Totals		

1

Jack Be Nimble
Nursery Rhymes Storybooks
11100 • 3 ¼″
Issued: 2000 • Susp.: 2000
Market Value: N/E

2

Jack-In-The-Box
10722 • 2 ¾″
Issued: 1999 • Current
Market Value: $____

3

Joyful Gathering
DC231 • 5″
Issued: 1994 • Susp.: 1997
Market Value: N/E

4

Color Change

Joyful Noise
DC409 • 3 ⅞″
Issued: 1996 • Susp.: 1997
Market Value: $26

5

Jumping Jack
10374 • 4″
Issued: 1998 • Current
Market Value: $____

6

Just For You
Love Notes
10679 • 2 ¾″
Issued: 1999 • Current
Market Value: $____

Cherubs

	Price Paid	Value
1.		
2.		
3.		
4.		
5.		
6.		
7.		
8.		
9.		
10.		
11.		
12.		
Totals		

7

Just Like Mommy
Early Release – Fall 1999
10866 • 3″
Issued: 2000 • Current
Market Value: $____

8

Just Married
10535 • 3 ¾″
Issued: 1998 • Current
Market Value: $____

9

Key To My Heart
10633 • 2 ⅜″
Issued: 1999 • Current
Market Value: $____

10

Keyboard
Band Of Angels
11199 • 2 ¾″
Issued: 2000 • Current
Market Value: $____

11

Kindergarten Cherub
10724 • 3 ½″
Issued: 1999 • Susp.: 2000
Market Value: N/E

12

King Of The Jungle
10183 • 4 ¼″
Issued: 1997 • Susp.: 1999
Market Value: N/E

1

A Kiss For Momma
DC402 • 3"
Issued: 1995 • Current
Market Value: $____

2

A Kiss In Time
DC309 • 4"
Issued: 1995 • Susp.: 1997
Market Value: $27

3

Kiss, Kiss
DC213 • 2"
Issued: 1995 • Susp.: 2000
Market Value: N/E

4

Kisses 'N Wishes
11212 • 3"
Issued: 2000 • Current
Market Value: $____

5

Kisses For Sale
10643 • 3 7/8"
Issued: 1999 • Current
Market Value: $____

6

Kitty And Me
DC051 • 3"
Issued: 1994 • Susp.: 1997
Market Value: $17

7

Kitty Pal
Dreamsicles Pals
10343 • 2 3/8"
Issued: 1998 • Current
Market Value: $____

8

Lady Bug
Early Release – Fall 1998
10595 • 3 1/4"
Issued: 1999 • Current
Market Value: $____

9

Lambie Pal
Dreamsicles Pals
10336 • 2 3/8"
Issued: 1998 • Current
Market Value: $____

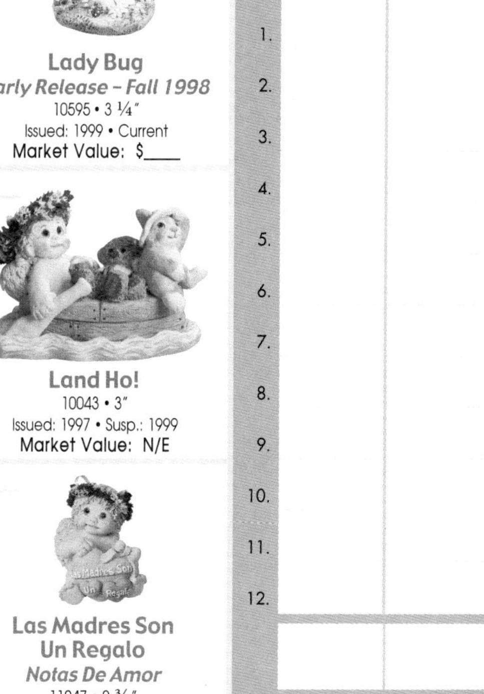

10

Land Ho!
10043 • 3"
Issued: 1997 • Susp.: 1999
Market Value: N/E

11

Language Of Love
11062 • 3 3/4"
Issued: 2000 • Current
Market Value: $____

12

Las Madres Son Un Regalo
Notas De Amor
11247 • 2 3/4"
Issued: 2000 • Current
Market Value: $____

Cherubs

	Price Paid	Value
1.		
2.		
3.		
4.		
5.		
6.		
7.		
8.		
9.		
10.		
11.		
12.		
Totals		

1

Let Your Light So Shine Before Men
Our Daily Blessings
11067 • 3 ¼″
Issued: 2000 • Current
Market Value: $____

2

Let's Bee Friends
10730 • 2 ¾″
Issued: 1999 • Current
Market Value: $____

3

Let's Chat
10735 • 3 ¼″
Issued: 1999 • Current
Market Value: $____

4

Let's Eat
Early Release – Fall 1997
10252 • 4″
Issued: TBA • Current
Market Value: $____

5

Let's Play Fetch
DC237 • 4 ½″
Issued: 1995 • Susp.: 1997
Market Value: $23

6

Let's Talk
11124 • 3 ¾″
Issued: 2000 • Current
Market Value: $____

Cherubs

	Price Paid	Value
1.		
2.		
3.		
4.		
5.		
6.		
7.		
8.		
9.		
10.		
11.		
12.		
Totals		

7

Life Is Good
DC119 (5119) • 5 ¼″
Issued: 1992 • Retired: 1996
Market Value: $32

8

Lily
Dreamsicles Garden
10552 • 3 ½″
Issued: 1998 • Current
Market Value: $____

9

Little Bo Peep
10375 • 3 ⅞″
Issued: 1998 • Susp.: 2000
Market Value: N/E

10

Little Cupid
DC212 • 2″
Issued: 1995 • Susp.: 2000
Market Value: N/E

11

Little Darlin'
DC146 • 2 ½″
Issued: 1992 • Retired: 1995
Market Value: $20

12
New

Little Ducky
11553 • 4 ½″
Issued: 2001 • Current
Market Value: $____

1

Little Leaguer
10366 • 3 1/8"
Issued: 1998 • Susp.: 2000
Market Value: N/E

2

Little One
10033 • 3 7/8"
Issued: 1997 • Susp.: 1999
Market Value: N/E

3

Little Star Chandler
10522 • 3 1/4"
Issued: 1998 • Susp.: 1999
Market Value: N/E

4

Littlest Angel
DC143 • 2 1/2"
Issued: 1992 • Retired: 1995
Market Value: $26

5

Logo Sculpture
DC003 • 7" (wide)
Issued: 1995 • Susp.: 1999
Market Value: $40

6

Look Who's New
11130 • 4 3/4"
Issued: 2000 • Current
Market Value: $____

7

The Lord Is My Shepherd
Our Daily Blessings
10686 • 3 1/4"
Issued: 1999 • Current
Market Value: $____

8

Los Bebes Son Preciosos
Notas De Amor
11244 • 2 7/8"
Issued: 2000 • Current
Market Value: $____

9

Lots Of Love
DC403 • 3"
Issued: 1995 • Susp.: 1999
Market Value: N/E

10
New

Love Birds
11492 • 4 1/8"
Issued: 2001 • Current
Market Value: $____

11

Love In Bloom (May)
The Calendar Collection
DC184 • 5"
Issued: 1994 • Retired: 1995
Market Value: $52

12
New

Love Is In Bloom
11504 • 2 1/2"
Issued: 2001 • Current
Market Value: $____

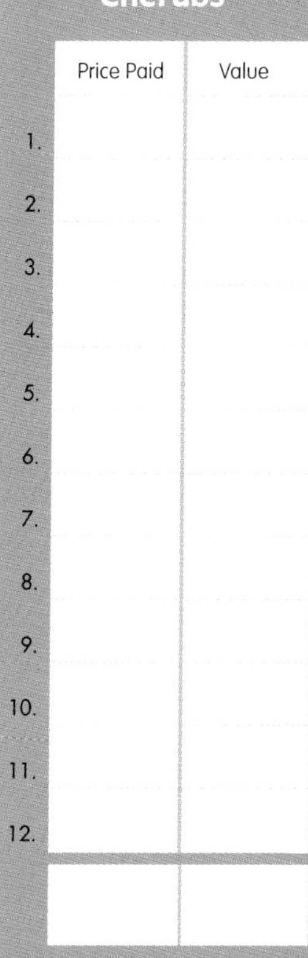

Cherubs

	Price Paid	Value
1.		
2.		
3.		
4.		
5.		
6.		
7.		
8.		
9.		
10.		
11.		
12.		
Totals		

1

Love Is In The Air
10992 • 3 ¼"
Issued: 2000 • Current
Market Value: $____

2

Love Letters
DC430 • 3 ¼"
Issued: 1997 • Susp.: 1999
Market Value: $25

3

Love Me Do
DC194 • 4 ¾"
Issued: 1995 • Retired: 1998
Market Value: $21

4

Love My Bunny
10367 • 4"
Issued: 1998 • Susp.: 1999
Market Value: N/E

5

Love My Kitty
DC130 • 3 ¾"
Issued: 1993 • Retired: 1997
Market Value: $25

6

Love My Lamb
10368 • 4 ½"
Issued: 1998 • Susp.: 1999
Market Value: N/E

Cherubs

	Price Paid	Value
1.		
2.		
3.		
4.		
5.		
6.		
7.		
8.		
9.		
10.		
11.		
12.		
Totals		

7

Love My Puppy
DC131 • 3 ¾"
Issued: 1993 • Retired: 1997
Market Value: $28

8

Love My Teddy
DC132 • 4"
Issued: 1993 • Retired: 1997
Market Value: $25

9

Love One Another
Our Daily Blessings
10687 • 3"
Issued: 1999 • Current
Market Value: $____

10

Love Poems
10637 • 3 ¼"
Issued: 1999 • Current
Market Value: $____

11

Love To Mom
DC717 • 2 ⅜"
Issued: 1997 • Current
Market Value: $____

12

Love You Bunches
11051 • 8 ¼"
Issued: 2000 • Current
Market Value: $____

1
New

Love You Bunches
11575 • 2 ⅝″
Issued: 2001 • Current
Market Value: $____

2

Love You Sew
10263 • 3″
Issued: 1998 • Retired: 1999
Market Value: N/E

3

Love's Little Messenger
10988 • 3 ¾″
Issued: 2000 • Current
Market Value: $____

4

Loverly
DC714 • 2 ⅝″
Issued: 1996 • Current
Market Value: $____

5

Loves Me, Loves Me Not
10644 • 3 ⅝″
Issued: 1999 • Susp.: 2000
Market Value: N/E

6

Lullaby
DC173 • 10″ (wide)
Issued: 1994 • Susp.: 1997
Market Value: $112

7

Lyrical Lute
10169 • 6 ½″
Issued: 1997 • Retired: 1998
Market Value: $30

8

Make A Joyful Noise
Our Daily Blessings
11071 • 4″
Issued: 2000 • Current
Market Value: $____

9

Make A Wish
DC118 • 5 ½″
Issued: 1992 • Susp.: 1999
Market Value: N/E

10

Making A Cake
DC418 • 4 ¼″
Issued: 1996 • Susp.: 1999
Market Value: N/E

11

Mama's Little Helper
10708 • 4″
Issued: 1999 • Current
Market Value: $____

12

Mary Contrary
10766 • 4″
Issued: 1999 • Susp.: 2000
Market Value: N/E

Cherubs

	Price Paid	Value
1.		
2.		
3.		
4.		
5.		
6.		
7.		
8.		
9.		
10.		
11.		
12.		
Totals		

1

Mary Had A Little Lamb
Nursery Rhymes Storybooks
11101 • 3 ¼"
Issued: 2000 • Susp.: 2000
Market Value: N/E

2

Matchmaker
10327 • 5 ⅝"
Issued: 1998 • Current
Market Value: $____

3

Me And My Shadow
DC116 • 5 ½"
Issued: 1993 • Retired: 1996
Market Value: $36

4

Me Haces Falta
Notas De Amor
11241 • 2 ¾"
Issued: 2000 • Current
Market Value: $____

5

Me Importas Tu
Notas De Amor
11242 • 3"
Issued: 2000 • Current
Market Value: $____

6

Mejores Amigos
Notas De Amor
11249 • 2 ¾"
Issued: 2000 • Current
Market Value: $____

7

Mellow Cello
10170 • 9 ½"
Issued: 1997 • Retired: 1998
Market Value: $40

8

Mermaid's Gift
10002 • 4"
Issued: 1996 • Susp.: 1997
Market Value: $46

9

A Message Just For You
11121 • 4 ½"
Issued: 2000 • Current
Market Value: $____

10
New

Message To Grandma
11424 • 3 ¾"
Issued: 2001 • Current
Market Value: $____

11
New

Message To Mom
11423 • 3 ¾"
Issued: 2001 • Current
Market Value: $____

12
New

Message To You
11426 • 3 ¾"
Issued: 2001 • Current
Market Value: $____

Cherubs

	Price Paid	Value
1.		
2.		
3.		
4.		
5.		
6.		
7.		
8.		
9.		
10.		
11.		
12.		
Totals		

1

Mini Ark – Elephant
10889 • 3 ¾"
Issued: 1999 • Susp.: 2000
Market Value: N/E

2

Mini Ark – Giraffe
10890 • 3 ¾"
Issued: 1999 • Susp.: 2000
Market Value: N/E

3

Mini Ark – Zebra
10891 • 3 ¾"
Issued: 1999 • Current
Market Value: $____

4

Mini Carousel – Bunny
10885 • 3 ¾"
Issued: 1999 • Current
Market Value: $____

5

Mini Carousel – Peacock
10887 • 3 ¾"
Issued: 1999 • Susp.: 2000
Market Value: N/E

6

Mini Carousel – Pony
10886 • 3 ¾"
Issued: 1999 • Current
Market Value: $____

7

Original 29

Mischief Maker
DC105 (5105) • 5"
Issued: 1991 • Retired: 1996
Market Value: $32

8

Miss Morningstar
DC141 • 7 ¼"
Issued: 1993 • Retired: 1996
Market Value: $50

9

Modesty
10870 • 3 ½"
Issued: 1999 • Susp.: 2000
Market Value: N/E

10

Mom Equals Love
11015 • 3"
Issued: 2000 • Current
Market Value: $____

11

Mom Has The Touch
11014 • 3 ¾"
Issued: 2000 • Current
Market Value: $____

12

Mom's Favorite
Early Release – Spring 1999
10805 • 3 ½"
Issued: 2000 • Current
Market Value: $____

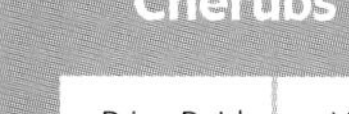

Cherubs

	Price Paid	Value
1.		
2.		
3.		
4.		
5.		
6.		
7.		
8.		
9.		
10.		
11.		
12.		
Totals		

1

Mom's Garden
10328 • 4 ½″
Issued: 1998 • Current
Market Value: $____

2
New

Mom's Special Rainbow
11573 • 4 ¼″
Issued: 2001 • Current
Market Value: $____

3

Mom's The Best
DC428 • 2 ⅜″
Issued: 1997 • Current
Market Value: $____

4

Mommy & Me
11433 • 3 ⅞″
Issued: 2000 • Current
Market Value: $____

5

Moms Are A Gift
Love Notes
10682 • 2 ⅞″
Issued: 1999 • Current
Market Value: $____

6
New

Moms Make Days Bright
11577 • 2 ¾″
Issued: 2001 • Current
Market Value: $____

7

Moms Rule
11012 • 3 ⅝″
Issued: 2000 • Current
Market Value: $____

8

Monkey Pal
Dreamsicles Pals
10337 • 2 ⅝″
Issued: 1998 • Current
Market Value: $____

9

Moon Dance
DC210 • 5 ½″
Issued: 1994 • Retired: 1997
Market Value: $43

10

Moonglow
DC235 • 3 ¾″
Issued: 1995 • Susp.: 1997
Market Value: $20

11

Moonstruck
Early Release – Fall 1997
10384 (10127) • 3 ⅜″
Issued: 1998 • Susp.: 1999
Market Value: N/E

12

Mother Goose
10764 • 4 ¾″
Issued: 1999 • Current
Market Value: $____

Cherubs

	Price Paid	Value
1.		
2.		
3.		
4.		
5.		
6.		
7.		
8.		
9.		
10.		
11.		
12.		
Totals		

1

Mother I Love You
10272 • 3 ¾"
Issued: 1998 • Current
Market Value: $____

2

Mother's Helper
Early Release – Fall 1997
10141 • 3 ⅛"
Issued: 1998 • Current
Market Value: $____

3
New

Mother's Little Angels
11582 • 7 ½" (wide)
Issued: 2001 • Current
Market Value: $____

4

Mother's Love
10881 • 3"
Issued: 1999 • Current
Market Value: $____

5

Mother-To-Be
10155 • 5 ¾"
Issued: 1997 • Susp.: 2000
Market Value: N/E

6

Music Makers
10382 • 3 ¼"
Issued: 1998 • Susp.: 1999
Market Value: N/E

7

My Angel Baby
Love Notes
11206 • 3"
Issued: 2000 • Current
Market Value: $____

8

My First Reader
DC087 • 3"
Issued: 1995 • Susp.: 1999
Market Value: N/E

9

My Funny Valentine
DC201 (5132) • 5 ½"
Issued: 1992 • Susp.: 1993
Market Value: $70

10
New

My Grandma
Thinking Of You
11506 • 2 ½"
Issued: 2001 • Current
Market Value: $____

11

My Love
Thinking Of You
11509 • 2 ⅜"
Issued: 2001 • Current
Market Value: $____

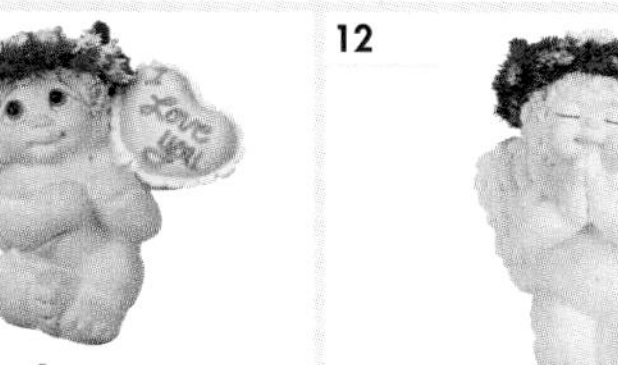

12

My Prayer
DC121 • 5 ½"
Issued: 1992 • Current
Market Value: $____

Cherubs

	Price Paid	Value
1.		
2.		
3.		
4.		
5.		
6.		
7.		
8.		
9.		
10.		
11.		
12.		
Totals		

1

My Shining Star
11172 • 2 ¾"
Issued: 2000 • Current
Market Value: $____

2

Nature's Bounty (August)
The Calendar Collection
DC187 • 4"
Issued: 1994 • Retired: 1995
Market Value: $52

3

Newborn Cherub
DC168 • 3" (wide)
Issued: 1994 • Susp.: 1996
Market Value: $33

4

Newlyweds
10534 • 4 ½"
Issued: 1998 • Current
Market Value: $____

5

'Nite 'Nite
DC238 • 4 ½"
Issued: 1995 • Susp.: 1997
Market Value: $23

6

No Place Like Home
11435 • 3 ¾"
Issued: 2000 • Current
Market Value: $____

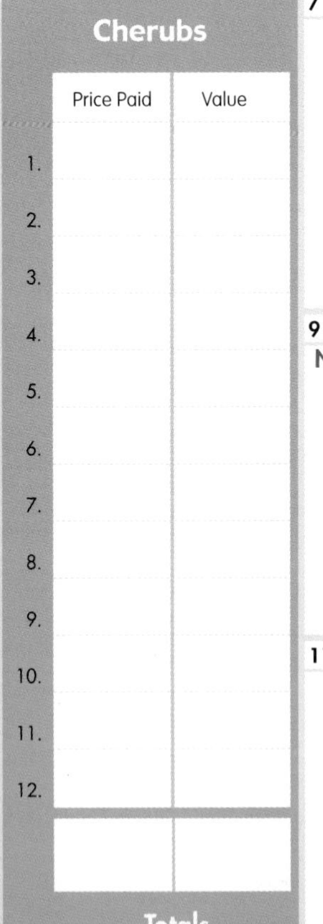

Cherubs

	Price Paid	Value
1.		
2.		
3.		
4.		
5.		
6.		
7.		
8.		
9.		
10.		
11.		
12.		
Totals		

7

Now Give Thanks (November)
The Calendar Collection
DC190 • 4 ¾"
Issued: 1994 • Retired: 1995
Market Value: $55

8

Color Change

Now I Lay Me . . .
DC406 • 4"
Issued: 1995 • Susp.: 1999
Market Value: $73

9

New

Number One Mom
11576 • 3 ¼"
Issued: 2001 • Current
Market Value: $____

10

Nurse
All Stars
11081 • 2 ¾"
Issued: 2000 • Current
Market Value: $____

11

A Nurse's Care
11422 • 3 ⅝"
Issued: 2000 • Current
Market Value: $____

12

Nursery Rhyme
DC229 • 7"
Issued: 1995 • Susp.: 1995
Market Value: $68

1

Ocean's Call
DC317 • 2 ½″
Issued: 1996 • Susp.: 2000
Market Value: N/E

2

Old Friends Are Best
11409 • 3 ¾″
Issued: 2000 • Current
Market Value: $____

3

On Bended Knee
DC196 • 2 ¼″
Issued: 1994 • Susp.: 2000
Market Value: N/E

4
New

On The Right Track
11580 • 4 ¼″
Issued: 2001 • Current
Market Value: $____

5

One Day At A Time
11063 • 4 ¼″
Issued: 2000 • Current
Market Value: $____

6

One World
DC306 • 3 ⅞″
Issued: 1995 • Retired: 1998
Market Value: $32

7

Our Little Angel
11194 • 4 ¼″
Issued: 2000 • Current
Market Value: $____

8
Color Change

Over The Rainbow
DC209 • 6″
Issued: 1994 • Susp.: 1997
Market Value: $26

9
P. S. I Love You
DC203 • 2 ¼″
Issued: 1993 • Retired: 1997
Market Value: $20

10
Panda Pal
Dreamsicles Pals
10334 • 2 ¼″
Issued: 1998 • Current
Market Value: $____

11

Pansies Carousel Horse
11477 • 4″
Issued: 2000 • Current
Market Value: $____

12

Patches
10711 • 3 ¼″
Issued: 1999 • Current
Market Value: $____

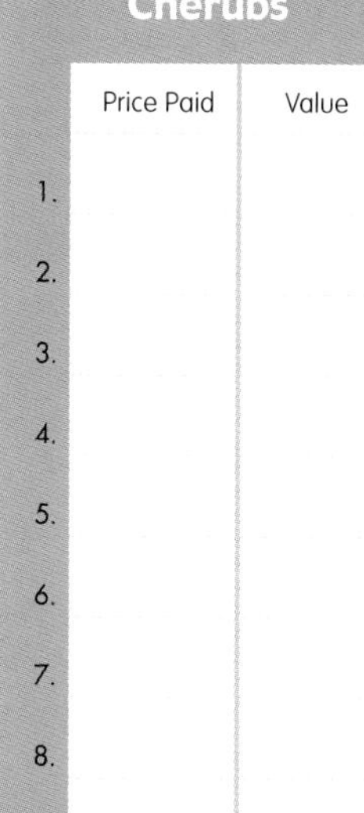

Cherubs

	Price Paid	Value
1.		
2.		
3.		
4.		
5.		
6.		
7.		
8.		
9.		
10.		
11.		
12.		
Totals		

1

Peaceful Dreams
10331 • 4 ¾"
Issued: 1998 • Retired: 1999
Market Value: N/E

2

Peacemaker
North Pole City Exclusive
10257 • 3 ¾"
Issued: 1997 • Current
Market Value: $____

3

Peacemaker II "United We Stand"
North Pole City Exclusive
10511 • 4 ⅛"
Issued: 1998 • Current
Market Value: $____

4

Penguin Pal
Dreamsicles Pals
10339 • 2 ⅝"
Issued: 1998 • Current
Market Value: $____

5

Penny For Your Thoughts
11178 • 2 ¾"
Issued: 2000 • Current
Market Value: $____

6

Pensando En Ti
Notas De Amor
11245 • 2 ¾"
Issued: 2000 • Susp.: 2000
Market Value: N/E

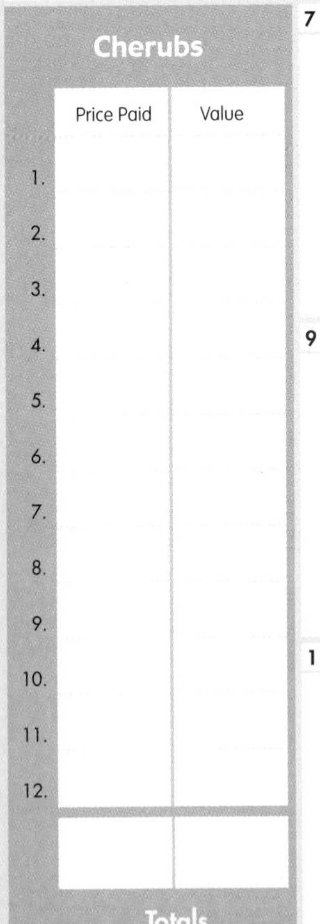

Cherubs

	Price Paid	Value
1.		
2.		
3.		
4.		
5.		
6.		
7.		
8.		
9.		
10.		
11.		
12.		
Totals		

7

Pep Rally
10726 • 3 ⅛"
Issued: 1999 • Current
Market Value: $____

8

Piano Lesson
DC413 • 5 ½"
Issued: 1995 • Susp.: 1997
Market Value: $53

9

Piece Of My Heart
DC195 • 3"
Issued: 1995 • Current
Market Value: $____

10

Piggy Pal
Dreamsicles Pals
10345 • 2 ¼"
Issued: 1998 • Current
Market Value: $____

11

Pillow Talk
11017 • 3"
Issued: 2000 • Current
Market Value: $____

12

Pink Logo Sculpture
DC001 • 6 ½" (wide)
Issued: 1992 • Retired: 1994
Market Value: $55

1

Pint-Sized Parade
DC323 • 3"
Issued: 1996 • Current
Market Value: $____

2

Playground Pony
10319 • 5 3/8"
Issued: 1998 • Current
Market Value: $____

3

Playmates
DC020 • 1 3/4"
Issued: 1996 • Current
Market Value: $____

4

Please Be Mine
10259 • 3 1/2"
Issued: 1998 • Retired: 1999
Market Value: N/E

5

A. POETRY IN MOTION Special Edition

B. POTERY IN MOTION Special Edition

Poetry In Motion (Special Edition)
DC113 • 5"
Issued: 1995 • Retired: 1997
Market Value: A. "Poetry" – $110 B. "Potery" – N/E

6

Police
All Stars
11083 • 2 3/4"
Issued: 2000 • Current
Market Value: $____

7

Pony Ride
11452 • 3 1/2"
Issued: 2000 • Current
Market Value: $____

8

Pool Pals (July)
The Calendar Collection
DC186 • 3 3/4"
Issued: 1994 • Retired: 1995
Market Value: $56

9

Poppy
Dreamsicles Garden
10783 • 3 7/8"
Issued: 1999 • Current
Market Value: $____

10

Pot Of Gold
Early Release – Fall 1997
10243 • 4 1/8"
Issued: TBA • Current
Market Value: $____

11

Prairie Pals
11436 • 4 1/8"
Issued: 2000 • Current
Market Value: $____

	Price Paid	Value
1.		
2.		
3.		
4.		
5.		
6.		
7.		
8.		
9.		
10.		
11.		
Totals		

1

Pray For Peace
10356 • 5″
Issued: 1998 • Susp.: 1999
Market Value: N/E

2

Prayer Time
DC148 • 3″
Issued: 1996 • Susp.: 1999
Market Value: N/E

3

Pretty Baby
11402 • 7″
Issued: 2000 • Current
Market Value: $____

4

Pretty In Pink
10987 • 3 1/2″
Issued: 2000 • Current
Market Value: $____

5

Pretty Posies
Early Release – Fall 1997
10140 • 3 1/8″
Issued: 1998 • Current
Market Value: $____

6

Prima Ballerina
10051 • 4″
Issued: 1997 • Susp.: 1999
Market Value: N/E

7

Pues Dios Asi Amo Al Mundo
Bendiciones
11257 • 3 1/4″
Issued: 2000 • Susp.: 2000
Market Value: N/E

8

Pumpkin Patch Cherub
DC206 • 3″
Issued: 1993 • Susp.: 2000
Market Value: N/E

9

Punkin Pal
11448 • 2 5/8″
Issued: 2000 • Current
Market Value: $____

10

Punkin Party
11446 • 3 1/4″
Issued: 2000 • Current
Market Value: $____

11

Punkin Patch
11447 • 3 3/4″
Issued: 2000 • Current
Market Value: $____

12

Puppy And Me
DC052 • 3″
Issued: 1994 • Susp.: 1997
Market Value: $17

Cherubs

	Price Paid	Value
1.		
2.		
3.		
4.		
5.		
6.		
7.		
8.		
9.		
10.		
11.		
12.		
Totals		

1

Purr-fect Pals
DC239 • 4 ½″
Issued: 1995 • Susp.: 1997
Market Value: $22

2

Quiet Time
11412 • 3 ½″
Issued: 2000 • Current
Market Value: $____

3

Ragamuffin
DC310 • 2 ¼″
Issued: 1995 • Susp.: 1999
Market Value: $____

4

Rainbow Rider
DC236 • 4″
Issued: 1995 • Susp.: 1997
Market Value: $23

5

A. © 1995 Cast Art Industries, Inc. DC311 Dreamsicles® "Rainbow's End" Made in Mexico

B. © 1995 Cast Art Industries, Inc. DC311 Dreamsicles® "Ranibow's End" Made in Mexico

Rainbow's End
DC311 • 2 ¼″
Issued: 1995 • Current
Market Value: A. "Rainbow's" – $____ B. "Ranibow's" – N/E

6

Range Rider
DC305 • 4″
Issued: 1995 • Retired: 1998
Market Value: $23

7

Reach For The Stars
10720 • 4 ¼″
Issued: 1999 • Current
Market Value: $____

8

Reach For The Stars
10721 • 4 ¼″
Issued: 1999 • Current
Market Value: $____

9

Read Me A Story
DC123 • 2 ¾″
Issued: 1995 • Current
Market Value: $____

10

Ready To Roll
DC424 • 4 ¼″
Issued: 1996 • Susp.: 1999
Market Value: N/E

11

Relay For Life
10650 • 4 ⅛″
Issued: 1999 • Current
Market Value: $____

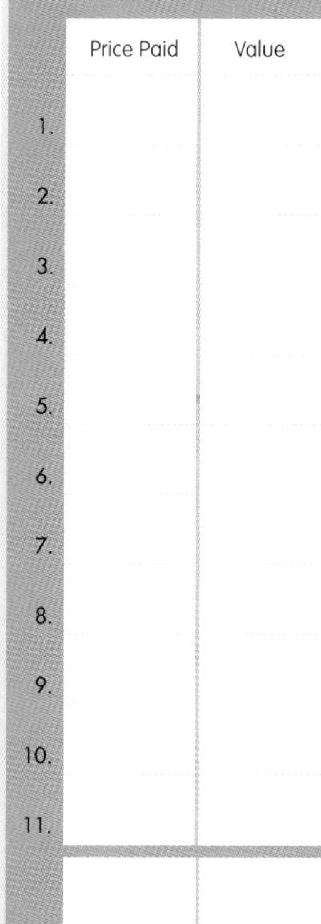

Cherubs

	Price Paid	Value
1.		
2.		
3.		
4.		
5.		
6.		
7.		
8.		
9.		
10.		
11.		
Totals		

1

Reward Yourself
11404 • 4″
Issued: 2000 • Current
Market Value: $____

2

A Ride In The Sky
11131 • 5 ½″
Issued: 2000 • Current
Market Value: $____

3

Ride Like The Wind (March)
The Calendar Collection
DC182 • 4 ½″
Issued: 1994 • Retired: 1995
Market Value: $52

4

Rising Star
Parade Of Gifts Exclusive
10516 • 4″
Issued: 1998 • Current
Market Value: $____

5

Rock-A-Bye
DC158 • 2 ¾″
Issued: 1995 • Susp.: 1999
Market Value: $20

6

Rock-A-Bye Baby
Early Release – Spring 1999
10788 • 3 ½″
Issued: 2000 • Current
Market Value: $____

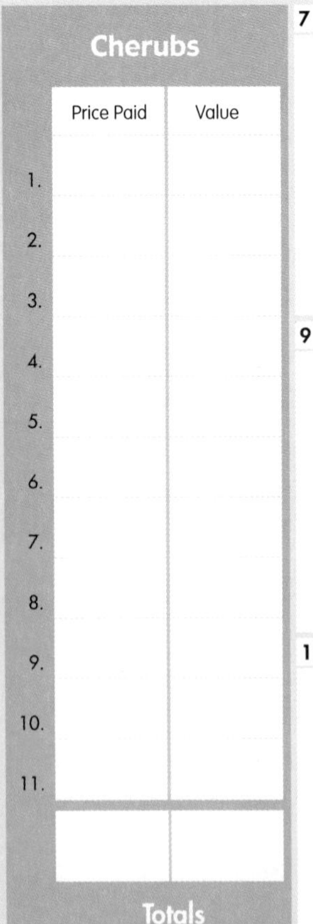

Cherubs

	Price Paid	Value
1.		
2.		
3.		
4.		
5.		
6.		
7.		
8.		
9.		
10.		
11.		
Totals		

7

Rock Away Rider
Early Release – Fall 1997
10123 • 3 ⅝″
Issued: TBA • Current
Market Value: $____

8

Rose
Dreamsicles Garden
10550 • 3 ½″
Issued: 1998 • Susp.: 2000
Market Value: $____

9

Rose Garden
DC347 • 4 ¼″
Issued: 1996 • Susp.: 1996
Market Value: $37

10

Roses Carousel Horse
11479 • 4″
Issued: 2000 • Current
Market Value: $____

11

Roses For You
10636 • 4 ½″
Issued: 1999 • Current
Market Value: $____

Rub-A-Dub-Dub
Early Release - Fall 1998
10495 • 3 ¼″
Issued: 1999 • Current
Market Value: $____

2

Saddle Up!
11066 • 5″
Issued: 2000 • Current
Market Value: $____

3

Safe In Her Arms
11092 • 6 ½″
Issued: 2000 • Current
Market Value: $____

Sailor Boy
10715 • 2 ⅞″
Issued: 1999 • Current
Market Value: $____

5

Saving For My Next Dreamsicles
11391 • N/A
Issued: 2000 • Current
Market Value: $____

6

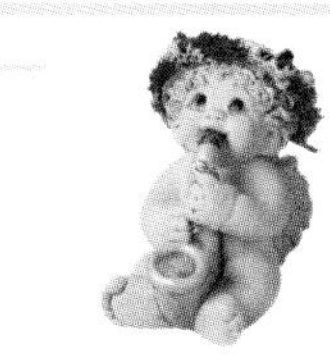

Saxophone
Band Of Angels
11198 • 2 ¾″
Issued: 2000 • Current
Market Value: $____

Say My Prayers
10878 • 6″
Issued: 1999 • Current
Market Value: $____

8

School Days (September)
The Calendar Collection
DC188 • 4 ½″
Issued: 1994 • Retired: 1995
Market Value: $52

Sealed With A Kiss
DC429 • 3 ½″
Issued: 1997 • Current
Market Value: $____

10

Searching For Hope
Fifth Avenue Exclusive
DC019 • 4 ¾″
Issued: 1997 • Retired: 1997
Market Value: $160

Seashore Surprise
11419 • 4″
Issued: 2000 • Current
Market Value: $____

12

Seat Of Honor
DC426 • 4″
Issued: 1996 • Susp.: 1999
Market Value: N/E

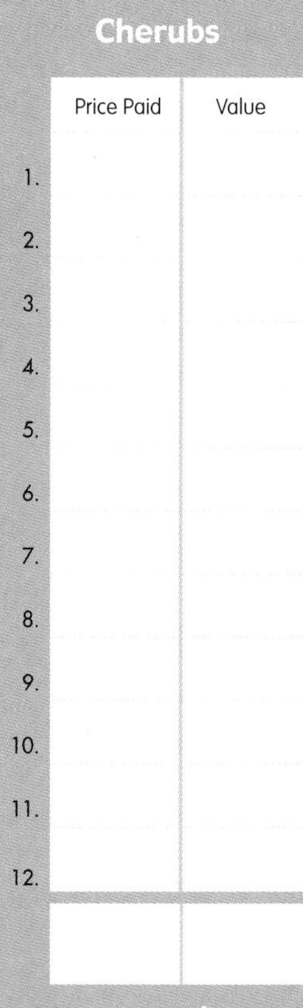

Cherubs

	Price Paid	Value
1.		
2.		
3.		
4.		
5.		
6.		
7.		
8.		
9.		
10.		
11.		
12.		
Totals		

1

See No Evil
10041 • 5 ½″
Issued: 1997 • Current
Market Value: $____

2

Serenity
10176 • 1 ⅞″
Issued: 1997 • Susp.: 1999
Market Value: N/E

3

Served With Love
Early Release – Fall 1999
10976 • 3 ¾″
Issued: TBA • Current
Market Value: $____

4

Share The Fun
DC178 • 3 ½″
Issued: 1994 • Susp.: 1997
Market Value: $25

5

Sharing
Early Release – Spring 2000
10978 • 3 ¾″
Issued: TBA • Current
Market Value: $____

6
New

She's The Best
11574 • 3 ¼″
Issued: 2001 • Current
Market Value: $____

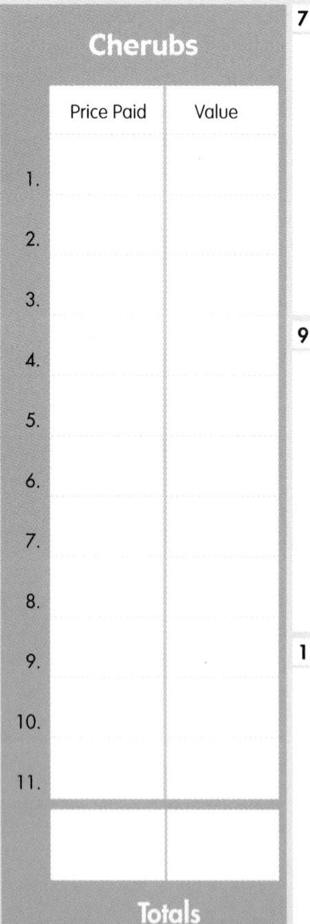

Cherubs

	Price Paid	Value
1.		
2.		
3.		
4.		
5.		
6.		
7.		
8.		
9.		
10.		
11.		
Totals		

7

Shipmates
10001 • 6″
Issued: 1996 • Susp.: 1997
Market Value: $32

8

Side By Side
DC169 • 4 ¾″
Issued: 1994 • Retired: 1995
Market Value: $47

9

Sign Of Love
10158 • 3″
Issued: 1997 • Current
Market Value: $____

10

Signing Figurine
DC074 • 3 ½″
Issued: 1997 • Current
Market Value: $____

11

Simply Pray
11123 • 4 ¼″
Issued: 2000 • Current
Market Value: $____

Cherubs

1

Sister I Love You
Expressions
10274 • 3 ¾″
Issued: 1998 • Current
Market Value: $____

2

Sisters
DC427 • 3 ⅛″
Issued: 1997 • Susp.: 2000
Market Value: N/E

3

Sisters
11431 • 3 ⅞″
Issued: 2000 • Current
Market Value: $____

4
Original 29

Sitting Pretty
DC101 (5101) • 3 ¾″
Issued: 1991 • Retired: 1996
Market Value: $25

5

Skateboard Heaven
11411 • 4 ⅜″
Issued: 2000 • Current
Market Value: $____

6
Color Change

Skater's Waltz
DC412 • 4 ½″
Issued: 1995 • Susp.: 1997
Market Value: $28

7
Color Change

Sleepover
DC421 • 4 ¾″
Issued: 1996 • Susp.: 1999
Market Value: $21

8

Sleepy Head
DC086 • 2 ¾″
Issued: 1995 • Susp.: 1999
Market Value: N/E

9
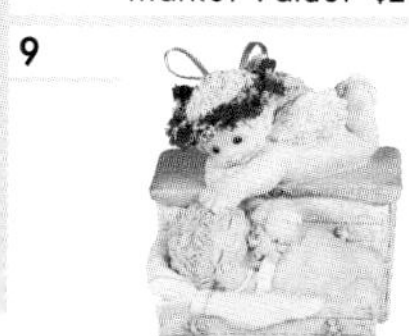

Sleepyhead
Early Release – Fall 1997
10150 • 3 ⅞″
Issued: TBA • Current
Market Value: $____

10

Sleigh Ride
DC122 • 5″
Issued: 1992 • Susp.: 1995
Market Value: $50

11
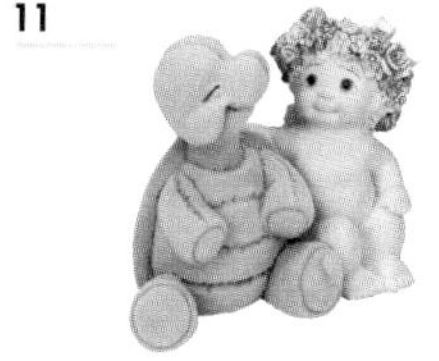

Slow But Sure
11454 • 3″
Issued: 2000 • Current
Market Value: $____

12

Slumber Party
10880 • 6″
Issued: 1999 • Current
Market Value: $____

	Price Paid	Value
1.		
2.		
3.		
4.		
5.		
6.		
7.		
8.		
9.		
10.		
11.		
12.		
Totals		

1

Color Change

Small Cherub With Hanging Ribbon
5104 • 4 ½″
Issued: 1991 • Susp.: 1992
Market Value: $90

2

Smile, Sunshine
11126 • 4 ½″
Issued: 2000 • Current
Market Value: $____

3

Snowflake
DC117 • 3 ¼″
Issued: 1994 • Susp.: 1996
Market Value: $22

4

Snuggle Baby
Baby 2000
11026 • 3″
Issued: 2000 • Current
Market Value: $____

5

Snuggle Blanket
DC082 • 2 ⅜″
Issued: 1995 • Susp.: 1999
Market Value: N/E

6

Snuggle Buddies
GCC Exclusive
DC017 • 5 ½″
Issued: 1996 • Closed: 1996
Market Value: $50

7

Soccer
All Stars
11076 • 2 ¾″
Issued: 2000 • Current
Market Value: $____

8

Sock Hop
DC222 • 3 ¾″
Issued: 1994 • Susp.: 1995
Market Value: $30

9

Soda-licious!
Early Release - Spring 1999
10696 • 3 ⅝″
Issued: 2000 • Current
Market Value: $____

10

Soft And Sweet
11403 • 7 ¼″ (wide)
Issued: 2000 • Current
Market Value: $____

11

Soldier Boy
10716 • 3 ⅜″
Issued: 1999 • Current
Market Value: $____

12

Solo Para Ti
Notas De Amor
11240 • 2 ¾″
Issued: 2000 • Current
Market Value: $____

Cherubs

	Price Paid	Value
1.		
2.		
3.		
4.		
5.		
6.		
7.		
8.		
9.		
10.		
11.		
12.		
Totals		

1

Someone Cares
Love Notes
10674 • 3″
Issued: 1999 • Current
Market Value: $____

2

Songbirds
Early Release – Fall 1997
10254 • 4″
Issued: 1998 • Susp.: 1999
Market Value: N/E

3

Speak No Evil
10042 • 5 ½″
Issued: 1997 • Current
Market Value: $____

4

Special Delivery (February)
The Calendar Collection
DC181 • 5″
Issued: 1994 • Retired: 1995
Market Value: $52

5
New

Special Mom
Thinking Of You
11510 • 2″
Issued: 2001 • Current
Market Value: $____

6

Special Occasions Cherub (set/5)
10167 • 6 ¼″
Issued: 1997 • Retired: 1999
Market Value: $40

7
New

Special You
Thinking Of You
11505 • 2 ½″
Issued: 2001 • Current
Market Value: $____

8

Spreading Happiness
10882 • 7 ¼″
Issued: 1999 • Current
Market Value: $____

9

Spring Cleaning
Early Release – Spring 1998
10407 • 4 ½″
Issued: 1998 • Current
Market Value: $____

10
New

Springtime Friends
11554 • 3 ¼″
Issued: 2001 • Current
Market Value: $____

11

Springtime Frolic (April)
The Calendar Collection
DC183 • 5″
Issued: 1994 • Retired: 1995
Market Value: $50

Cherubs

	Price Paid	Value
1.		
2.		
3.		
4.		
5.		
6.		
7.		
8.		
9.		
10.		
11.		
Totals		

1

Stairway To The Stars
DC348 • 5 3/8"
Issued: 1996 • Susp.: 1996
Market Value: $33

2

Standing Ovation
10163 • 4 1/4"
Issued: 1997 • Current
Market Value: $____

3

Star Baby
11389 • 2"
Issued: 2000 • Current
Market Value: $____

4

Star Bright
DC084 • 2 1/4"
Issued: 1995 • Susp.: 1999
Market Value: N/E

5

Star Gazers
DC308 • 4"
Issued: 1995 • Susp.: 1997
Market Value: $37

6

A Star In One
DC318 • 3 1/4"
Issued: 1996 • Susp.: 1997
Market Value: $26

7

Star Makers
DC344 • 4 1/2"
Issued: 1996 • Susp.: 1998
Market Value: $35

8

Star Performer
11134 • 4 3/4"
Issued: 2000 • Current
Market Value: $____

9

Star Power
Early Release – Fall 1997
10128 • 3 3/4"
Issued: TBA • Susp.: 1997
Market Value: $32

10

Stardust
10385 • 3 3/4"
Issued: 1998 • Susp.: 1999
Market Value: N/E

11

Starkeeping
DC360 • 3 5/8"
Issued: 1996 • Susp.: 1996
Market Value: $40

12

Starlight, Starbright
DC708 • 2"
Issued: 1995 • Susp.: 1997
Market Value: $16

Cherubs

	Price Paid	Value
1.		
2.		
3.		
4.		
5.		
6.		
7.		
8.		
9.		
10.		
11.		
12.		
Totals		

1

Stolen Kiss
DC162 • 2 ¼"
Issued: 1994 • Current
Market Value: $____

2
New

Stop And Smell The Roses
11495 • 3 ⅛"
Issued: 2001 • Current
Market Value: $____

3

Straight From The Heart
DC314 • 5 ⅞"
Issued: 1996 • Susp.: 1997
Market Value: $23

4

String Serenade
10168 • 6 ¾"
Issued: 1997 • Retired: 1998
Market Value: $34

5

A Stroll In The Park
10357 • 6 ¼"
Issued: 1998 • Current
Market Value: $____

6

Sucking My Thumb
DC156 • 2"
Issued: 1994 • Retired: 1995
Market Value: $22

7

Sugar 'N Spice
DC327 • 3 ⅛"
Issued: 1996 • Susp.: 1999
Market Value: N/E

8
Color Change

Sugarfoot
DC167 • 5"
Issued: 1994 • Retired: 1998
Market Value: $33

9

Summer Memories
11065 • 4"
Issued: 2000 • Current
Market Value: $____

10

Sun Shower
Early Release – Fall 1997
10383 (10126) • 3 ½"
Issued: 1998 • Susp.: 1999
Market Value: N/E

11

Sunday Stroll
DC400 • 3 ⅞"
Issued: 1995 • Susp.: 1999
Market Value: N/E

12

Sunflower
DC221 • 2 ½"
Issued: 1996 • Current
Market Value: $____

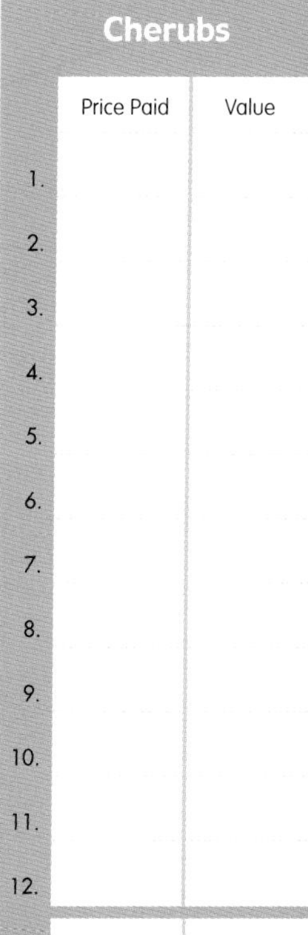

Cherubs

	Price Paid	Value
1.		
2.		
3.		
4.		
5.		
6.		
7.		
8.		
9.		
10.		
11.		
12.		
Totals		

1

Sunflower
Dreamsicles Garden
10782 • 4″
Issued: 1999 • Susp.: 2000
Market Value: N/E

2

Sunflower Carousel Horse
11478 • 4″
Issued: 2000 • Current
Market Value: $____

3

Sunny Days
11127 • 3 ¾″
Issued: 2000 • Current
Market Value: $____

4

Super Star
DC704 • 6″
Issued: 1995 • Susp.: 1997
Market Value: $25

5

Surprise!
Lil' Wonders
11181 • 2 ¾″
Issued: 2000 • Current
Market Value: $____

6

Surprise Gift
DC152 • 2″
Issued: 1994 • Retired: 1995
Market Value: $19

7

Swan Lake
DC163 • 3 ½″
Issued: 1995 • Susp.: 1999
Market Value: N/E

8

Sweet Blessings
11053 • 11 ½″
Issued: 2000 • Current
Market Value: $____

9

Sweet Bouquet
DC081 • 2 ¼″
Issued: 1995 • Susp.: 1999
Market Value: N/E

10

Sweet Chariot
DC345 • 4″
Issued: 1996 • Susp.: 1999
Market Value: N/E

11

Cherubs

	Price Paid	Value
1.		
2.		
3.		
4.		
5.		
6.		
7.		
8.		
9.		
10.		
11.		
Totals		

Cherubs

1

Color Change

Sweet Charity
DC411 • 4 ¼"
Issued: 1995 • Susp.: 1997
Market Value: $28

2

Sweet Dreams
DC125 • 11"
Issued: 1993 • Retired: 1995
Market Value: $60

3

Sweet Gingerbread
DC223 • 3 ¾"
Issued: 1994 • Susp.: 1995
Market Value: $30

4

New

Sweet Heart
11501 • 3 ½"
Issued: 2001 • Current
Market Value: $____

5

Sweet Licks
10694 • 3 ¼"
Issued: 2000 • Current
Market Value: $____

6

Sweet Pea
10038 • 3 ¾"
Issued: 1997 • Susp.: 1999
Market Value: N/E

7

Sweet Sentiments
Early Release – Spring 1998
10406 • 3 ⅝"
Issued: TBA • Current
Market Value: $____

8

Sweet Sixteen
10731 • 3 ⅞"
Issued: 1999 • Current
Market Value: $____

9

Sweeter Than Candy
11020 • 3 ½"
Issued: 2000 • Current
Market Value: $____

10

New

Sweeter When Shared
11502 • 3 ⅝"
Issued: 2001 • Current
Market Value: $____

11

Sweethearts
DC200 • 6"
Issued: 1994 • Susp.: 1997
Market Value: $43

12

Sweetie
10876 • 7"
Issued: 1999 • Current
Market Value: $____

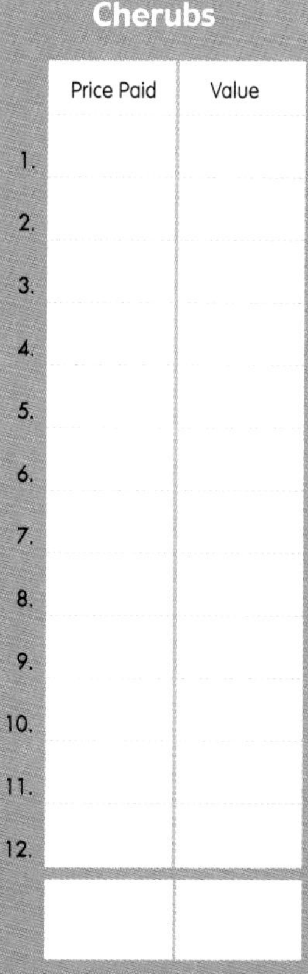

Cherubs

	Price Paid	Value
1.		
2.		
3.		
4.		
5.		
6.		
7.		
8.		
9.		
10.		
11.		
12.		
Totals		

1

Sweets For My Sweet
10993 • 3 ¾"
Issued: 2000 • Current
Market Value: $____

2

Sweetums
10161 • 3"
Issued: 1997 • Current
Market Value: $____

3

Swimming For Hope
Fifth Avenue Exclusive
DC016 • 5"
Issued: 1996 • Retired: 1996
Market Value: $120

4

Color Change

Swing On A Star
DC208 • 5 ½"
Issued: 1994 • Susp.: 1997
Market Value: $40

5

Swingtime
10044 • 4"
Issued: 1997 • Susp.: 1999
Market Value: N/E

6

Taking Aim
DC432 • 6" (wide)
Issued: 1997 • Retired: 1998
Market Value: $35

7

Taking Good Care
11122 • 4 ½"
Issued: 2000 • Current
Market Value: $____

8

Taste Of Honey (LE-5,000)
GoCollect.com Exclusive
11390 • N/A
Issued: 2000 • Current
Market Value: $____

9

Tea Party
GCC Exclusive
DC015 • 3"
Issued: 1996 • Retired: 1996
Market Value: $57

10

Tea Time
10705 • 3 ⅛"
Issued: 1999 • Current
Market Value: $____

11

Teacher
All Stars
11082 • 2 ¾"
Issued: 2000 • Current
Market Value: $____

Cherubs

	Price Paid	Value
1.		
2.		
3.		
4.		
5.		
6.		
7.		
8.		
9.		
10.		
11.		
Totals		

1

Teacher's Pet
DC124 • 5″
Issued: 1993 • Retired: 1997
Market Value: $36

2

Team Player
10164 • 3 ¾″
Issued: 1997 • Current
Market Value: $____

3

Teddy And Me
DC053 • 3″
Issued: 1994 • Susp.: 1997
Market Value: $22

4
New

Teddy Love
11494 • 4″
Issued: 2001 • Current
Market Value: $____

5

Tender Loving Care
DC247 • 3 ¼″
Issued: 1995 • Susp.: 1997
Market Value: $22

6

A Tender Touch
11004 • 3 ¼″
Issued: 2000 • Current
Market Value: $____

7

Tennis
All Stars
11077 • 2 ¾″
Issued: 2000 • Current
Market Value: $____

8

Thank You
Love Notes
10675 • 3"
Issued: 1999 • Current
Market Value: $____

9

Thanks A Bunch
Love Notes
11207 • 2 ¾″
Issued: 2000 • Current
Market Value: $____

10

Thanks To You
DC316 • 3 ⅜″
Issued: 1996 • Susp.: 1998
Market Value: $20

11

Thanksgiving Cherubs
DC207 • 3 ¼″
Issued: 1994 • Susp.: 2000
Market Value: N/E

12

Think It Over
10874 • 4″
Issued: 1999 • Susp.: 2000
Market Value: N/E

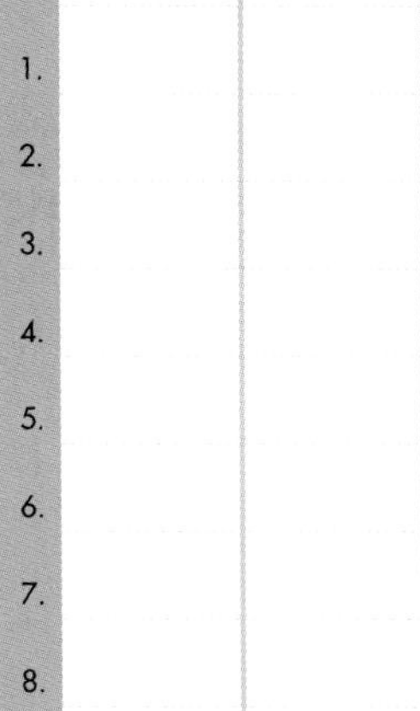

Cherubs

	Price Paid	Value
1.		
2.		
3.		
4.		
5.		
6.		
7.		
8.		
9.		
10.		
11.		
12.		
Totals		

1

Thinking Of You
DC129 • 9″
Issued: 1993 • Retired: 1997
Market Value: $63

2

Thinking Of You
Love Notes
10676 • 2 ¾″
Issued: 1999 • Current
Market Value: $____

3

Thinking Of You
Love Notes
11204 • 2 ¾″
Issued: 2000 • Current
Market Value: $____

4

Thoughtfully Yours
11193 • 3″
Issued: 2000 • Current
Market Value: $____

5
New

Thoughts Of You
11493 • 5 ¼″
Issued: 2001 • Current
Market Value: $____

6

Three Amigos
DC179 • 3 ¼″
Issued: 1994 • Susp.: 1997
Market Value: $22

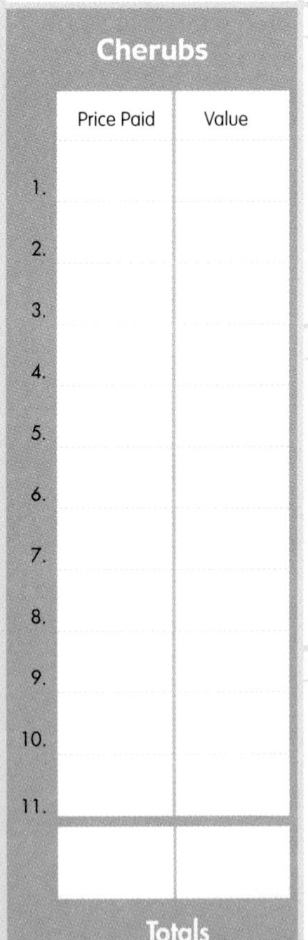

Cherubs

	Price Paid	Value
1.		
2.		
3.		
4.		
5.		
6.		
7.		
8.		
9.		
10.		
11.		
Totals		

7

Three Wheelin'
DC401 • 4″
Issued: 1995 • Susp.: 1998
Market Value: $20

8

Tiger By The Tail
10182 • 4 ¼″
Issued: 1997 • Susp.: 1999
Market Value: N/E

9
New

Timeless Story
11556 • 4 ⅜″
Issued: 2001 • Current
Market Value: $____

10

Tiny Dancer
DC165 • 4 ½″
Issued: 1993 • Retired: 1997
Market Value: $23

11

Tippy Toes
11133 • 4 ¾″
Issued: 2000 • Current
Market Value: $____

1

To Mom, From Me
11013 • 3 ½″
Issued: 2000 • Current
Market Value: $____

2

To Start Your Day
10707 • 4 ⅜″
Issued: 1999 • Current
Market Value: $____

3

Together Again
Early Release – Fall 1997
10246 • 4″
Issued: TBA • Susp.: 1997
Market Value: $19

4

Toy Treasures
Early Release – Fall 1998
10514 • 3 ⅝″
Issued: 1999 • Current
Market Value: $____

5

The Toymaker
10654 • 4 ¼″
Issued: 2000 • Current
Market Value: $____

6

Treats For Two
10699 • 3 ½″
Issued: 1999 • Current
Market Value: $____

7

True Friends
11050 • 10 ½″
Issued: 2000 • Current
Market Value: $____

8

Tweet-Hearts
10991 • 3 ⅝″
Issued: 2000 • Current
Market Value: $____

9

Twice The Fun
Early Release – Fall 1998
10505 • 4 ¼″
Issued: TBA • Current
Market Value: $____

10

Twinkle Toes
DC091 • 2 ¼″
Issued: 1995 • Susp.: 1999
Market Value: N/E

11

Twinkle, Twinkle
DC700 • 3 ½″
Issued: 1995 • Retired: 1997
Market Value: $23

12

Twins
11430 • 3 ⅞″
Issued: 2000 • Current
Market Value: $____

Cherubs

	Price Paid	Value
1.		
2.		
3.		
4.		
5.		
6.		
7.		
8.		
9.		
10.		
11.		
12.		
Totals		

1

Two's Company
10727 • 3 ¾″
Issued: 1999 • Current
Market Value: $____

2

Twosome
DC149 • 5″
Issued: 1996 • Susp.: 1997
Market Value: $31

3

Un Amigo Te Ama Todo El Tiempo
Bendiciones
11260 • 2 ¾″
Issued: 2000 • Current
Market Value: $____

4

Un Angel Te Cuida
Notas De Amor
11246 • 2 ⅞″
Issued: 2000 • Susp.: 2000
Market Value: N/E

5

Under The Big Top
DA251 • 5″
Issued: 1996 • Susp.: 1998
Market Value: $30

6

Unicorn Pal
Dreamsicles Pals
10338 • 2 ½″
Issued: 1998 • Current
Market Value: $____

7

Unlock My Heart
10632 • 2 ⅜″
Issued: 1999 • Current
Market Value: $____

8

Up All Night
DC155 • 2″
Issued: 1994 • Retired: 1995
Market Value: $23

9

Upsy Daisy!
DC085 • 2 ⅛″
Issued: 1995 • Susp.: 1999
Market Value: N/E

10
New

Valentine Wishes
11500 • 4″
Issued: 2001 • Current
Market Value: $____

11

Vintage 2000
11089 • 4 ½″
Issued: 2000 • Current
Market Value: $____

12

Violet
Dreamsicles Garden
10549 • 3 ½″
Issued: 1998 • Current
Market Value: $____

Cherubs

	Price Paid	Value
1.		
2.		
3.		
4.		
5.		
6.		
7.		
8.		
9.		
10.		
11.		
12.		
Totals		

1

Violin
Band Of Angels
11200 • 2 ¾"
Issued: 2000 • Current
Market Value: $____

2

Vitality
10172 • 2 ¼"
Issued: 1997 • Susp.: 1999
Market Value: N/E

3

Warm Fuzzies
11088 • 5 ⅓"
Issued: 2000 • Current
Market Value: $____

4

Warming Up
10875 • 3 ¼"
Issued: 1999 • Current
Market Value: $____

5

We Are Winning
10380 • 3 ⅝"
Issued: 1998 • Current
Market Value: $____

6

We'll Always Be Friends
11003 • 3 ⅜"
Issued: 2000 • Current
Market Value: $____

7

We'll Be Forever Friends
Parade Of Gifts Exclusive
10979 • 3 ½"
Issued: 1999 • Current
Market Value: $____

8
New

We'll Stick Together
11571 • 4 ⅝"
Issued: 2001 • Current
Market Value: $____

9

We're Best Friends
DC715 • 6"
Issued: 1996 • Susp.: 1997
Market Value: $30

10

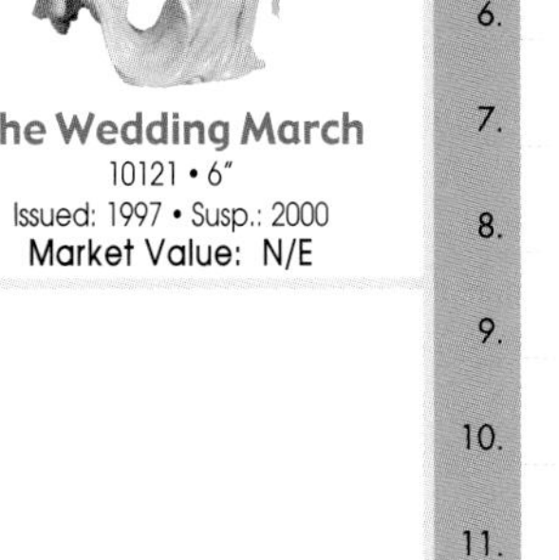

The Wedding March
10121 • 6"
Issued: 1997 • Susp.: 2000
Market Value: N/E

11

Wedding Rehearsal
DC134 • 5"
Issued: 1994 • Susp.: 1999
Market Value: $22

	Price Paid	Value
1.		
2.		
3.		
4.		
5.		
6.		
7.		
8.		
9.		
10.		
11.		
Totals		

1

What More Can I Say?
11016 • 4 ¼″
Issued: 2000 • Current
Market Value: $____

2

What Would Jesus Do?
10725 • 3 ¼″
Issued: 1999 • Current
Market Value: $____

3

Where Love Grows
10638 • 3 ¾″
Issued: 1999 • Current
Market Value: $____

4

Wild Blue Yonder
10718 • 3 ⅛″
Issued: 1999 • Current
Market Value: $____

5

Wildflower
DC107 (5107) • 3 ½″
Issued: 1991 • Retired: 1996
Market Value: $26

6

Will You Be Mine?
11018 • 3 ½″
Issued: 2000 • Current
Market Value: $____

Cherubs

	Price Paid	Value
1.		
2.		
3.		
4.		
5.		
6.		
7.		
8.		
9.		
10.		
11.		
Totals		

7

Windy City
European Imports Exclusive
10151 • 5 ½″
Issued: 1997 • Current
Market Value: $____

8

Color Change

A Wing And A Prayer
DC410 • 4 ¾″
Issued: 1995 • Susp.: 1998
Market Value: N/E

9

Winger
DC319 • 3 ¼″
Issued: 1996 • Susp.: 1997
Market Value: $19

10

Winning Colors
Early Release – Fall 1998
10515 • 4″
Issued: 1999 • Current
Market Value: $____

11

Winter Ride
10177 • 5 ¾″
Issued: 1997 • Susp.: 1998
Market Value: $24

1

Winter Wonderland (January)
The Calendar Collection
DC180 • 5 ½″
Issued: 1994 • Retired: 1995
Market Value: $55

2

Wish I May
10872 • 5″
Issued: 1999 • Current
Market Value: $____

3

Wish You Were Here
10075 • 4 ⅛″
Issued: 1997 • Retired: 1999
Market Value: N/E

4

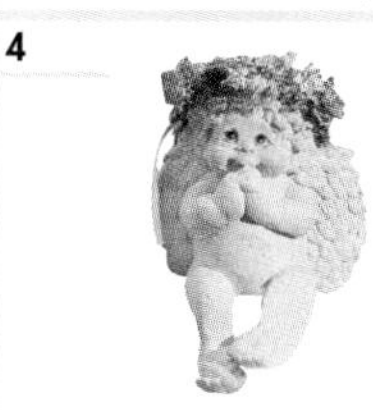

Wishin' On A Star
DC120 • 4 ¼″
Issued: 1993 • Retired: 1998
Market Value: $22

5

Wishing 'N Hoping
DC328 • 3 ¼″
Issued: 1996 • Susp.: 1999
Market Value: $16

6

Color Change

Wishing Well
DC423 • 6 ¼″
Issued: 1996 • Retired: 1998
Market Value: $42

7

Wistful Thinking
DC707 • 2″
Issued: 1995 • Retired: 1998
Market Value: $21

8

With This Ring
11116• 4 ½″
Issued: 2000 • Current
Market Value: $____

9

The Woodcarvers
10631 • 4″
Issued: 1999 • Current
Market Value: $____

10

You Are Loved
Love Notes
11209 • 2 ⅝″
Issued: 2000 • Current
Market Value: $____

11

You Are My Sunshine
Love Notes
10680 • 2 ¾″
Issued: 1999 • Current
Market Value: $____

Cherubs

	Price Paid	Value
1.		
2.		
3.		
4.		
5.		
6.		
7.		
8.		
9.		
10.		
11.		
Totals		

1

You Are My Sunshine
10728 • 3 ½″
Issued: 1999 • Current
Market Value: $____

2

You Caught My Heart
10985 • 3 ¼″
Issued: 2000 • Current
Market Value: $____

3

You're A Catch
11019 • 4″
Issued: 2000 • Current
Market Value: $____

4

You're My Shining Star
10712 • 5 ½″
Issued: 1999 • Susp.: 2000
Market Value: N/E

5

You're So Tweet
10723 • 3 ¼″
Issued: 1999 • Current
Market Value: $____

6

You're Special
10275 • 3 ¾″
Issued: 1998 • Current
Market Value: $____

7

You've Got A Friend
DC170 • 6″
Issued: 1994 • Susp.: 1997
Market Value: $47

8

You've Got Mail
10989 • 4 ¼″
Issued: 2000 • Current
Market Value: $____

9

Young Love
DC214 • 2″
Issued: 1995 • Susp.: 2000
Market Value: N/E

10

Number Zero
DC071 • 3″
Issued: 1996 • Susp.: 1999
Market Value: N/E

11

First Birthday
DC061 • 2 ½″
Issued: 1995 • Susp.: 1999
Market Value: N/E

12

Second Birthday
DC062 • 2 ½″
Issued: 1995 • Susp.: 1999
Market Value: N/E

Cherubs

	Price Paid	Value
1.		
2.		
3.		
4.		
5.		
6.		
7.		
8.		
9.		

Birthday Cherubs

	Price Paid	Value
10.		
11.		
12.		
Totals		

1

Third Birthday
DC063 • 2 ½"
Issued: 1995 • Susp.: 1999
Market Value: N/E

2

Fourth Birthday
DC064 • 2 ½"
Issued: 1995 • Susp.: 1999
Market Value: N/E

3

Fifth Birthday
DC065 • 2 ¾"
Issued: 1995 • Susp.: 1999
Market Value: N/E

4

Sixth Birthday
DC066 • 2 ¾"
Issued: 1995 • Susp.: 1999
Market Value: N/E

5

Seventh Birthday
DC067 • 3"
Issued: 1995 • Susp.: 1999
Market Value: N/E

6

Eighth Birthday
DC068 • 3"
Issued: 1995 • Susp.: 1999
Market Value: N/E

7

Ninth Birthday
DC069 • 3"
Issued: 1995 • Susp.: 1999
Market Value: N/E

8

Calendar Collectibles – January
10536 • 4"
Issued: 1998 • Current
Market Value: $____

9

Calendar Collectibles – February
10537 • 3 ¾"
Issued: 1998 • Current
Market Value: $____

10
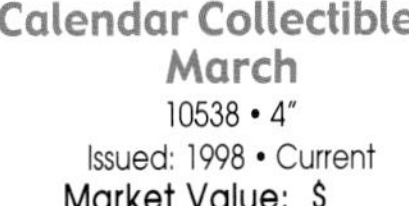
Calendar Collectibles – March
10538 • 4"
Issued: 1998 • Current
Market Value: $____

Birthday Cherubs

	Price Paid	Value
1.		
2.		
3.		
4.		
5.		
6.		
7.		
Calendar Collectibles		
8.		
9.		
10.		
Totals		

1

Calendar Collectibles – April
10539 • 3 ¾"
Issued: 1998 • Current
Market Value: $____

2

Calendar Collectibles – May
10540 • 3 ½"
Issued: 1998 • Current
Market Value: $____

3

Calendar Collectibles – June
10541 • 3 ¾"
Issued: 1998 • Current
Market Value: $____

4

Calendar Collectibles – July
10542 • 3 ¼"
Issued: 1998 • Current
Market Value: $____

5

Calendar Collectibles – August
10543 • 3 ½"
Issued: 1998 • Current
Market Value: $____

6

Calendar Collectibles – September
10544 • 3 ⅞"
Issued: 1998 • Current
Market Value: $____

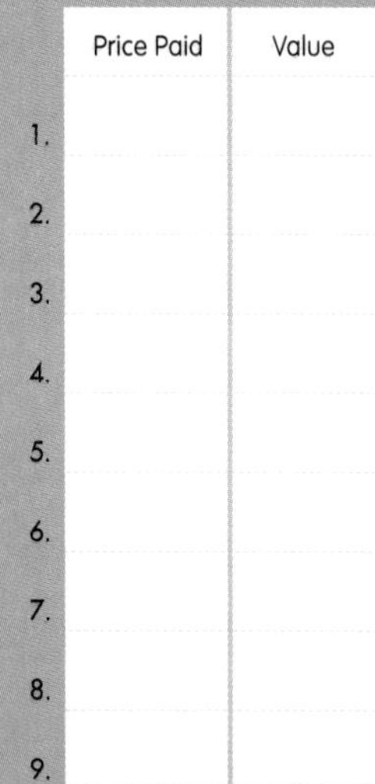

Calendar Collectibles

	Price Paid	Value
1.		
2.		
3.		
4.		
5.		
6.		
7.		
8.		
9.		

Gemstone Collection

	Price Paid	Value
10.		
11.		
Totals		

7

Calendar Collectibles – October
10545 • 3 ¼"
Issued: 1998 • Current
Market Value: $____

8

Calendar Collectibles – November
10546 • 3 ⅜"
Issued: 1998 • Current
Market Value: $____

9

Calendar Collectibles – December
10547 • 3 ⅜"
Issued: 1998 • Current
Market Value: $____

10

Garnet (January)
DC434 • 3 ⅝"
Issued: 1997 • Susp.: 1999
Market Value: N/E

11

Amethyst (February)
DC435 • 3 ½"
Issued: 1997 • Susp.: 1999
Market Value: N/E

1

Aquamarine (March)
DC436 • 3 ½"
Issued: 1997 • Susp.: 1999
Market Value: N/E

2

Diamond (April)
DC437 • 3 ¾"
Issued: 1997 • Susp.: 1999
Market Value: N/E

3

Emerald (May)
DC438 • 3 ¼"
Issued: 1997 • Susp.: 1999
Market Value: N/E

4

Alexandrite (June)
DC439 • 3 ½"
Issued: 1997 • Susp.: 1999
Market Value: N/E

5

Ruby (July)
DC440 • 3 ¼"
Issued: 1997 • Susp.: 1999
Market Value: N/E

6

Peridot (August)
DC441 • 3 ⅝"
Issued: 1997 • Susp.: 1999
Market Value: N/E

7

Sapphire (September)
DC442 • 3 ¾"
Issued: 1997 • Susp.: 1999
Market Value: N/E

8

Rose Quartz (October)
DC443 • 3 ½"
Issued: 1997 • Susp.: 1999
Market Value: N/E

9

A.

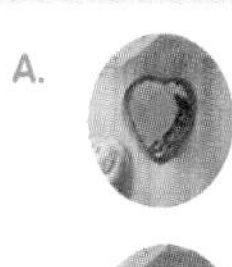

B.

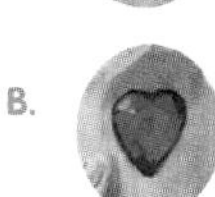

Topaz (November)
DC444 • 3 ¾"
Issued: 1997 • Susp.: 1999
Market Value: A. Yellow Stone – N/E B. Blue Stone – N/E

10

Turquoise (December)
DC445 • 3 ½"
Issued: 1997 • Susp.: 1999
Market Value: N/E

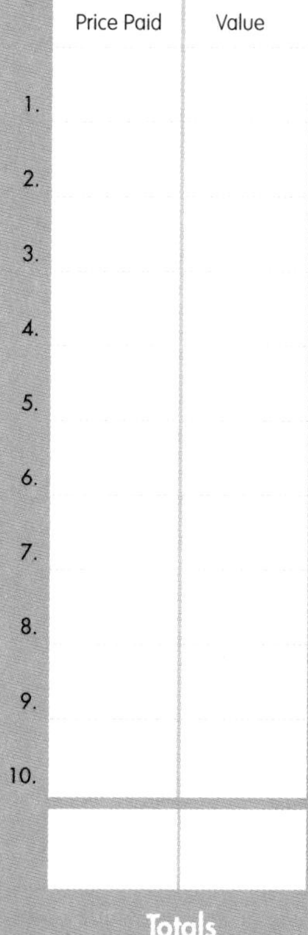

Gemstone Collection

	Price Paid	Value
1.		
2.		
3.		
4.		
5.		
6.		
7.		
8.		
9.		
10.		
Totals		

1

The Flying Lesson – Golden Halo (LE-10,000)
10935 • 6 ½"
Issued: 1999 • Susp.: 2000
Market Value: N/E

2

Golden A Child's Prayer
10798 • 2 ½"
Issued: 1999 • Susp.: 2000
Market Value: N/E

3

Golden Baby Love
10800 • 2 ½"
Issued: 1999 • Current
Market Value: $____

4

Golden Best Pals
10659 • 4 ¾"
Issued: 1999 • Susp.: 1999
Market Value: $18

5

Golden Bright Eyes
Early Release – Fall 1999
10933 • 3 ½"
Issued: TBA • Current
Market Value: $____

6

Golden Bundle Of Joy
10795 • 2 ½"
Issued: 1999 • Susp.: 2000
Market Value: N/E

Golden Halo Collection

	Price Paid	Value
1.		
2.		
3.		
4.		
5.		
6.		
7.		
8.		
9.		
10.		
11.		
12.		
Totals		

7

Golden Cherub And Child
10656 • 5 ½"
Issued: 1999 • Current
Market Value: $____

8

Golden Forever Friends
10658 • 4 ½"
Issued: 1999 • Current
Market Value: $____

9

Golden Heavenly Dreamer
10661 • 5 ½"
Issued: 1999 • Current
Market Value: $____

10

Golden Little Darlin'
10799 • 2 ½"
Issued: 1999 • Current
Market Value: $____

11

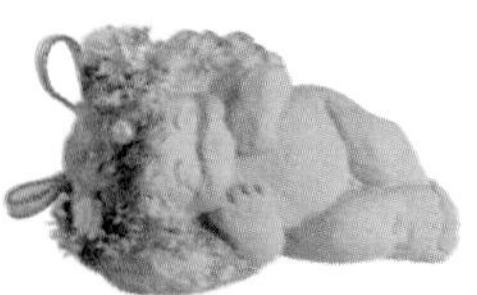

Golden Little Dream
10797 • 2 ½"
Issued: 1999 • Susp.: 2000
Market Value: N/E

12

Golden Littlest Angel
10796 • 2 ½"
Issued: 1999 • Current
Market Value: $____

1

Golden Make A Wish
10663 • 5 ½″
Issued: 1999 • Susp.: 2000
Market Value: N/E

2

Golden Mischief Maker
10660 • 5″
Issued: 1999 • Susp.: 1999
Market Value: $14

3

Golden Sitting Pretty
10657 • 3 ¾″
Issued: 1999 • Current
Market Value: $____

4

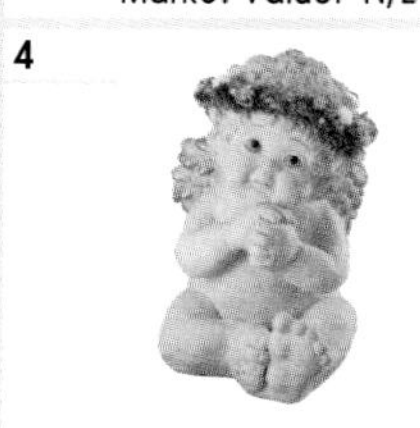

Golden Thinking Of You
10932 • 9″
Issued: 1999 • Susp.: 2000
Market Value: N/E

5

Golden Tiny Dancer
I.C.E. Exclusive
10934 • 4 ½″
Issued: 1999 • Current
Market Value: $____

6

Golden Wildflower
10662 • 3 ½″
Issued: 1999 • Susp.: 2000
Market Value: N/E

7

Quilted Numbers – 0
11160 • 2 ¾″
Issued: 2000 • Current
Market Value: $____

8

Quilted Numbers – 1
11151 • 3″
Issued: 2000 • Current
Market Value: $____

9

Quilted Numbers – 2
11152 • 3″
Issued: 2000 • Current
Market Value: $____

10

Quilted Numbers – 3
11153 • 2 ¾″
Issued: 2000 • Current
Market Value: $____

11

Quilted Numbers – 4
11154 • 2 ¼″
Issued: 2000 • Current
Market Value: $____

12

Quilted Numbers – 5
11155 • 3″
Issued: 2000 • Current
Market Value: $____

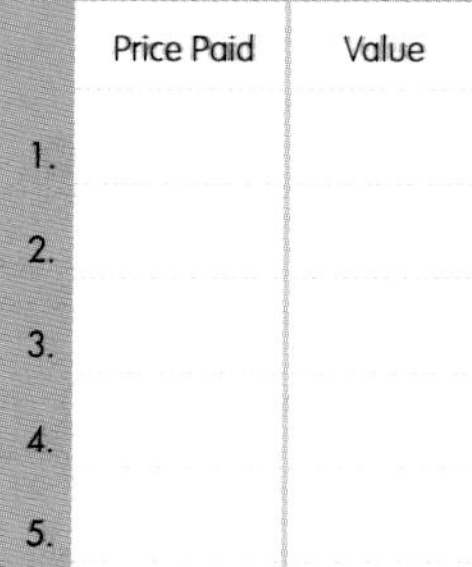

Golden Halo Collection

	Price Paid	Value
1.		
2.		
3.		
4.		
5.		
6.		
Quilted Numbers Collection		
7.		
8.		
9.		
10.		
11.		
12.		
Totals		

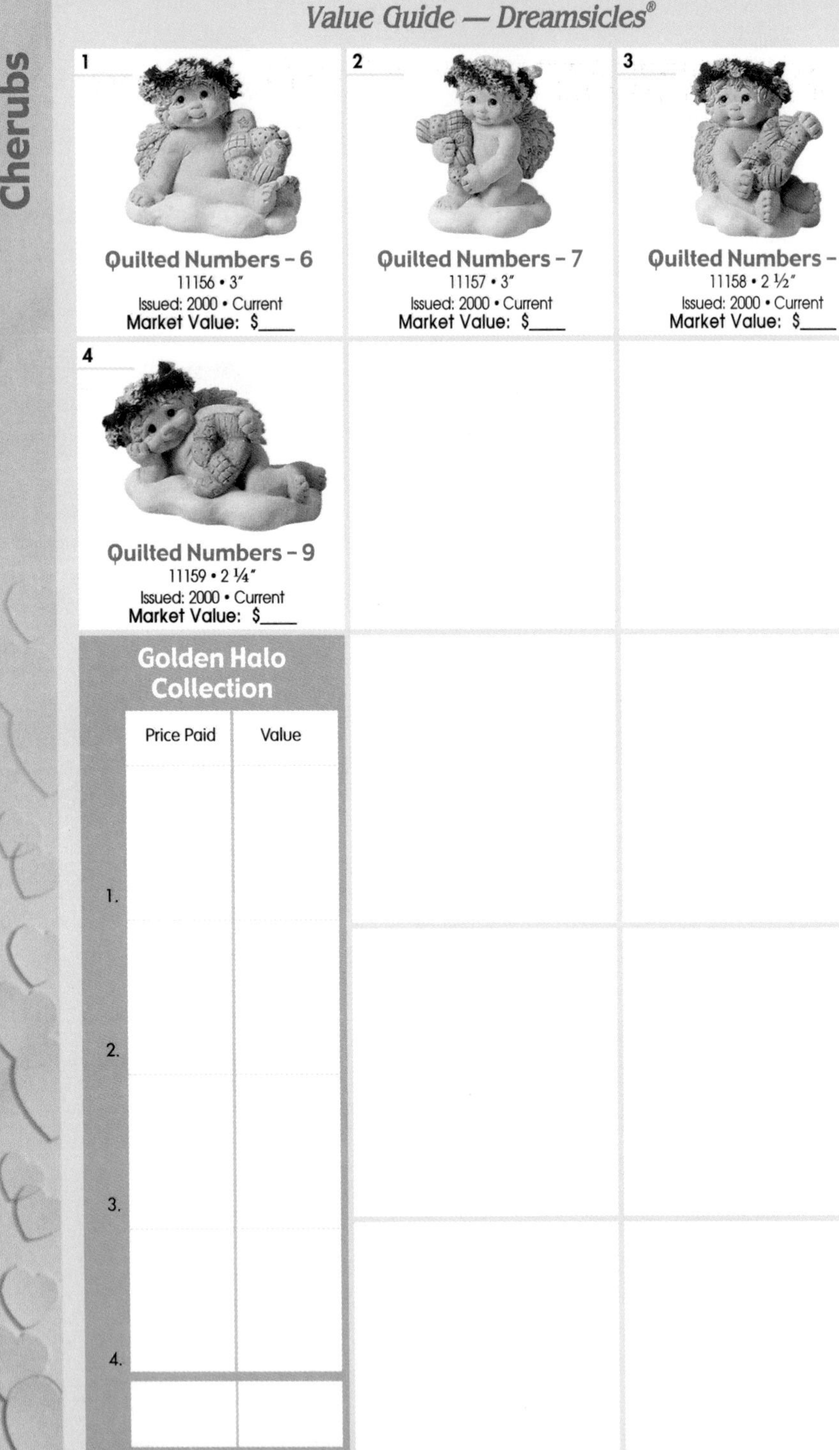

1
Quilted Numbers – 6
11156 • 3"
Issued: 2000 • Current
Market Value: $____

2
Quilted Numbers – 7
11157 • 3"
Issued: 2000 • Current
Market Value: $____

3
Quilted Numbers – 8
11158 • 2 ½"
Issued: 2000 • Current
Market Value: $____

4
Quilted Numbers – 9
11159 • 2 ¼"
Issued: 2000 • Current
Market Value: $____

Golden Halo Collection

	Price Paid	Value
1.		
2.		
3.		
4.		
Totals		

Holiday Cherubs

The colorful red ribbons and berries on the wreaths of these adorable holiday-themed Dreamsicles cherubs are sure to enchant collectors the whole year through. Be sure to catch the newest little angels in stores soon!

1

Away In A Manger
10430 • 6″
Issued: 1998 • Current
Market Value: $____

2

Baby And Me
DX054 • 3″
Issued: 1994 • Susp.: 1997
Market Value: $19

3

Baby Love
DX147 • 2 ½″
Issued: 1992 • Retired: 1995
Market Value: $25

4

Baby's First Christmas
DX242 • 3″
Issued: 1994 • Susp.: 1997
Market Value: $22

5

Bear Hugs
10436 • 3″
Issued: 1998 • Susp.: 1999
Market Value: N/E

6

Bearing Gifts
DX255 • 2 ½″
Issued: 1996 • Susp.: 1999
Market Value: N/E

7

Bedtime Prayer
DX703 • 3″
Issued: 1995 • Susp.: 1997
Market Value: $17

8

Bedtime Story
10857 • 4″
Issued: 1999 • Susp.: 1999
Market Value: N/E

9

Best Buddies
DX159 • 3 ¾″
Issued: 1995 • Susp.: 1996
Market Value: $22

10

Best Pals
DX103 • 4 ¾″
Issued: 1991 • Retired: 1994
Market Value: $46

Holiday Cherubs

	Price Paid	Value
1.		
2.		
3.		
4.		
5.		
6.		
7.		
8.		
9.		
10.		
Totals		

1

Birdie And Me
DX056 • 2 ½"
Issued: 1994 • Susp.: 1997
Market Value: $16

2

Bluebird On My Shoulder
DX115 • 6"
Issued: 1992 • Retired: 1995
Market Value: $50

3

Born This Day
DX230 • 4"
Issued: 1994 • Susp.: 1998
Market Value: $32

4

Bright Eyes
DX108 • 3 ½"
Issued: 1991 • Susp.: 1996
Market Value: $18

5

Bundle Of Joy
DX142 • 2 ½"
Issued: 1992 • Retired: 1995
Market Value: $22

6

Bunny And Me
DX055 • 2 ⅝"
Issued: 1994 • Susp.: 1997
Market Value: $16

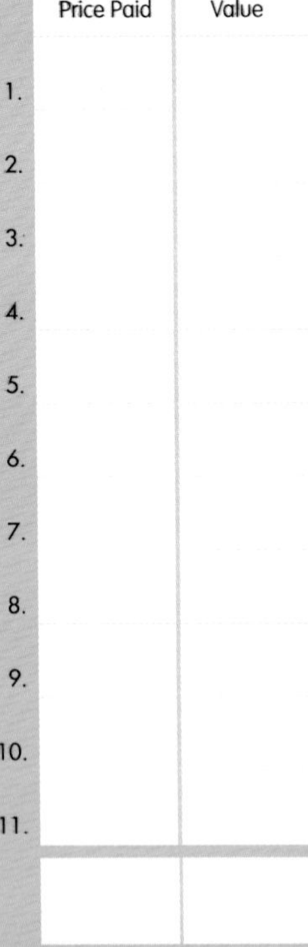

Holiday Cherubs

	Price Paid	Value
1.		
2.		
3.		
4.		
5.		
6.		
7.		
8.		
9.		
10.		
11.		
Totals		

7

Candy Cane
Tiny Tots
11338 • 2 ¼"
Issued: 2000 • Current
Market Value: $____

8

Caroler #1
DX216 • 6 ½"
Issued: 1992 • Retired: 1995
Market Value: $46

9

Caroler #2
DX217 • 6 ½"
Issued: 1992 • Retired: 1995
Market Value: $46

10

Caroler #3
DX218 • 6 ½"
Issued: 1992 • Retired: 1995
Market Value: $46

11

The Carolers
10469 • 3 ¾"
Issued: 1998 • Susp.: 1999
Market Value: N/E

1

Catch A Snowflake
10815 • 4″
Issued: 1999 • Susp.: 1999
Market Value: N/E

2

Cheerful Givers
10624 • 3 ½″
Issued: 1999 • Current
Market Value: $____

3

Cherub And Child
DX100 • 5 ½″
Issued: 1991 • Retired: 1995
Market Value: $55

4

A Child's Prayer
DX145 • 2 ½″
Issued: 1992 • Retired: 1995
Market Value: $17

5

Chimney Cherub
Early Release – Fall 1998
10507 • 4″
Issued: 1999 • Current
Market Value: $____

6

Christmas Blessings
11346 • 5 ⅛″
Issued: 2000 • Current
Market Value: $____

7

Christmas Cradle
10808 • 3 ¼″
Issued: 1999 • Current
Market Value: $____

8

Christmas Cutie
10845 • 3 ¾″
Issued: 1999 • Current
Market Value: $____

9

Christmas Devotion
10852 • 3″
Issued: 1999 • Susp.: 2000
Market Value: N/E

10

Christmas Faith
10851 • 3″
Issued: 1999 • Current
Market Value: $____

11

Christmas Morning
DX710 • 3 ½″
Issued: 1995 • Susp.: 1997
Market Value: N/E

12

Christmas Surprise!
11326 • 5 ½″
Issued: 2000 • Current
Market Value: $____

Holiday Cherubs

	Price Paid	Value
1.		
2.		
3.		
4.		
5.		
6.		
7.		
8.		
9.		
10.		
11.		
12.		
Totals		

1

Christmas Trim
DX711 • 2"
Issued: 1996 • Susp.: 1997
Market Value: $16

2

Come Let Us Adore Him
DX475 • 8 1/4"
Issued: 1995 • Susp.: 1997
Market Value: $110

3

Cookies
Tiny Tots
DX256 • 2 1/4"
Issued: 2000 • Current
Market Value: $____

4

Counting The Days
10807 • 6 1/2"
Issued: 1999 • Current
Market Value: $____

5

Cute And Cuddly
11341 • 2 3/4"
Issued: 2000 • Susp.: 2000
Market Value: N/E

6

Daydreamin'
10850 • 6 1/2"
Issued: 1999 • Susp.: 1999
Market Value: N/E

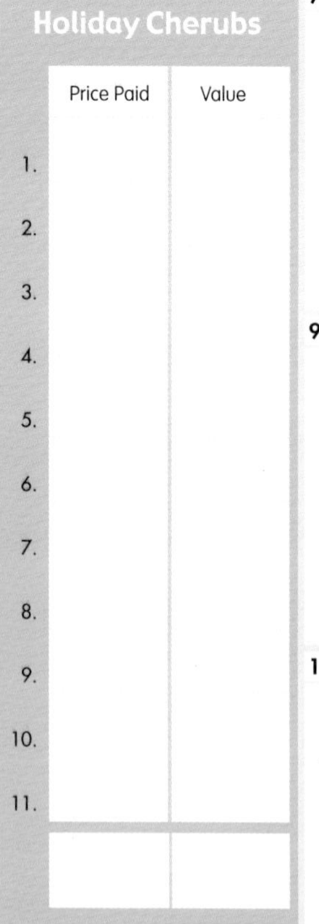

Holiday Cherubs

	Price Paid	Value
1.		
2.		
3.		
4.		
5.		
6.		
7.		
8.		
9.		
10.		
11.		
Totals		

7

Deck The Halls
10434 • 2 3/4"
Issued: 1998 • Susp.: 1999
Market Value: N/E

8

Dream A Little Dream
DX144 • 2 1/2"
Issued: 1992 • Retired: 1995
Market Value: $19

9

Follow Your Star
DX257 • 2 1/2"
Issued: 1996 • Susp.: 1998
Market Value: $26

10

Forever Friends
DX102 • 4 1/2"
Issued: 1991 • Retired: 1994
Market Value: $50

11

Forever Yours
DX110 • 10"
Issued: 1991 • Retired: 1995
Market Value: $75

1

Forty Winks
DX233 • 3 ½"
Issued: 1995 • Susp.: 1996
Market Value: $26

2

Free Bird
DX234 • 3 ¾"
Issued: 1995 • Susp.: 1996
Market Value: $20

3

Fun For All
11321 • 3"
Issued: 2000 • Current
Market Value: $____

4

Fuzzy Wuzzy
11342 • 3 ½"
Issued: 2000 • Susp.: 2000
Market Value: N/E

5

Gift Wrapped
10437 • 2 ½"
Issued: 1998 • Susp.: 1999
Market Value: N/E

6

Gifts For All
11324 • 7 ½" wide
Issued: 2000 • Current
Market Value: $____

7

Gingerbread House
DX254 • 2 ⅝"
Issued: 1996 • Susp.: 1999
Market Value: N/E

8

Gingerbread House
Tiny Tots
11333 • 2 ¼"
Issued: 2000 • Current
Market Value: $____

9

God's Word
10855 • 3 ⅜"
Issued: 1999 • Current
Market Value: $____

10

The Good Book
10856 • 3 ⅜"
Issued: 1999 • Current
Market Value: $____

11

Good Shepherd
DX104 • 4"
Issued: 1994 • Susp.: 1997
Market Value: $35

12

Good Will Towards Men
10811 • 4 ⅝"
Issued: 1999 • Current
Market Value: $____

Holiday Cherubs

	Price Paid	Value
1.		
2.		
3.		
4.		
5.		
6.		
7.		
8.		
9.		
10.		
11.		
12.		
Totals		

1

Grandma's Or Bust
DX227 • 4"
Issued: 1995 • Susp.: 1996
Market Value: $23

2

Granny's Cookies
DX228 • 2 ½"
Issued: 1995 • Susp.: 1996
Market Value: $17

3

The Greatest Gift Of All
10809 • 4 ⅛"
Issued: 1999 • Current
Market Value: $____

4

Happy Feet
DX164 • 3"
Issued: 1995 • Susp.: 1996
Market Value: $19

5

He Is Born
11348 • 5 ½"
Issued: 2000 • Current
Market Value: $____

6

Heart
Tiny Tots
11334 • 2 ½"
Issued: 2000 • Current
Market Value: $____

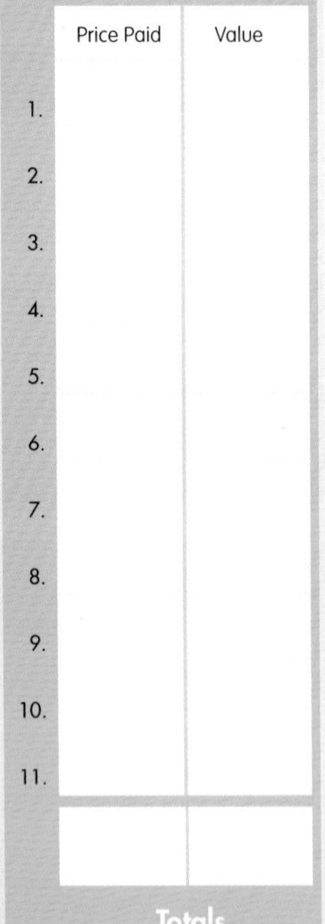

Holiday Cherubs

	Price Paid	Value
1.		
2.		
3.		
4.		
5.		
6.		
7.		
8.		
9.		
10.		
11.		
Totals		

7

Hearth And Home
Early Release – Fall 1999
10977 • 3 ¾"
Issued: 2000 • Current
Market Value: $____

8

Heavenly Dreamer
DX106 • 5 ½"
Issued: 1991 • Retired: 1996
Market Value: $32

9

Heavenly Hearth
11312 • 5 ½"
Issued: 2000 • Current
Market Value: $____

10

Hello Dolly
DX702 • 3 ½"
Issued: 1995 • Susp.: 1997
Market Value: $20

11

Herald Angel
10431 • 3 ¼"
Issued: 1998 • Susp.: 1999
Market Value: N/E

1

Here Comes Trouble
DX214 • 8″
Issued: 1992 • Susp.: 1997
Market Value: N/E

2

Here's Looking At You
DX172 • 4″
Issued: 1994 • Retired: 1995
Market Value: $42

3

Holiday Buddies
10185 • 3 ⅝″
Issued: 1997 • Susp.: 1999
Market Value: N/E

4

Holiday Home
10819 • 3 ⅜″
Issued: 1999 • Current
Market Value: $____

5

Holiday Pals
DX709 • 3 ¾″
Issued: 1995 • Susp.: 1997
Market Value: N/E

6

Hooked On You
Early Release – Fall 1998
10623 • 3 ¾″
Issued: 2000 • Current
Market Value: $____

7

Hugabye Baby
DX701 • 3″
Issued: 1995 • Retired: 1997
Market Value: $19

8

Huggy Bear
11323 • 5 ½″
Issued: 2000 • Current
Market Value: $____

9

Hushaby Baby
DX303 • 3 ¾″
Issued: 1995 • Susp.: 1996
Market Value: $23

10

I Love Mommy
DX226 • 2 ¾″
Issued: 1995 • Susp.: 1996
Market Value: $20

11

I Love You
DX225 • 4 ½″
Issued: 1995 • Susp.: 1996
Market Value: N/E

12

Jesus Loves Me
11345 • 5 ½″
Issued: 2000 • Current
Market Value: $____

Holiday Cherubs

	Price Paid	Value
1.		
2.		
3.		
4.		
5.		
6.		
7.		
8.		
9.		
10.		
11.		
12.		
Totals		

1

Jingle Bell Rock
Early Release – Fall 1998
10615 • 4 ½"
Issued: 1999 • Current
Market Value: $____

2

Jingle Bells
10818 • 4 ¼"
Issued: 1999 • Current
Market Value: $____

3

The Joy Of Giving
10812 • 3 ½"
Issued: 1999 • Current
Market Value: $____

4

Joy Ride
10429 • 3 ¾"
Issued: 1998 • Susp.: 1999
Market Value: N/E

5

Joyful Gathering
DX231 • 5"
Issued: 1994 • Susp.: 1998
Market Value: N/E

6

Kitty And Me
DX051 • 3"
Issued: 1994 • Susp.: 1997
Market Value: $16

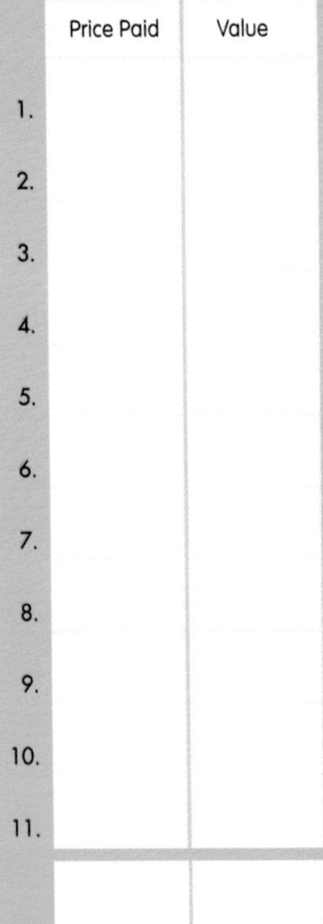

Holiday Cherubs

	Price Paid	Value
1.		
2.		
3.		
4.		
5.		
6.		
7.		
8.		
9.		
10.		
11.		
Totals		

7

Let's Play Fetch
DX237 • 4 ½"
Issued: 1995 • Susp.: 1996
Market Value: $22

8

Life Is Good
DX119 • 5 ¼"
Issued: 1992 • Retired: 1996
Market Value: $32

9

The Light Of The World
11349 • 5"
Issued: 2000 • Current
Market Value: $____

10

Lighting The Tree (w/blinking L.E.D. lights)
11314 • 6 ½"
Issued: 2000 • Susp.: 2000
Market Value: N/E

11

Little Darlin'
DX146 • 2 ½"
Issued: 1992 • Retired: 1995
Market Value: $20

1

Littlest Angel
DX143 • 2 ½″
Issued: 1992 • Retired: 1995
Market Value: $20

2

Love My Kitty
DX130 • 3 ¾″
Issued: 1993 • Retired: 1996
Market Value: $32

3

Love My Puppy
DX131 • 3 ¾″
Issued: 1993 • Retired: 1996
Market Value: $32

4

Love My Teddy
DX132 • 4″
Issued: 1993 • Retired: 1996
Market Value: $32

5

Make A Wish
DX118 • 5 ½″
Issued: 1992 • Susp.: 1996
Market Value: $19

6

Makin' A List #2
10465 • 5 ¼″
Issued: 1998 • Susp.: 1999
Market Value: N/E

7

Making Christmas Memories
11313 • 4 ¼″
Issued: 2000 • Current
Market Value: $____

8

Color Change

Mall Santa
DX258 • 6″
Issued: 1996 • Retired: 1998
Market Value: $42

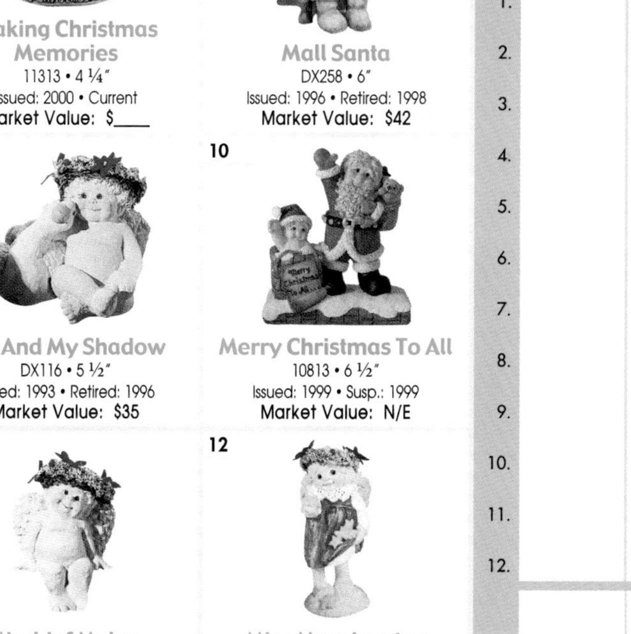

9

Me And My Shadow
DX116 • 5 ½″
Issued: 1993 • Retired: 1996
Market Value: $35

10

Merry Christmas To All
10813 • 6 ½″
Issued: 1999 • Susp.: 1999
Market Value: N/E

11

Mischief Maker
DX105 • 5″
Issued: 1991 • Retired: 1996
Market Value: $30

12

Miss Morningstar
DX141 • 7 ¼″
Issued: 1993 • Retired: 1996
Market Value: $50

Holiday Cherubs

	Price Paid	Value
1.		
2.		
3.		
4.		
5.		
6.		
7.		
8.		
9.		
10.		
11.		
12.		
Totals		

1

Moon Dance
DX210 • 5 ½″
Issued: 1995 • Retired: 1996
Market Value: $46

2

Moonglow
DX235 • 3 ¾″
Issued: 1995 • Susp.: 1996
Market Value: $19

3

My Special Friends
Early Release – Fall 1999
10865 • 4″
Issued: 2000 • Current
Market Value: $____

4

Musical Rest
10432 • 2 ⅜″
Issued: 1998 • Susp.: 1999
Market Value: N/E

5

My Big Buddy
11343 • 3″
Issued: 2000 • Susp.: 2000
Market Value: N/E

6

My Prayer
DX121 • 5 ½″
Issued: 1992 • Susp.: 1999
Market Value: N/E

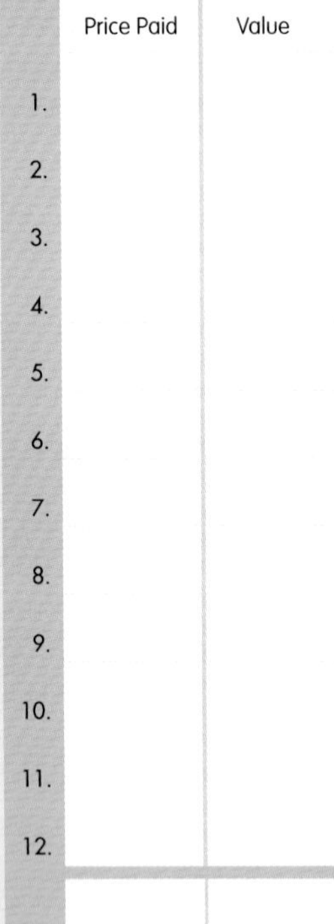

Holiday Cherubs

	Price Paid	Value
1.		
2.		
3.		
4.		
5.		
6.		
7.		
8.		
9.		
10.		
11.		
12.		
Totals		

7

Naughty Or Nice?
10848 • 7 ¼″
Issued: 1999 • Susp.: 1999
Market Value: N/E

8

Newborn Cherub
DX168 • 3″ wide
Issued: 1994 • Susp.: 1996
Market Value: $23

9

'Nite 'Nite
DX238 • 4 ½″
Issued: 1995 • Susp.: 1996
Market Value: $23

10

Noel
DX712 • 2 ⅜″
Issued: 1996 • Susp.: 1997
Market Value: $13

11

North Pole Cherub
Early Release – Fall 1998
10467 • 4 ⅜″
Issued: TBA • Current
Market Value: $____

12

Northern Exposure
DC420 • 5 ½″
Issued: 1996 • Susp.: 1997
Market Value: $56

1

Nursery Rhyme
DX229 • 7"
Issued: 1995 • Susp.: 1995
Market Value: $72

2

Oh Little Star
DX713 • 2 ¼"
Issued: 1996 • Susp.: 1997
Market Value: $13

3

Open Me First
DC243 • 3 ¼"
Issued: 1994 • Susp.: 1996
Market Value: $36

4

Open Me First
DX243 • 3 ¼"
Issued: 1994 • Susp.: 1997
Market Value: $37

5

Over The Rainbow
DX209 • 6"
Issued: 1995 • Susp.: 1996
Market Value: N/E

6

Peace
10816 • 4 ¾"
Issued: 1999 • Current
Market Value: $____

7

Peace On Earth
10859 • 4"
Issued: 1999 • Susp.: 1999
Market Value: N/E

8

Poetry In Motion
Special Edition
DX113 • 5"
Issued: 1995 • Retired: 1997
Market Value: $120

9

Praying
Tiny Tots
11336 • 3"
Issued: 2000 • Current
Market Value: $____

10

Puppy And Me
DX052 • 3"
Issued: 1994 • Susp.: 1997
Market Value: $19

11

Purr-fect Pals
DX239 • 4 ½"
Issued: 1995 • Susp.: 1996
Market Value: $23

Holiday Cherubs

	Price Paid	Value
1.		
2.		
3.		
4.		
5.		
6.		
7.		
8.		
9.		
10.		
11.		
Totals		

1

Rainbow Rider
DX236 • 4"
Issued: 1995 • Susp.: 1996
Market Value: $23

2

Range Rider
DX305 • 4"
Issued: 1995 • Susp.: 1996
Market Value: $23

3

Color Change

Read Me A Story
DX123 • 2 ¾"
Issued: 1995 • Susp.: 1996
Market Value: $18

4

Ready For Santa
11318 • 4"
Issued: 2000 • Current
Market Value: $____

5

Rejoice
10817 • 6"
Issued: 1999 • Susp.: 1999
Market Value: N/E

6

Remembering You
10849 • 10"
Issued: 1999 • Susp.: 1999
Market Value: N/E

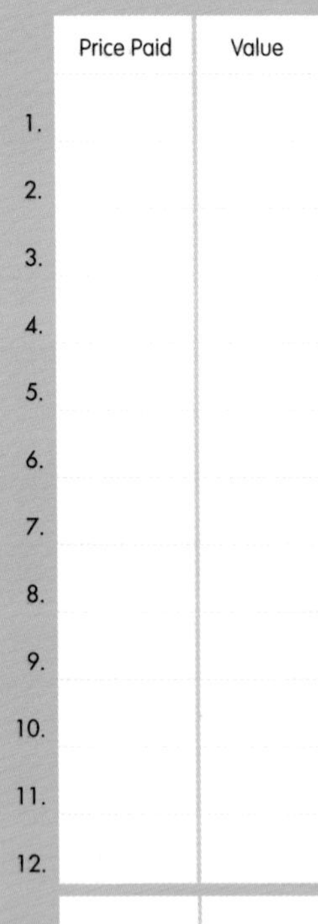

Holiday Cherubs

	Price Paid	Value
1.		
2.		
3.		
4.		
5.		
6.		
7.		
8.		
9.		
10.		
11.		
12.		
Totals		

7

Santa At Prayer
10843 • 6 ½"
Issued: 1999 • Susp.: 1999
Market Value: $50

8

Color Change

Santa Baby
DX256 • 2 ¼"
Issued: 1996 • Current
Market Value: $____

9

Santa's Elves
10820 • 4"
Issued: 1999 • Susp.: 1999
Market Value: N/E

10

Santa's Little Helper
DX109 • 4"
Issued: 1991 • Retired: 1997
Market Value: $15

11

Santa's Shop
10186 • 4 ½"
Issued: 1997 • Susp.: 1998
Market Value: N/E

12

Santa's Surprise
10823 • 5 ½"
Issued: 1999 • Susp.: 1999
Market Value: N/E

1

Season Of Joy
10427 • 2 ½″
Issued: 1999 • Susp.: 1999
Market Value: N/E

2

Season Of Love
10425 • 3 ¼″
Issued: 1999 • Susp.: 1999
Market Value: N/E

3

Season Of Peace
10426 • 2 ¾″
Issued: 1999 • Susp.: 1999
Market Value: N/E

4

Share The Fun
DX178 • 3 ½″
Issued: 1994 • Susp.: 1996
Market Value: $26

5

Side By Side
DX169 • 4 ¾″
Issued: 1994 • Retired: 1995
Market Value: $62

6

Silent Prayer
10847 • 4 ¾″
Issued: 1999 • Susp.: 1999
Market Value: N/E

7

Sing Noel
10438 • 3″
Issued: 1999 • Susp.: 1999
Market Value: N/E

8

Sittin' Pretty
11325 • 3 ¾″
Issued: 2000 • Current
Market Value: $____

9

Sitting Pretty
DX101 • 3 ¾″
Issued: 1991 • Retired: 1996
Market Value: $26

10

Sleigh Ride
DX122 • 5″
Issued: 1992 • Susp.: 1997
Market Value: $50

11

Small Cherub With Hanging Ribbon
5104C • 4 ½″
Issued: 1991 • Susp.: 1992
Market Value: $92

Holiday Cherubs

	Price Paid	Value
1.		
2.		
3.		
4.		
5.		
6.		
7.		
8.		
9.		
10.		
11.		
Totals		

1

Snow Ball
10470 • 6 ¼"
Issued: 1999 • Susp.: 1999
Market Value: N/E

2

Snow Ride
10468 • 4 ½"
Issued: 1999 • Susp.: 1999
Market Value: N/E

3

Snowball
Tiny Tots
11335 • 2 ½"
Issued: 2000 • Current
Market Value: $____

4

Snowbound
Early Release – Fall 1997
10120 • 4 ½"
Issued: TBA • Current
Market Value: $____

5

Snowflake
DX117 • 3 ¼"
Issued: 1994 • Current
Market Value: $____

6

Snuggle Up!
11320 • 3 ¼"
Issued: 2000 • Current
Market Value: $____

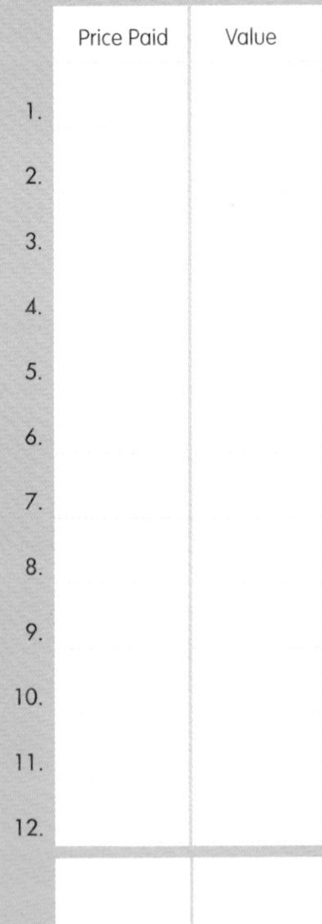

Holiday Cherubs

	Price Paid	Value
1.		
2.		
3.		
4.		
5.		
6.		
7.		
8.		
9.		
10.		
11.		
12.		
Totals		

7

Starlight, Starbright
DX708 • 2"
Issued: 1995 • Susp.: 1997
Market Value: $16

8

Stocking Stuffer
10435 • 2 ⅞"
Issued: 1998 • Susp.: 1999
Market Value: N/E

9

Stolen Kiss
DX162 • 2 ¼"
Issued: 1994 • Susp.: 1996
Market Value: $22

10

Super Star
DX704 • 6"
Issued: 1995 • Susp.: 1997
Market Value: N/E

11

Swan Lake
DX163 • 3 ½"
Issued: 1995 • Susp.: 1996
Market Value: $22

12

Sweet Dreams
DX125 • 11"
Issued: 1993 • Retired: 1995
Market Value: $55

1

Sweet Stuff
10433 • 2 ½″
Issued: 1999 • Susp.: 1999
Market Value: N/E

2

Swing On A Star
DX208 • 5 ½″
Issued: 1995 • Susp.: 1996
Market Value: $40

3

Teacher's Pet
DX124 • 5″
Issued: 1993 • Retired: 1997
Market Value: $36

4

Teddy And Me
DX053 • 3″
Issued: 1994 • Susp.: 1997
Market Value: $20

5

Thinking Of You
DX129 • 9″
Issued: 1993 • Retired: 1997
Market Value: $72

6

Three Amigos
DX179 • 3 ¼″
Issued: 1994 • Susp.: 1996
Market Value: $20

7

Time To Tumble
Tumbling Santas
11329 • 2 ½″
Issued: 2000 • Current
Market Value: $____

8

Tiny Tumbler
Tumbling Santas
11330 • 2 ½″
Issued: 2000 • Current
Market Value: $____

9

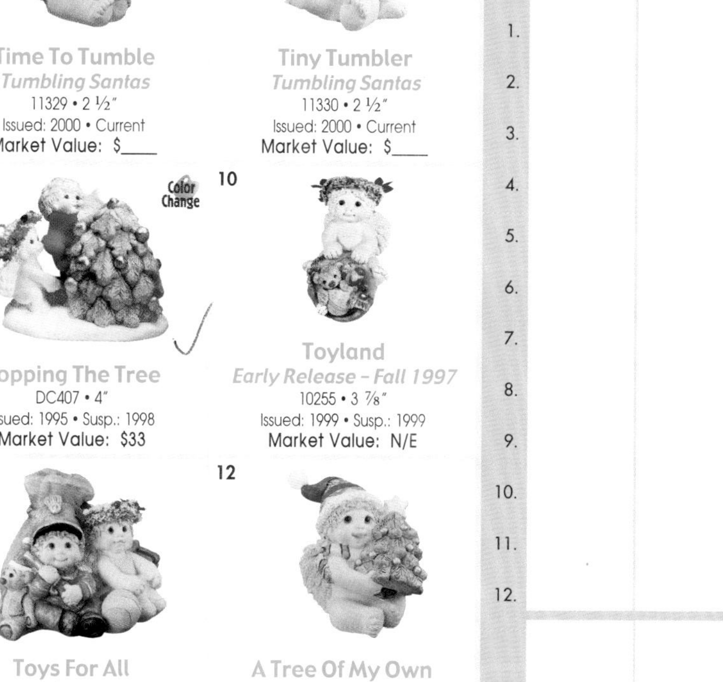

Topping The Tree
DC407 • 4″
Issued: 1995 • Susp.: 1998
Market Value: $33

10

Toyland
Early Release – Fall 1997
10255 • 3 ⅞″
Issued: 1999 • Susp.: 1999
Market Value: N/E

11

Toys For All
11311 • 3″
Issued: 2000 • Current
Market Value: $____

12

A Tree Of My Own
11319 • 3″
Issued: 2000 • Current
Market Value: $____

Holiday Cherubs

	Price Paid	Value
1.		
2.		
3.		
4.		
5.		
6.		
7.		
8.		
9.		
10.		
11.		
12.		
Totals		

1

Tumbled Out
Tumbling Santas
11328 • 2"
Issued: 2000 • Current
Market Value: $____

2

Tumbling Toes
Tumbling Santas
11331 • 2 ¾"
Issued: 2000 • Current
Market Value: $____

3

Turkey Tales
11327 • 3"
Issued: 2000 • Current
Market Value: $____

4

Twinkle, Twinkle
DX700 • 3 ½"
Issued: 1995 • Retired: 1997
Market Value: $23

5

Under The Mistletoe
DX253 • 4 ⅛"
Issued: 1996 • Susp.: 1998
Market Value: $24

6

Up On Top
10814 • 4 ¼"
Issued: 1999 • Current
Market Value: $____

Holiday Cherubs

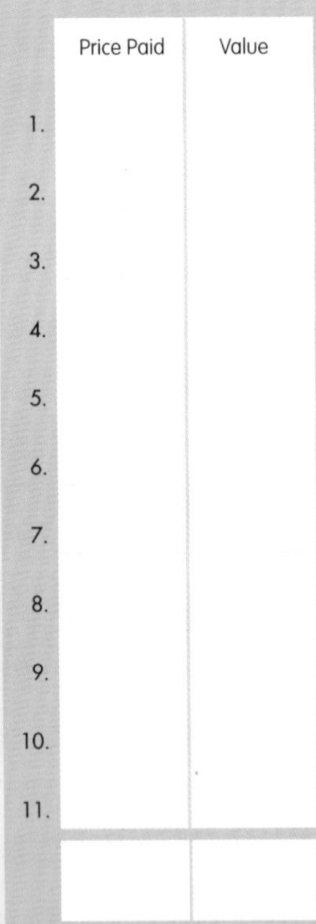

	Price Paid	Value
1.		
2.		
3.		
4.		
5.		
6.		
7.		
8.		
9.		
10.		
11.		
Totals		

7

Visions Of Sugarplums
DX300 • 5 ½"
Issued: 1996 • Susp.: 1998
Market Value: $45

8

Warm And Fuzzy
11340 • 3 ½"
Issued: 2000 • Current
Market Value: $____

9

Where Is Santa?
10846 • 4 ½"
Issued: 1999 • Current
Market Value: $____

10

Who Needs Reindeer?
10821 • 5 ½"
Issued: 1999 • Current
Market Value: $____

11

Wildflower
DX107 • 3 ½"
Issued: 1991 • Retired: 1996
Market Value: $26

1

Wishin' On A Star
DX120 • 4 ¼"
Issued: 1993 • Susp.: 1996
Market Value: $20

2

Wistful Thinking
DX707 • 2"
Issued: 1995 • Susp.: 1997
Market Value: $20

3

You've Got A Friend
DX170 • 6"
Issued: 1994 • Susp.: 1996
Market Value: $47

4

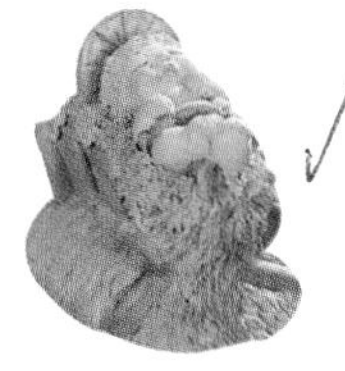

Baby Jesus
DX488 • 2 ½"
Issued: 1995 • Current
Market Value: $____

5

Balthazar
DX481 • 3"
Issued: 1995 • Current
Market Value: $____

6

Bethlehem Inn
DX474 • 9 ½"
Issued: 1996 • Current
Market Value: $____

7

Camel
DX477 • 4"
Issued: 1995 • Current
Market Value: $____

8

Cow
DX480 • 4 ¾"
Issued: 1995 • Current
Market Value: $____

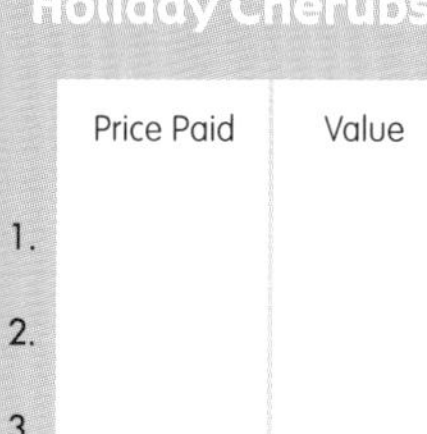

9

Donkey
DX478 • 3 ¾"
Issued: 1995 • Current
Market Value: $____

10

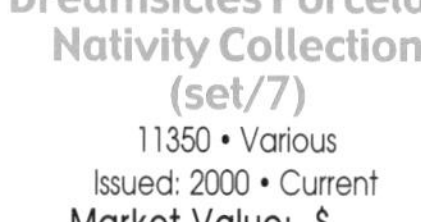

Dreamsicles Porcelain Nativity Collection (set/7)
11350 • Various
Issued: 2000 • Current
Market Value: $____

11

Elephant
DX476 • 4"
Issued: 1995 • Current
Market Value: $____

12

Gaspar
DX483 • 3 ⅛"
Issued: 1995 • Current
Market Value: $____

Holiday Cherubs

	Price Paid	Value
1.		
2.		
3.		
Nativity		
4.		
5.		
6.		
7.		
8.		
9.		
10.		
11.		
12.		
Totals		

1

Girl With Goose
10477 • 3 ½"
Issued: 1998 • Current
Market Value: $____

2

Horse
DX479 • 4"
Issued: 1995 • Current
Market Value: $____

3

Joseph
DX485 • 3 ½"
Issued: 1995 • Current
Market Value: $____

4

Little Drummer Boy
10479 • 2 ⅞"
Issued: 1998 • Current
Market Value: $____

5

Little Town Of Bethlehem Assortment (set/5)
11356 • Various
Issued: 2000 • Current
Market Value: $____

6

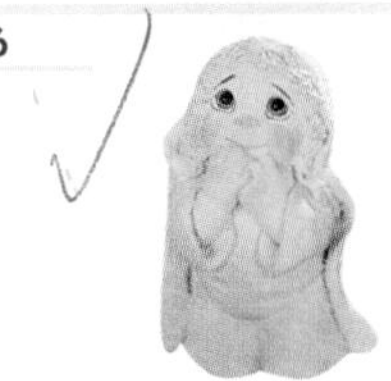

Mary
DX484 • 2 ⅞"
Issued: 1995 • Current
Market Value: $____

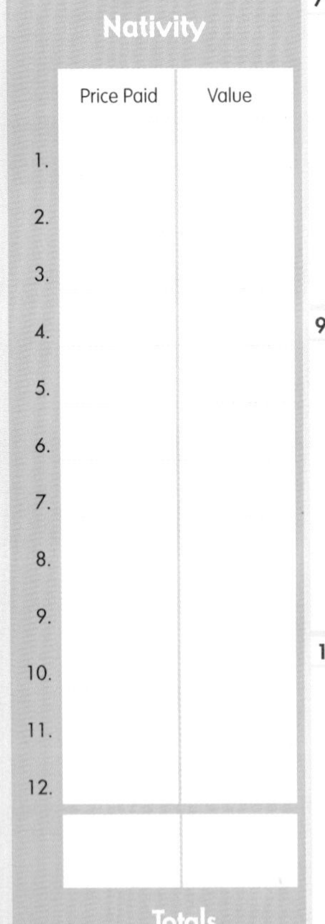

Nativity

	Price Paid	Value
1.		
2.		
3.		
4.		
5.		
6.		
7.		
8.		
9.		
10.		
11.		
12.		
Totals		

7

Melchior
DX482 • 3 ½"
Issued: 1995 • Current
Market Value: $____

8

Miniature Nativity Assortment (set/7)
10489 • Various
Issued: 1998 • Susp.: 1999
Market Value: N/E

9

Nativity Collection (set/15)
DX489 • Various
Issued: 1995 • Current
Market Value: $____

10

Shepherd And Sheep
DX486 • 3 ¾"
Issued: 1995 • Current
Market Value: $____

11

Shepherd With Staff
10478 • 3 ⅞"
Issued: 1998 • Current
Market Value: $____

12

Three Lambs (set/3)
DX487 • 2"
Issued: 1995 • Current
Market Value: $____

Animals & Other Figurines

In addition to the charming cherubs, the Dreamsicles family includes an adorable line of animals such as bears, pigs and bunnies, as well as other figurines such as witches and cheerleaders.

1

Beary Sweet
DA455 • 5″
Issued: 1994 • Susp.: 1996
Market Value: $32

2 Original 29

Buddy Bear
DA451 (5051) • 2 ½″
Issued: 1991 • Retired: 1994
Market Value: $20

3

Clara Bear
DA454 • 5 ½″
Issued: 1995 • Susp.: 1996
Market Value: $25

4

Country Bear
DA458 • 5″
Issued: 1993 • Susp.: 1996
Market Value: $28

5 Original 29

Mama Bear
DA452 (5052) • 3 ½″
Issued: 1991 • Retired: 1994
Market Value: $22

6

Pierre The Bear
DA453 • 4″
Issued: 1993 • Susp.: 1996
Market Value: $35

7

Pierre The Bear
DX453 • 4″
Issued: 1993 • Susp.: 1996
Market Value: $35

8

Teddy Bear
DA456 (5056) • 4 ½″
Issued: 1992 • Susp.: 1995
Market Value: $32

9

Wedding Bears
DA457 (5057) • 5 ¼″
Issued: 1992 • Susp.: 1996
Market Value: $37

10

Dodo
DA482 (5082) • 3 ½″
ssued: 1992 • Retired: 1994
Market Value: $52

11

Lazy Bones
DA605 • 3″
Issued: 1992 • Susp.: 1993
Market Value: $45

12

Papa Pelican
DA602 • 8 ½″
Issued: 1992 • Retired: 1994
Market Value: $50

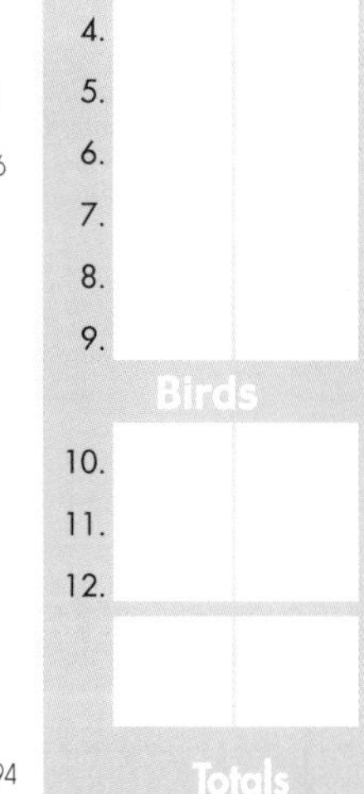

Bears	Price Paid	Value
1.		
2.		
3.		
4.		
5.		
6.		
7.		
8.		
9.		
Birds		
10.		
11.		
12.		
Totals		

1

Pelican Jr.
DA601 • 5″
Issued: 1992 • Susp.: 1996
Market Value: $37

2

Auntie Bunny
DA120 • 4 ½″
Issued: 1995 • Susp.: 1997
Market Value: $40

3

Bigfoot Bunny
DA121 • 11″
Issued: 1995 • Susp.: 1997
Market Value: $50

4

Binky
10025 • 2″
Issued: 1997 • Current
Market Value: $____

5

Bunny Bouquet
10024 • 6″
Issued: 1997 • Current
Market Value: $____

6

Bunny Gardener
DA128 • 4 ¼″
Issued: 1995 • Susp.: 1997
Market Value: $14

7 Original 29

Bunny Hop
DA105 (5005) • 5 ¼″
Issued: 1991 • Retired: 1995
Market Value: $40

8

Bunny Trail
DA125 • 4″
Issued: 1995 • Susp.: 1997
Market Value: $14

9

A Chorus Line
10027 • 2 ⅝″
Issued: 1997 • Current
Market Value: $____

10

Colors Of Spring
DA126 • 3 ¼″
Issued: 1995 • Susp.: 1997
Market Value: N/E

11

Cupid's Helper
DA203 • 2 ¼″
Issued: 1995 • Current
Market Value: $____

12

Dimples
DA100 (5000) • 2 ¼″
Issued: 1991 • Retired: 1995
Market Value: $15

13

Easter Surprise
DA115 • 4 ¼″
Issued: 1993 • Susp.: 1997
Market Value: $24

	Price Paid	Value
Birds		
1.		
Bunnies		
2.		
3.		
4.		
5.		
6.		
7.		
8.		
9.		
10.		
11.		
12.		
13.		
Totals		

1

Egg-citing
DA131 • 2″
Issued: 1995 • Current
Market Value: $____

2

Gathering Flowers
DA320 (5320) • 4 ½″
Issued: 1991 • Retired: 1995
Market Value: $46

3

Gathering Flowers
DX320 • 4 ½″
Issued: 1991 • Retired: 1993
Market Value: $46

4

Helga
DA112 (5012) • 3 ¼″
Issued: 1992 • Retired: 1995
Market Value: $30

5 Original 29

Hippity Hop
DA106 (5006) • 9″
Issued: 1991 • Retired: 1994
Market Value: $50

6

Hitchin' A Ride
DA321 (5321)• 4 ½″
Issued: 1991 • Susp.: 1997
Market Value: $42

7 Original 29

Honey Bun
DA101 (5001) • 2 ¼″
Issued: 1991 • Retired: 1995
Market Value: $16

8

Hop
10999 • 2 ¼″
Issued: 2000 • Current
Market Value: $____

9

Jump
11000 • 2 ¾″
Issued: 2000 • Current
Market Value: $____

10

Just For You
DA132 • 2″
Issued: 1995 • Current
Market Value: $____

11

King Rabbit
DA124 (5024) • 18″
Issued: 1991 • Retired: 1994
Market Value: $125

12

Little Sister
DA110 (5010) • 3 ¼″
Issued: 1992 • Susp.: 1997
Market Value: $24

13

Mom Hugs Best
11002 • 3 ⅞″
Issued: 2000 • Current
Market Value: $____

14 Original 29

Mr. Bunny
DA107 (5007) • 6 ¼″
Issued: 1991 • Retired: 1994
Market Value: $42

Bunnies

	Price Paid	Value
1.		
2.		
3.		
4.		
5.		
6.		
7.		
8.		
9.		
10.		
11.		
12.		
13.		
14.		
Totals		

1 Original 29

Mrs. Bunny
DA108 (5008) • 5 ½″
Issued: 1991 • Retired: 1994
Market Value: $42

2

Pal Joey
DA104 • 4 ¾″
Issued: 1993 • Retired: 1995
Market Value: $36

3

Party Bunny
DA116 • 4 ¼″
Issued: 1993 • Susp.: 1995
Market Value: $23

4

Pumpkin Harvest
DA322 (5322) • 4 ½″
Issued: 1991 • Retired: 1994
Market Value: $32

5

St. Peter Rabbit
DA243 • 8″
Issued: 1992 • Retired: 1994
Market Value: $70

6 Original 29

Santa Bunny
DX203 (5003) • 8 ½″
Issued: 1991 • Retired: 1994
Market Value: $65

7

Sarge
DA111 (5011) • 3 ¼″
Issued: 1992 • Retired: 1995
Market Value: $20

8

Scooter Bunny
DA129 • 2 ½″
Issued: 1995 • Susp.: 1997
Market Value: $15

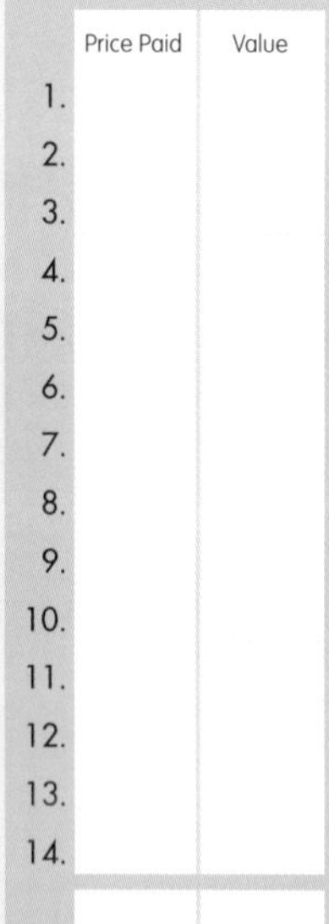

Bunnies

	Price Paid	Value
1.		
2.		
3.		
4.		
5.		
6.		
7.		
8.		
9.		
10.		
11.		
12.		
13.		
14.		
Totals		

9

Sir Hareold
DA123 (5023) • 10 ½″
Issued: 1992 • Retired: 1996
Market Value: $75

10

Skip
10998 • 3 ¼″
Issued: 2000 • Current
Market Value: $____

11

Soap Box Bunny
DA221 (5303) • 4″
Issued: 1991 • Retired: 1995
Market Value: $41

12

Sonny Boy
DA109 (5009) • 3 ¼″
Issued: 1992 • Susp.: 1997
Market Value: $26

13

Steppin' Out
DA130 • 2 ½″
Issued: 1995 • Current
Market Value: $____

14

Sweetie Pie
10026 • 2 ¼″
Issued: 1997 • Current
Market Value: $____

1

Original 29

Tiny Bunny
DA102 (5002) • 3"
Issued: 1991 • Retired: 1995
Market Value: $22

2

A Tisket, A Tasket
DA114 • 4 ½"
Issued: 1993 • Susp.: 1997
Market Value: $22

3

Tuckered Out
DA127 • 4 ¾"
Issued: 1995 • Current
Market Value: $____

4

Uncle Bunny
DA119 • 5"
Issued: 1995 • Susp.: 1997
Market Value: $35

5

Cat Nap
DA551 (5351) • 5 ½"
Issued: 1992 • Susp.: 1995
Market Value: $20

6

The Cat's Meow
DA552 (5352) • 5"
Issued: 1992 • Susp.: 1995
Market Value: $23

7

Cute As A Button
DA553 (5353) • 4"
Issued: 1992 • Susp.: 1995
Market Value: $29

8

Fat Cat
DA555 (5355) • 5 ¼"
Issued: 1992 • Retired: 1994
Market Value: $42

9

Pretty Kitty
DA554 (5354) • 5 ½"
Issued: 1992 • Susp.: 1995
Market Value: $32

10

Go, Team Go! – Blue
11168 • 3"
Issued: 2000 • Current
Market Value: $____

11

Go, Team Go! – Green
11164 • 3"
Issued: 2000 • Current
Market Value: $____

12

Go, Team Go! – Maroon
11169 • 3"
Issued: 2000 • Current
Market Value: $____

13

Go, Team Go! – Orange
11166 • 3"
Issued: 2000 • Current
Market Value: $____

	Price Paid	Value
Bunnies		
1.		
2.		
3.		
4.		
Cats		
5.		
6.		
7.		
8.		
9.		
Cheerleaders		
10.		
11.		
12.		
13.		
Totals		

1

Go, Team Go! – Purple
11170 • 3″
Issued: 2000 • Current
Market Value: $____

2

Go, Team Go! – Red
11167 • 3″
Issued: 2000 • Current
Market Value: $____

3

Go, Team Go! – Yellow
11165 • 3″
Issued: 2000 • Current
Market Value: $____

4

An Apple A Day
10531 • 4 ½″
Issued: 1998 • Susp.: 1999
Market Value: N/E

5

Cafe Au Lait
10533 • 3 ½″
Issued: 1998 • Susp.: 1999
Market Value: N/E

6

Carnation
DA379 (5179) • 4″
Issued: 1991 • Retired: 1996
Market Value: $22

7

Cow Belle
10532 • 5 ⅜″
Issued: 1998 • Susp.: 1999
Market Value: N/E

8

Cowpokes
DA384 • 4 ¾″
Issued: 1995 • Susp.: 1997
Market Value: $15

Cheerleaders

	Price Paid	Value
1.		
2.		
3.		

Cows

	Price Paid	Value
4.		
5.		
6.		
7.		
8.		
9.		
10.		
11.		
12.		
13.		
14.		
Totals		

9

Original 29

Dairy Delight
DA381 (5181) • 5 ½″
Issued: 1991 • Retired: 1995
Market Value: $43

10

Daisy
DA376 • 2 ½″
Issued: 1995 • Susp.: 1997
Market Value: $25

11

Get Along Little Dogie
DA378 (5178) • 3 ½″
Issued: 1991 • Susp.: 1997
Market Value: $22

12

Henrietta
DA383 • 7″ wide
Issued: 1994 • Retired: 1996
Market Value: $42

13

Hey Diddle Diddle
DA380 (5180) • 5 ¼″
Issued: 1991 • Retired: 1996
Market Value: $34

14

Moo Cow
DA377 • 4″
Issued: 1993 • Susp.: 1997
Market Value: $20

1

Santa Cow
DX455 • 4 ¾″
Issued: 1995 • Susp.: 1997
Market Value: $33

2 Original 29

Sweet Cream
DA382 (5182) • 7 ¼″
Issued: 1991 • Retired: 1996
Market Value: $48

3

Hound Dog
DA568 • 3″
Issued: 1992 • Retired: 1994
Market Value: $30

4

Man's Best Friend
DA560 • 3 ½″
Issued: 1992 • Retired: 1994
Market Value: $24

5

Puppy Love
DA562 • 3 ½″
Issued: 1992 • Retired: 1994
Market Value: $22

6

Red Rover
DA566 • 5 ½″
Issued: 1992 • Retired: 1994
Market Value: $26

7

Scooter
DA567 • 3″
Issued: 1992 • Retired: 1994
Market Value: $29

8

Baby Jumbo
10028 • 3 ⅛″
Issued: 1997 • Susp.: 1998
Market Value: $15

9

Balancing Act
10584 • 4 ⅜″
Issued: 1998 • Susp.: 1999
Market Value: N/E

10

Bubbles
10585 • 3 ¼″
Issued: 1998 • Susp.: 1999
Market Value: N/E

11 Color Change

Center Ring
DA250 • 3″
Issued: 1996 • Susp.: 1998
Market Value: N/E

12 Color Change

Elephant Walk
DA253 • 5 ½″
Issued: 1996 • Susp.: 1998
Market Value: N/E

13

Forgetful
11231 • 2 ½″
Issued: 2000 • Current
Market Value: $____

14

Intermission
DA254 • 2 ¼″
Issued: 1996 • Susp.: 1998
Market Value: N/E

	Price Paid	Value
Cows		
1.		
2.		
Dogs		
3.		
4.		
5.		
6.		
7.		
Elephants		
8.		
9.		
10.		
11.		
12.		
13.		
14.		
Totals		

1

Peanut Gallery
DA256 • 3 ¼″
Issued: 1996 • Susp.: 1998
Market Value: N/E

2

Color Change

Showtime
DA255 • 5″
Issued: 1996 • Susp.: 1998
Market Value: N/E

3

Trunkful Of Love
10029 • 3 ¼″
Issued: 1997 • Susp.: 1998
Market Value: N/E

4

Blowfish
DA608 • 1″
Issued: 1992 • Susp.: 1993
Market Value: $36

5

Double Fish
DA611 • 2 ½″
Issued: 1992 • Susp.: 1993
Market Value: $26

6

Largemouth Bass
DA609 • 3″
Issued: 1992 • Susp.: 1993
Market Value: $26

7

Needlenose Fish
DA610 • 3 ½″
Issued: 1992 • Susp.: 1993
Market Value: $35

8

All Smiles
10929 • 2 ⅞″
Issued: 1999 • Current
Market Value: $____

9

Boo!
10587 • 5″
Issued: 1998 • Current
Market Value: $____

10

Boo Babies (set/4)
DA655 • 2″
Issued: 1994 • Current
Market Value: $____

11

Boo Who?
DA650 (5650) • 4 ½″
Issued: 1991 • Retired: 1996
Market Value: $32

12

Ghostly Assortment
10973 • 3 ½″
Issued: 1999 • Susp.: 2000
Market Value: N/E

13

Goblins Galore
DA656 • 7 ¼″ (wide)
Issued: 1995 • Current
Market Value: $____

14

Halloween Surprise
10928 • 4 ¾″
Issued: 1999 • Susp.: 2000
Market Value: N/E

	Price Paid	Value
Elephants		
1.		
2.		
3.		
Fish		
4.		
5.		
6.		
7.		
Ghosts & Goblins		
8.		
9.		
10.		
11.		
12.		
13.		
14.		
Totals		

1

Swept Away
10930 • 3 ½″
Issued: 1999 • Current
Market Value: $____

2

Trick Or Treat
DA651 (5651) • 4 ½″
Issued: 1991 • Retired: 1996
Market Value: $40

3

Original 29

Lambie Pie
DA328 (5028) • 4″
Issued: 1991 • Retired: 1994
Market Value: $22

4

Original 29

Mutton Chops
DA326 (5026) • 2 ½″
Issued: 1991 • Retired: 1994
Market Value: $20

5

Socrates The Sheep
5029 • 5″
Issued: 1991 • Susp.: 1992
Market Value: $90

6

Original 29

Wooley Bully
DA327 (5027) • 2 ¾″
Issued: 1991 • Retired: 1994
Market Value: $20

7

Batter Up
10070 • 3″
Issued: 1997 • Susp.: 1997
Market Value: N/E

8

Cheesecake
10074 • 2 ¾″
Issued: 1997 • Susp.: 1997
Market Value: N/E

9

Color Me Happy
10069 • 3″
Issued: 1997 • Susp.: 1997
Market Value: N/E

10

Family Reunion
10072 • 3″
Issued: 1997 • Susp.: 1997
Market Value: N/E

11

Fancy Dance
10071 • 3″
Issued: 1997 • Susp.: 1997
Market Value: N/E

12

Let It Snow
DA473 • 3″
Issued: 1994 • Susp.: 1997
Market Value: $18

13

Original 29

Mother Mouse
DA477 (5077) • 4″
Issued: 1991 • Retired: 1994
Market Value: $32

14

Mouse-O'-Lantern
DA472 • 3″
Issued: 1993 • Susp.: 1997
Market Value: $17

	Price Paid	Value
Ghosts & Goblins		
1.		
2.		
Lambs & Sheep		
3.		
4.		
5.		
6.		
Mice		
7.		
8.		
9.		
10.		
11.		
12.		
13.		
14.		
Totals		

1

Mouse On Skis
DA475 (5300) • 4 ½″
Issued: 1991 • Susp.: 1993
Market Value: $40

2 Original 29

P. J. Mouse
DA476 (5076) • 2 ¾″
Issued: 1991 • Retired: 1994
Market Value: $28

3

Sleigh Bells Ring
DA474 • 2 ¾″
Issued: 1994 • Susp.: 1997
Market Value: $42

4

Sweet On You
10073 • 2 ½″
Issued: 1997 • Susp.: 1997
Market Value: N/E

5

Little Drummer Boy
DX241 • 6″
Issued: 1992 • Susp.: 1996
Market Value: $46

6 Original 29

Musician With Cymbals
5154 • 7 ¼″
Issued: 1991 • Susp.: 1992
Market Value: $110

7 Original 29

Musician With Drums
5152 • 8″
Issued: 1991 • Susp.: 1992
Market Value: $120

8 Original 29

Musician With Flute
5153 • 7 ½″
Issued: 1991 • Susp.: 1992
Market Value: $110

9 Original 29

Musician With Trumpet
5151 • 7″
Issued: 1991 • Susp.: 1992
Market Value: $100

10

Hambone
DA344 (5044) • 3 ¼″
Issued: 1991 • Retired: 1996
Market Value: $22

11

Hamlet
DA342 (5042) • 4 ¼″
Issued: 1991 • Retired: 1996
Market Value: $22

12

Kitchen Pig
DA345 (5045) • 8 ½″
Issued: 1991 • Susp.: 1995
Market Value: $63

13

Momma Pig
DA347 • 4 ½″
Issued: 1994 • Susp.: 1996
Market Value: $25

14

Pappy Pig
DA346 • 4 ¾″
Issued: 1994 • Susp.: 1996
Market Value: $30

	Price Paid	Value
Mice		
1.		
2.		
3.		
4.		
Musicians		
5.		
6.		
7.		
8.		
9.		
Pigs		
10.		
11.		
12.		
13.		
14.		
Totals		

1

Piglet
DA343 (5043) • 3"
Issued: 1991 • Retired: 1996
Market Value: $28

2 Original 29

Pigmalion
DA340 (5040) • 2"
Issued: 1991 • Retired: 1995
Market Value: $23

3 Original 29

Pigtails
DA341 (5041) • 2"
Issued: 1991 • Retired: 1995
Market Value: $22

4

Pintsize Pigs
DA349 • 3 ½"
Issued: 1994 • Susp.: 1996
Market Value: $32

5

Preppie Pig
DA348 • 4 ½"
Issued: 1994 • Susp.: 1996
Market Value: $26

6 Color Change

Elf Help
DX259 • 3 ¼"
Issued: 1996 • Susp.: 1997
Market Value: N/E

7

Father Christmas
DX246 • 8 ½"
Issued: 1993 • Susp.: 1997
Market Value: $60

8

Father Christmas #2
10463 • 8"
Issued: 1998 • Susp.: 1999
Market Value: N/E

9

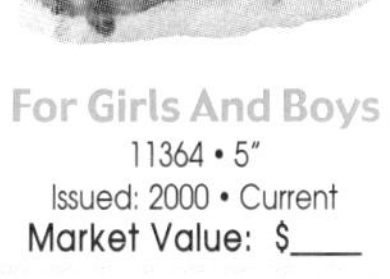

For Girls And Boys
11364 • 5"
Issued: 2000 • Current
Market Value: $____

10

Giant Santa
10422 • 14"
Issued: 1998 • Susp.: 1999
Market Value: N/E

11

Greetings
11363 • 4 ½"
Issued: 2000 • Current
Market Value: $____

12

Here Comes Santa Claus
DX245 • 18"
Issued: 1991 • Susp.: 1997
Market Value: N/E

13

Ho Ho Ho
11322 • 8 ½"
Issued: 2000 • Current
Market Value: $____

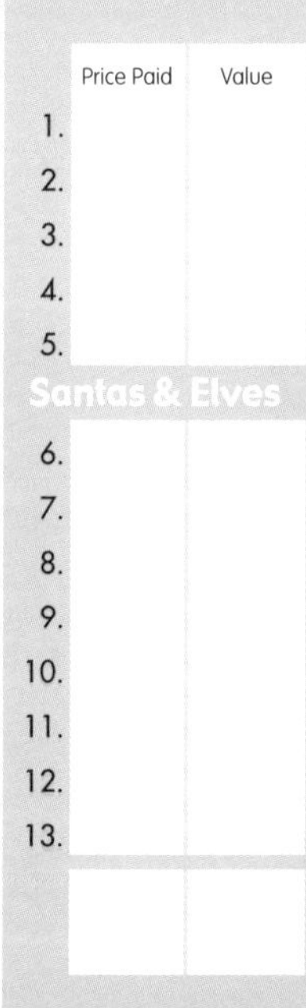

Pigs

	Price Paid	Value
1.		
2.		
3.		
4.		
5.		
Santas & Elves		
6.		
7.		
8.		
9.		
10.		
11.		
12.		
13.		
Totals		

1

Jolly Old Santa
DX244 • 7 ½″
Issued: 1992 • Susp.: 1997
Market Value: $42

2

Jolly Old Santa #2
10464 • 7″
Issued: 1998 • Susp.: 1999
Market Value: N/E

3

Noble Fir
11366 • 4″
Issued: 2000 • Current
Market Value: $____

4

Right On Track
11368 • 8″ (wide)
Issued: 2000 • Current
Market Value: $____

5

Santa's Elf
DX240 • 5 ½″
Issued: 1991 • Retired: 1996
Market Value: $42

6

Taking A Break
11365 • 3 ¼″
Issued: 2000 • Current
Market Value: $____

7

Up On The Rooftop
10423 • 5 ¾″
Issued: 1998 • Susp.: 1999
Market Value: $____

8

Woodland Santa
10810 • 7″
Issued: 1999 • Current
Market Value: $____

Santas & Elves

	Price Paid	Value
1.		
2.		
3.		
4.		
5.		
6.		
7.		
8.		
Witches		
9.		
10.		
11.		
12.		
13.		
14.		
Totals		

9

Be-Witching
DA652 • 5″
Issued: 1993 • Current
Market Value: $____

10

Halloween Ride
DA659 • 4″
Issued: 1994 • Susp.: 2000
Market Value: N/E

11

Hocus Pocus
10927 • 5″
Issued: 1999 • Current
Market Value: $____

12

13

Pumpkin Seed
DA662 • 3″
Issued: 1994 • Current
Market Value: $____

Pumpkin Seed
10606 • 3″
Issued: 1998 • Current
Market Value: $____

14

Spellbound
10589 • 6 ⅛″
Issued: 1998 • Current
Market Value: $____

1

Sweeping Beauty
DA661 • 2 ½″
Issued: 1994 • Current
Market Value: $____

2

Sweeping Beauty
10605 • 2 ½″
Issued: 1998 • Current
Market Value: $____

3

Wicked Witch
10592 • 12″
Issued: 1998 • Current
Market Value: $____

4

Witch
DA660 (5660) • 5″
Issued: 1991 • Current
Market Value: $____

5

Witch's Brew
DA654 • 4″
Issued: 1994 • Current
Market Value: $____

6

Witch's Potion
10588 • 6 ¾″
Issued: 1998 • Current
Market Value: $____

7 Original 29

Armadillo
5176 • 3 ½″
Issued: 1991 • Susp.: 1992
Market Value: N/E

8

Be Merry
10822 • 2 ½″
Issued: 1999 • Current
Market Value: $____

9

Beach Baby
DA615 • 6 ½″
Issued: 1992 • Retired: 1994
Market Value: $46

10

Big Shot
11229 • 3″
Issued: 2000 • Current
Market Value: $____

11

Boom Boom
11228 • 3″
Issued: 2000 • Current
Market Value: $____

12

Bundle Up
10473 • 3 ½″
Issued: 1998 • Susp.: 1999
Market Value: N/E

13

Photo Unavailable

Circus Ring
11230 • 1″
Issued: 2000 • Current
Market Value: $____

14

Crabby
DA607 • 2 ½″
Issued: 1992 • Susp.: 1993
Market Value: $32

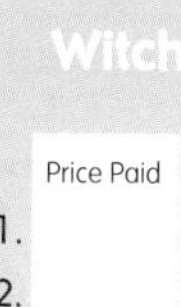

Witches

	Price Paid	Value
1.		
2.		
3.		
4.		
5.		
6.		
Other Figurines		
7.		
8.		
9.		
10.		
11.		
12.		
13.		
14.		
Totals		

1

Dilly
10599 • 3″
Issued: 1998 • Susp.: 1999
Market Value: N/E

2

Dino
DA480 (5080) • 4 ¼″
Issued: 1992 • Retired: 1994
Market Value: $55

3

Frankie
10920 • 8″
Issued: 1999 • Current
Market Value: $____

4

Free Ride
DA631 (5031) • 3 ½″
Issued: 1992 • Susp.: 1996
Market Value: $50

5

Happy Sailing
DA220 (5301) • 3 ¾″
Issued: 1991 • Retired: 1994
Market Value: $30

6

Heads Up
11226 • 3 ½″
Issued: 2000 • Susp.: 2000
Market Value: N/E

7

Li'l Chick
DA385 • 2″
Issued: 1993 • Susp.: 1995
Market Value: $19

8

Li'l Duck
DA388 • 2″
Issued: 1993 • Susp.: 1995
Market Value: $19

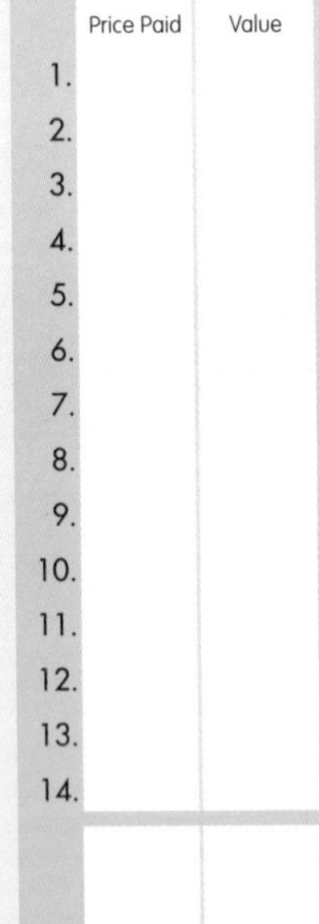

Other Figurines

	Price Paid	Value
1.		
2.		
3.		
4.		
5.		
6.		
7.		
8.		
9.		
10.		
11.		
12.		
13.		
14.		
Totals		

9

Little Giggles
11225 • 2 ½″
Issued: 2000 • Susp.: 2000
Market Value: N/E

10

Mom's Taxi
10736 • 3 ¾″
Issued: 1999 • Current
Market Value: $____

11

Naptime
DA556 • 2 ¾″
Issued: 1996 • Susp.: 1996
Market Value: $26

12

Octopus' Garden
DA606 • 4″
Issued: 1992 • Susp.: 1993
Market Value: $45

13 Color Change

Opening Night
DA252 • 4″
Issued: 1996 • Susp.: 1998
Market Value: $26

14

Prancer
DX202 • 8″
Issued: 1991 • Susp.: 1997
Market Value: $60

1

Rhino
DA481 (5081) • 4″
Issued: 1992 • Retired: 1994
Market Value: $45

2

Ricky Raccoon
5170 • 6 ½″
Issued: 1991 • Susp.: 1992
Market Value: $90

3

Scarecrow & Friends
DA653 • 3″
Issued: 1993 • Susp.: 2000
Market Value: N/E

4

Scary Noises
10925 • 4 ½″
Issued: 1999 • Current
Market Value: $____

5

Scary Stories
10926 • 4 ½″
Issued: 1999 • Current
Market Value: $____

6

Sledding
10472 • 4″
Issued: 1998 • Susp.: 1999
Market Value: N/E

7

Slow Poke
DA630 (5030) • 4 ½″
Issued: 1992 • Susp.: 1995
Market Value: $45

8

Snowman
DX252 • 3 ½″
Issued: 1991 • Susp.: 1996
Market Value: $21

9

Splash
DA616 • 6 ¼″
Issued: 1993 • Retired: 1994
Market Value: $62

10

Tender Toes
11227 • 2 ¾″
Issued: 2000 • Current
Market Value: $____

11

Three On A Sled
DX454 • 4″
Issued: 1994 • Susp.: 1997
Market Value: $30

12

Water Ballet
10006 • 5″
Issued: 1996 • Susp.: 1997
Market Value: $30

13

Winter's Comin'
DA471 (5171) • 4 ½″
Issued: 1991 • Susp.: 1993
Market Value: $43

Other Figurines

	Price Paid	Value
1.		
2.		
3.		
4.		
5.		
6.		
7.		
8.		
9.		
10.		
11.		
12.		
13.		
Totals		

Dreamsicles Kids™

These charming sculptures portray children at play, capturing their youthful innocence. Although no new pieces have been introduced recently, the popularity of the Dreamsicles Kids endures .

1 Color Change

All I Want
DK040 • 3 ⅜"
Issued: 1996 • Susp.: 1997
Market Value: $20

2

Anticipation (I.C.E. Figurine)
SP002 • 4 ¼"
Issued: 1997 • Current
Market Value: $____

3

Apple Dumpling
10059 • 3 ⅞"
Issued: 1997 • Susp.: 1998
Market Value: N/E

4

Apple Polisher
10058 • 4 ⅛"
Issued: 1997 • Susp.: 1998
Market Value: N/E

5

Arctic Pals
10178 • 2 ¾"
Issued: 1997 • Susp.: 1998
Market Value: N/E

6

Baby Bunny
10065 • 4"
Issued: 1997 • Current
Market Value: $____

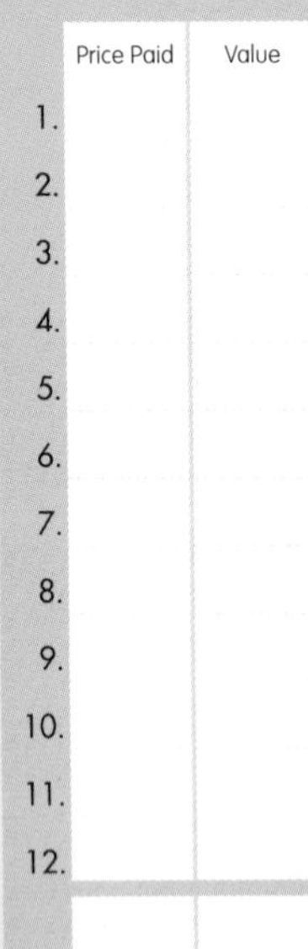

Dreamsicles Kids™

	Price Paid	Value
1.		
2.		
3.		
4.		
5.		
6.		
7.		
8.		
9.		
10.		
11.		
12.		
Totals		

7 Color Change

Bear Back Rider
DK025 • 4 ½"
Issued: 1996 • Susp.: 1997
Market Value: N/E

8

Beggars' Night
10204 • 4 ¼"
Issued: 1997 • Current
Market Value: $____

9

Bewitched
10601 • 5 ¼"
Issued: 1998 • Current
Market Value: $____

10

By The Sea
10055 • 3 ½"
Issued: 1997 • Susp.: 1998
Market Value: N/E

11

Child's Play
DK018 • 2 ⅞"
Issued: 1996 • Susp.: 1998
Market Value: $18

12

Coconut Kids
10008 • 3"
Issued: 1996 • Susp.: 1997
Market Value: N/E

1

Come All Ye Faithful
DK033 • 3 ¾″
Issued: 1996 • Susp.: 1997
Market Value: N/E

2

Dances With Bears
DK036 • 3 ⅝″
Issued: 1996 • Susp.: 1997
Market Value: N/E

3

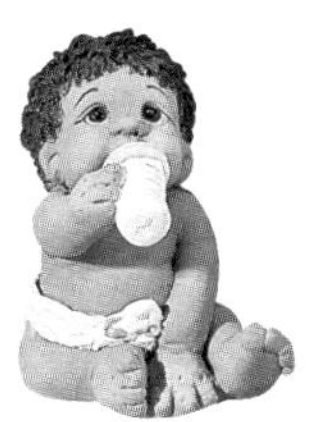

Diaper Dandy
DK017 • 2 ¾″
Issued: 1996 • Susp.: 1997
Market Value: N/E

4

Dream Team
10090 • 3″
Issued: 1997 • Current
Market Value: $____

5

Dreamsicles Kids Logo
DK001 • 4 ¼″
Issued: 1996 • Susp.: 1997
Market Value: $40

6

Egg-citement
10066 • 4 ⅛″
Issued: 1997 • Current
Market Value: $____

7

Favorite Toy
10188 • 4 ½″
Issued: 1997 • Susp.: 1998
Market Value: $16

8

The First Noel
DK032 • 3 ½″
Issued: 1996 • Susp.: 1997
Market Value: N/E

9

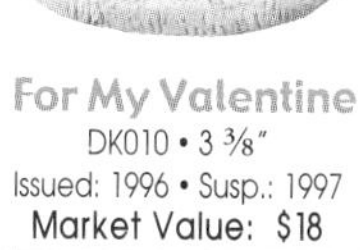

For My Valentine
DK010 • 3 ⅜″
Issued: 1996 • Susp.: 1997
Market Value: $18

10

Free Kittens
DK038 • 2 ⅞″
Issued: 1996 • Retired: 1998
Market Value: $20

11

Free Puppies
DK039 • 2 ¾″
Issued: 1996 • Retired: 1998
Market Value: $18

12

Frosty Friends
10179 • 2 ½″
Issued: 1997 • Susp.: 1998
Market Value: $16

13

Here's My List
DK022 • 3 ½″
Issued: 1996 • Susp.: 1997
Market Value: $21

Dreamsicles Kids™

	Price Paid	Value
1.		
2.		
3.		
4.		
5.		
6.		
7.		
8.		
9.		
10.		
11.		
12.		
13.		
Totals		

1

Color Change

High Chair High Jinks
DK030 • 3 3/8"
Issued: 1996 • Susp.: 1997
Market Value: $20

2

Honey Bunny
DK016 • 2 1/4"
Issued: 1996 • Current
Market Value: $____

3

Hug A Bunny
DK015 • 4"
Issued: 1996 • Susp.: 1997
Market Value: N/E

4

Hula Honeys
10011 • 3 1/2"
Issued: 1996 • Susp.: 1997
Market Value: N/E

5

Color Change

Joy To The World
DK031 • 4"
Issued: 1996 • Susp.: 1997
Market Value: N/E

6

Color Change

Junior Nurse
DK029 • 3"
Issued: 1996 • Current
Market Value: $____

7

Kissing Booth
DK042 • 3 3/8"
Issued: 1997 • Susp.: 1998
Market Value: $24

8

Color Change

Light The Candles
DK026 • 2 3/4"
Issued: 1996 • Susp.: 1997
Market Value: $16

9

Lion's Share
DA663 • 4 1/4"
Issued: 1996 • Current
Market Value: $____

10

Love You, Mom
DK011 • 3 3/4"
Issued: 1996 • Susp.: 1998
Market Value: $18

11

Mama's Girl
DK019 • 2 3/4"
Issued: 1996 • Susp.: 1997
Market Value: N/E

12

Mush You Huskies
10180 • 12" (wide)
Issued: 1997 • Susp.: 1998
Market Value: N/E

13

My A-B-C's
DK012 • 3"
Issued: 1996 • Susp.: 1997
Market Value: N/E

Dreamsicles Kids™

	Price Paid	Value
1.		
2.		
3.		
4.		
5.		
6.		
7.		
8.		
9.		
10.		
11.		
12.		
13.		
Totals		

1

Nutcracker Sweet
10189 • 3 ¼″
Issued: 1997 • Susp.: 1998
Market Value: $11

2

Ocean Friends
10010 • 5 ½″
Issued: 1996 • Susp.: 1997
Market Value: $30

3

Piggy Bank
DK024 • 3″
Issued: 1996 • Susp.: 1997
Market Value: N/E

4 Color Change

Please, Santa
DK023 • 3 ½″
Issued: 1996 • Susp.: 1997
Market Value: $16

5

Pop Goes The Weasel
DK014 • 2 ½″
Issued: 1996 • Susp.: 1997
Market Value: N/E

6

Potty Break
10056 • 3″
Issued: 1997 • Susp.: 1998
Market Value: $10

7

Potty Time
10057 • 3″
Issued: 1997 • Susp.: 1998
Market Value: $13

8

Pull Toy
DK027 • 4 ¼″
Issued: 1996 • Retired: 1998
Market Value: $20

9

Punkin
10203 • 4 ½″
Issued: 1997 • Current
Market Value: $____

10

Rhyme Time
DK013 • 2 ¾″
Issued: 1996 • Susp.: 1997
Market Value: $18

11

Sand, Sun And Fun
10054 • 2 ⅞″
Issued: 1997 • Susp.: 1998
Market Value: N/E

12 Color Change

Silent Night
DK034 • 3 ⅜″
Issued: 1996 • Susp.: 1997
Market Value: $16

13 Color Change

Snowball Fight
DK037 • 3 ⅝″
Issued: 1996 • Susp.: 1997
Market Value: N/E

Dreamsicles Kids™

	Price Paid	Value
1.		
2.		
3.		
4.		
5.		
6.		
7.		
8.		
9.		
10.		
11.		
12.		
13.		
Totals		

1

Spilt Milk
10053 • 4 ¼"
Issued: 1997 • Susp.: 1997
Market Value: N/E

2

Sunken Treasure
10009 • 3 ½"
Issued: 1996 • Susp.: 1997
Market Value: $18

3

Surf's Up
10007 • 3 ½"
Issued: 1996 • Susp.: 1997
Market Value: $22

4

Three Bears
DK035 • 2 ½"
Issued: 1996 • Susp.: 1997
Market Value: N/E

5

Three Musketeers
DA664 • 4"
Issued: 1996 • Current
Market Value: $____

6

Toddlin' Tyke
DK020 • 3"
Issued: 1996 • Susp.: 1998
Market Value: N/E

7 Color Change

Visit With Santa
DK021 • 3 ¾"
Issued: 1996 • Susp.: 1997
Market Value: $26

8

Witchcraft
10602 • 6 ½"
Issued: 1998 • Current
Market Value: $____

Dreamsicles Kids™

	Price Paid	Value
1.		
2.		
3.		
4.		
5.		
6.		
7.		
8.		
9.		
Totals		

9 Color Change

Young Pups
DK028 • 3 ¼"
Issued: 1996 • Susp.: 1997
Market Value: N/E

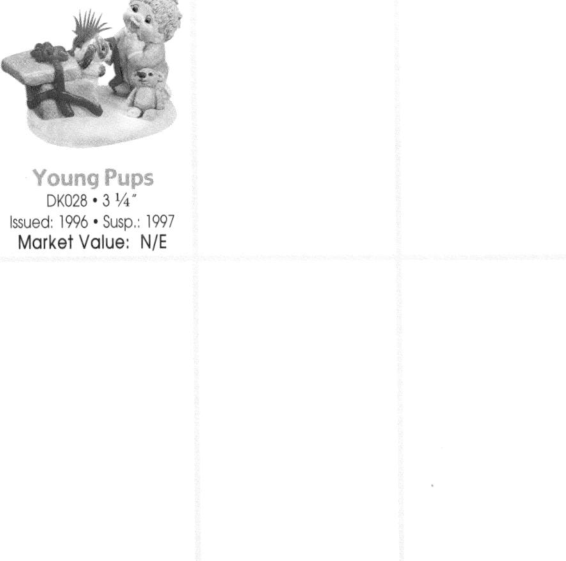

Heavenly Classics™

First introduced in 1995, all Heavenly Classics figurines have been retired or suspended.

1

All God's Creatures
HC357 • 7 ¼"
Issued: 1995 • Susp.: 1997
Market Value: $75

2

Bundles Of Love
HC370 • 8"
Issued: 1996 • Susp.: 1996
Market Value: $1,000

3

Crowning Glory
HC359 • 7"
Issued: 1996 • Susp.: 1997
Market Value: $70

4

Devoted Companions
HC365 • 4 ½"
Issued: 1996 • Susp.: 1997
Market Value: $30

5

Dreamboat
10060 • 7"
Issued: 1997 • Retired: 1997
Market Value: $110

6

First Flight
HC369 • 9 ½"
Issued: 1996 • Susp.: 1997
Market Value: $110

7

Footsteps
HC367 • 5"
Issued: 1996 • Susp.: 1997
Market Value: $30

8

Color Change

A Gift Of Love
HC366 • 4 ½"
Issued: 1996 • Susp.: 1997
Market Value: $30

9

God Bless The Child
HC352 (DC352) • 10"
Issued: 1995 • Susp.: 1997
Market Value: $85

10

Heartwarming
HC360 • 6 ½"
Issued: 1996 • Susp.: 1997
Market Value: $85

11

Higher Learning
HC353 (DC353) • 6 ½"
Issued: 1995 • Susp.: 1997
Market Value: $105

12

Hush Little Baby
HC361 • 7 ¼"
Issued: 1996 • Susp.: 1997
Market Value: $58

13

Making Memories
HC381 • 11"
Issued: 1996 • Susp.: 1996
Market Value: $110

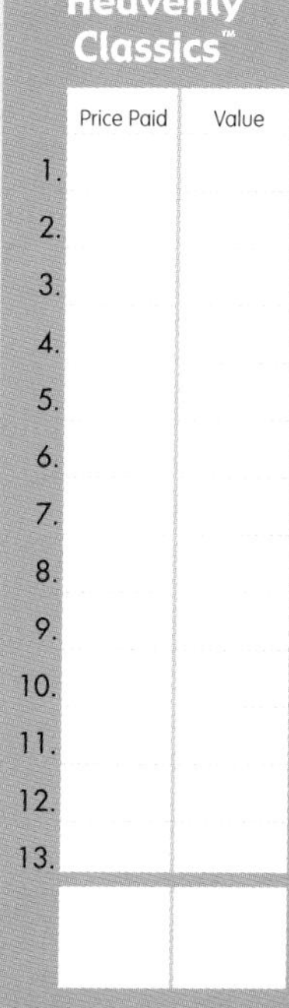

Heavenly Classics™

	Price Paid	Value
1.		
2.		
3.		
4.		
5.		
6.		
7.		
8.		
9.		
10.		
11.		
12.		
13.		
Totals		

1

Making Memories
10096 • 11″
Issued: 1997 • Susp.: 1997
Market Value: $110

2

Music Appreciation
HC354 (DC354) • 5 ½″
Issued: 1995 • Susp.: 1997
Market Value: $110

3

Nature's Blessing
HC364 • 3 ¾″
Issued: 1996 • Susp.: 1997
Market Value: $50

4

New Beginnings
10251 • 6 ¼″
Issued: 1997 • Susp.: 1998
Market Value: $45

5

Ode To Joy
HC362 • 6 ¾″
Issued: 1996 • Susp.: 1997
Market Value: $65

6

On Wings Of Love
HC355 (DC355) • 9 ½″
Issued: 1995 • Susp.: 1997
Market Value: $110

7

Our Father
HC356 • 4 ¾″
Issued: 1995 • Susp.: 1997
Market Value: $48

8

Power Of Love
HC363 • 6″
Issued: 1996 • Susp.: 1997
Market Value: $50

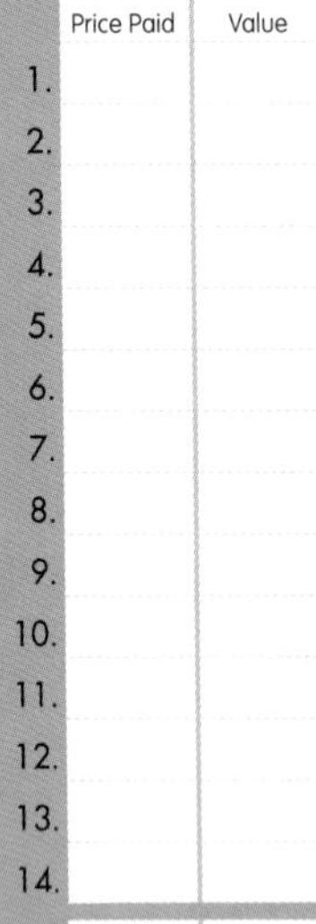

Heavenly Classics™

	Price Paid	Value
1.		
2.		
3.		
4.		
5.		
6.		
7.		
8.		
9.		
10.		
11.		
12.		
13.		
14.		
Totals		

9

Reach For The Stars
HC382 • 7″
Issued: 1996 • Susp.: 1996
Market Value: $85

10

Reverence
HC350 (DC350) • 7 ½″
Issued: 1995 • Susp.: 1997
Market Value: $135

11

Sleep Little Angel
HC368 • 5 ¾″
Issued: 1996 • Susp.: 1997
Market Value: $80

12

Sounds Of Heaven
10250 • 7 ¼″
Issued: 1997 • Susp.: 1998
Market Value: $48

13

Starry Starry Night
HC358 • 8 ½″
Issued: 1995 • Susp.: 1997
Market Value: $80

14

Winter's Kiss
HC383 • 4 ¾″
Issued: 1996 • Susp.: 1996
Market Value: $45

Northern Lights™

Debuting in 1999, the Northern Lights collection features pieces in wintry tones of white, blue and purple.

1

Alexandrite (June)
Birthstone Collection
60042 • 3″
Issued: 2000 • Current
Market Value: $____

2

All Dressed Up
60761 • 7″
Issued: 2000 • Current
Market Value: $____

3

Amethyst (February)
Birthstone Collection
60038 • 3″
Issued: 2000 • Current
Market Value: $____

4

Aquamarine (March)
Birthstone Collection
60039 • 3″
Issued: 2000 • Current
Market Value: $____

5

Aurora
Early Release – Fall 1999
60028 • 4 ¼″
Issued: 2000 • Current
Market Value: $____

6

Bear With Me
Parade Of Gifts Exclusive
60081 • N/A
Issued: 2000 • Current
Market Value: $____

7

Bearing Gifts
60257 • 7″
Issued: 1999 • Current
Market Value: $____

8

Blue Cheese
60765 • 7 ¼″
Issued: 2000 • Current
Market Value: $____

9

Blue Spruce
60520 • 5″
Issued: 2000 • Current
Market Value: $____

10

Bully Moose
60750 • 6 ½″
Issued: 1999 • Current
Market Value: $____

11

Bully Moose Jr.
60141 • 5 ⅜″ wide
Issued: 2000 • Current
Market Value: $____

12

Bunny Slope
60002 • 4″
Issued: 1999 • Current
Market Value: $____

Northern Lights™

	Price Paid	Value
1.		
2.		
3.		
4.		
5.		
6.		
7.		
8.		
9.		
10.		
11.		
12.		
Totals		

1

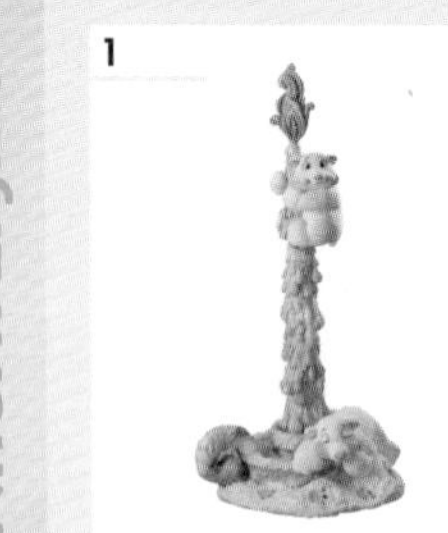

Candle Caper
60766 • 9″
Issued: 2000 • Current
Market Value: $____

2

Catch Of The Day
60054 • 3″
Issued: 2000 • Current
Market Value: $____

3

Checkin' It Twice
60255 • 9 ¾″
Issued: 1999 • Current
Market Value: $____

4

Clean Sweep
60500 • 3 ⅛″
Issued: 1999 • Current
Market Value: $____

5

Clean Up Crew
60620 • 4 ⅝″
Issued: 2000 • Current
Market Value: $____

6

Crystal Deer
60095 • 3 ½″
Issued: 2000 • Current
Market Value: $____

7

Crystal Duet
60014 • 4″
Issued: 1999 • Current
Market Value: $____

8

Crystal Town
60612 • 3 ⅜″
Issued: 2000 • Current
Market Value: $____

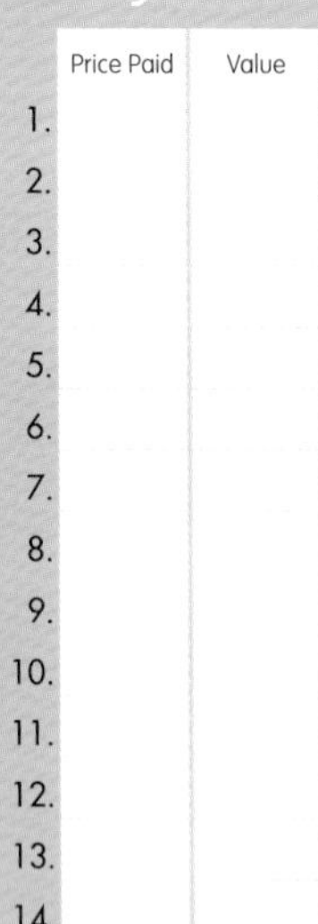

Northern Lights™

	Price Paid	Value
1.		
2.		
3.		
4.		
5.		
6.		
7.		
8.		
9.		
10.		
11.		
12.		
13.		
14.		
Totals		

9

Diamond (April)
Birthstone Collection
60040 • 3″
Issued: 2000 • Current
Market Value: $____

10

Dolphin Dreams
60126 • 3 ½″
Issued: 2000 • Current
Market Value: $____

11

Elf In Training
60302 • 3 ½″
Issued: 2000 • Current
Market Value: $____

12

Emerald (May)
Birthstone Collection
60041 • 3″
Issued: 2000 • Current
Market Value: $____

13

Fantasy Ride
60301 • 4″
Issued: 2000 • Current
Market Value: $____

14

Father Frost
60252 • 7 ½″
Issued: 1999 • Current
Market Value: $____

1

Father Noel
60251 • 8 ¾″
Issued: 1999 • Current
Market Value: $____

2

For Girls And Boys
60261 • 5″
Issued: 2000 • Current
Market Value: $____

3

Fountain Frolic
60146 • 3 ¾″
Issued: 2000 • Current
Market Value: $____

4

Frosty Fairways
60063 • 4″
Issued: 2000 • Current
Market Value: $____

5

Frosty Treat
60510 • 3 ¾″
Issued: 1999 • Current
Market Value: $____

6

Fruitful Winter
60519 • 4″
Issued: 2000 • Current
Market Value: $____

7

Garnet (January)
Birthstone Collection
60037 • 3″
Issued: 2000 • Current
Market Value: $____

8

A Gift For You
60140 • 3″
Issued: 2000 • Current
Market Value: $____

9

Gliding All The Way
60017 • 2 ¾″
Issued: 1999 • Current
Market Value: $____

10

Goal In One
60061 • 3 ½″
Issued: 2000 • Current
Market Value: $____

11

Graceful Passage
60128 • 3 ½″
Issued: 2000 • Current
Market Value: $____

12

Greetings
60260 • 4 ½″
Issued: 2000 • Current
Market Value: $____

13

Guide My Way
60008 • 6 ¾″
Issued: 1999 • Current
Market Value: $____

14

Guiding Light
60011 • 3 ⅞″
Issued: 1999 • Current
Market Value: $____

Northern Lights™

	Price Paid	Value
1.		
2.		
3.		
4.		
5.		
6.		
7.		
8.		
9.		
10.		
11.		
12.		
13.		
14.		
Totals		

1

Happy Skier
60142 • 1 ⅞"
Issued: 2000 • Current
Market Value: $____

2

Having A Ball
60026 • 2 ¾"
Issued: 2000 • Current
Market Value: $____

3

High Hopes
60760 • 7 ½"
Issued: 2000 • Current
Market Value: $____

4

Hold On Tight
Early Release – Fall 1999
60027 • 4 ⅛"
Issued: 2000 • Current
Market Value: $____

5

Holiday On Ice
60521 • 4"
Issued: 2000 • Current
Market Value: $____

6

Hoop Shot
60307 • 3 ¼"
Issued: 2000 • Current
Market Value: $____

7

Ice Castle
60502 • 3 ⅜"
Issued: 1999 • Current
Market Value: $____

8

Ice Fishing
60504 • 3 ½"
Issued: 1999 • Current
Market Value: $____

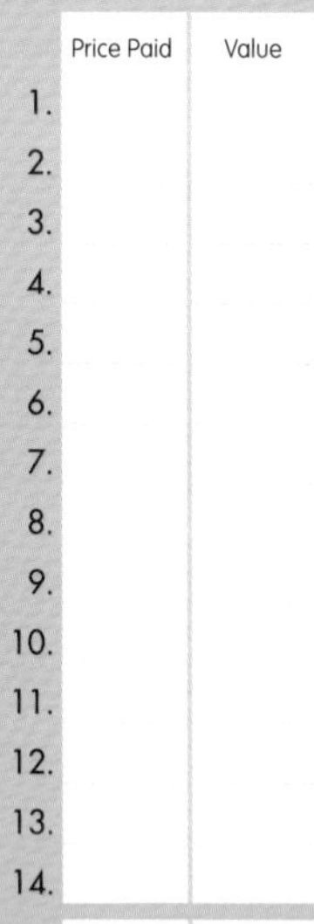

Northern Lights™

	Price Paid	Value
1.		
2.		
3.		
4.		
5.		
6.		
7.		
8.		
9.		
10.		
11.		
12.		
13.		
14.		
Totals		

9

Ice Gliding
60136 • 3 ⅛"
Issued: 2000 • Current
Market Value: $____

10

Ice Sculpture
60503 • 4"
Issued: 1999 • Current
Market Value: $____

11

Iceberg Chorus
60752 • 2 ¾"
Issued: 1999 • Current
Market Value: $____

12

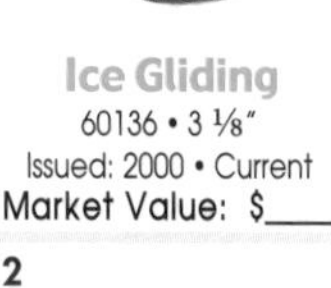

Icy Delights
60618 • 3 ¾"
Issued: 2000 • Current
Market Value: $____

13

It's Clear To See . . .
60032 • 3 ½"
Issued: 2000 • Current
Market Value: $____

14

Joy
60094 • 4 ¼"
Issued: 2000 • Current
Market Value: $____

1

Lacing Up
60139 • 2″
Issued: 2000 • Current
Market Value: $____

2

Let's Be Lovebirds
60030 • 4″
Issued: 2000 • Current
Market Value: $____

3

Little Love
60096 • 2″
Issued: 2000 • Current
Market Value: $____

4

Little Snowflake
60003 • 3 3/8″
Issued: 1999 • Current
Market Value: $____

5

Littlest Snowball
60514 • 2 1/2″
Issued: 2000 • Current
Market Value: $____

6

Love Blooms Eternal
60029 • 3 1/4″
Issued: 2000 • Current
Market Value: $____

7

Love Match
60062 • 3 3/4″
Issued: 2000 • Current
Market Value: $____

8

Love Some "Bunny"
60016 • 3″
Issued: 1999 • Current
Market Value: $____

9

Love Ya
60756 • 6 1/2″
Issued: 2000 • Current
Market Value: $____

10

Lover's Lane
60757 • 5″
Issued: 2000 • Current
Market Value: $____

11

Makin' A Snowman
60004 • 3 3/8″
Issued: 1999 • Current
Market Value: $____

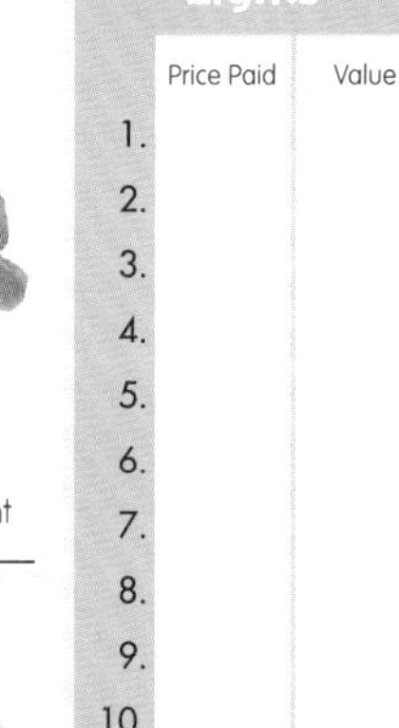

Northern Lights™

	Price Paid	Value
1.		
2.		
3.		
4.		
5.		
6.		
7.		
8.		
9.		
10.		
11.		
12.		
13.		
14.		
Totals		

12

Merrily, Merrily
60508 • 3 1/2″
Issued: 1999 • Current
Market Value: $____

13

Merry Skaters
60256 • 6″
Issued: 1999 • Current
Market Value: $____

14

Millennium 2000
60069 • 3 1/4″
Issued: 2000 • Current
Market Value: $____

1

Miss Starlight
60759 • 7″
Issued: 2000 • Current
Market Value: $____

2

Mrs. Frosty
60610 • 3 ⅛″
Issued: 2000 • Current
Market Value: $____

3

Nick The Stick
60258 • 7″
Issued: 1999 • Current
Market Value: $____

4

Noble Fir
60263 • 4″
Issued: 2000 • Current
Market Value: $____

5

Northern Crossing (LE-10,000)
60013 • 4 ½″
Issued: 1999 • Current
Market Value: $____

6

Northern Lights Nativity Collection (set/6)
60107 • Various
Issued: 2000 • Current
Market Value: $____

7

Northern Lights Numbers – 1
60056 • 3″
Issued: 2000 • Current
Market Value: $____

8

Northern Lights Numbers – 2
60057 • 3 ½″
Issued: 2000 • Current
Market Value: $____

9

Northern Lights Numbers – 3
60058 • 3 ½″
Issued: 2000 • Current
Market Value: $____

10

Off We Go
60611 • 3 ½″
Issued: 2000 • Current
Market Value: $____

11

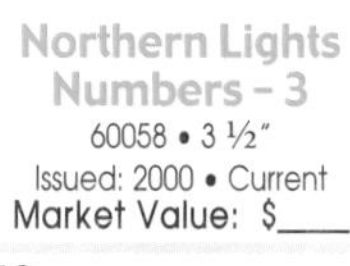

Once Upon A Winter's Day . . .
60052 • 2 ⅞″
Issued: 2000 • Current
Market Value: $____

12

Paddling Home
60615 • 3 ½″
Issued: 2000 • Current
Market Value: $____

13

Penguin Pals
60751 • 5 ⅜″
Issued: 1999 • Current
Market Value: $____

Northern Lights™

	Price Paid	Value
1.		
2.		
3.		
4.		
5.		
6.		
7.		
8.		
9.		
10.		
11.		
12.		
13.		
Totals		

1

Penguins On Parade
60524 • 4 ¾″
Issued: 2000 • Current
Market Value: $____

2

Peppermint Penguin
60763 • 6 ¼″
Issued: 2000 • Current
Market Value: $____

3

Peridot (August)
Birthstone Collection
60044 • 3″
Issued: 2000 • Current
Market Value: $____

4

Piled High
60754 • 7 ½″
Issued: 1999 • Current
Market Value: $____

5

Pleasant Dreams
60129 • 4 ¼″
Issued: 2000 • Current
Market Value: $____

6

Polar Painters
60619 • 5 ¾″
Issued: 2000 • Current
Market Value: $____

7

Polar Pals
60010 • 5 ½″
Issued: 1999 • Current
Market Value: $____

8

Powder Puff
60009 • 3 ¾″
Issued: 1999 • Current
Market Value: $____

9

Ready, Set, Go!
60051 • 3″
Issued: 2000 • Current
Market Value: $____

10

Right On Track
60265 • 8″ (wide)
Issued: 2000 • Current
Market Value: $____

11

Rockin' Reindeer
60005 • 4 ¾″
Issued: 1999 • Current
Market Value: $____

12

Rose Quartz (October)
Birthstone Collection
60046 • 3″
Issued: 2000 • Current
Market Value: $____

13

Ruby (July)
Birthstone Collection
60043 • 3″
Issued: 2000 • Current
Market Value: $____

14

Saint Nick
60250 • 15″
Issued: 1999 • Current
Market Value: $____

Northern Lights™

	Price Paid	Value
1.		
2.		
3.		
4.		
5.		
6.		
7.		
8.		
9.		
10.		
11.		
12.		
13.		
14.		
Totals		

1

Santa's Sleigh Ride (LE-5,000)
GoCollect.com Exclusive
60097 • N/A
Issued: 2000 • Current
Market Value: $____

2

Sapphire (September)
Birthstone Collection
60045 • 3″
Issued: 2000 • Current
Market Value: $____

3

Shy Snowguy
60144 • 2 ¼″
Issued: 2000 • Current
Market Value: $____

4

Sisters Make Best Friends
60124 • 3 ½″
Issued: 2000 • Current
Market Value: $____

5

Sitting Bully
GCC Exclusive
60755 • 3 ¼″
Issued: 1999 • Current
Market Value: $____

6

Skating Away
60070 • 4 ¼″
Issued: 2000 • Current
Market Value: $____

7

Ski Bunny
60762 • 8 ¼″
Issued: 2000 • Current
Market Value: $____

8

Ski School
60501 • 3 ½″
Issued: 1999 • Current
Market Value: $____

Northern Lights™

	Price Paid	Value
1.		
2.		
3.		
4.		
5.		
6.		
7.		
8.		
9.		
10.		
11.		
12.		
13.		
14.		
Totals		

9

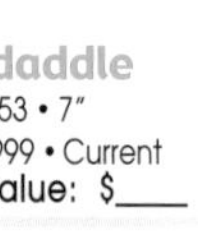

Ski-daddle
60253 • 7″
Issued: 1999 • Current
Market Value: $____

10

Sleddin'
60007 • 4 ⅝″
Issued: 1999 • Retired: 2000
Market Value: N/E

11

Slip And Slide
60506 • 4 ¾″
Issued: 1999 • Current
Market Value: $____

12

Snow Angel
60025 • 4 ½″
Issued: 1999 • Current
Market Value: $____

13

Snow Buddy
60512 • 15 ¼″
Issued: 2000 • Current
Market Value: $____

14

Snow Tackle
60305 • 3 ½″
Issued: 2000 • Current
Market Value: $____

Northern Lights™

1

Snowball Friends
60516 • 3 ¼"
Issued: 2000 • Current
Market Value: $____

2

Snowball Fun
60507 • 4 ¼"
Issued: 1999 • Current
Market Value: $____

3

Snowball Game
60060 • 3 ¾"
Issued: 2000 • Current
Market Value: $____

4

Snowball Ride
60515 • 3 ½"
Issued: 2000 • Current
Market Value: $____

5

Snowball Scoop
60517 • 3 ½"
Issued: 2000 • Current
Market Value: $____

6

Snowball Serve
60306 • 3 ½"
Issued: 2000 • Current
Market Value: $____

7

Snowball Sweep
60518 • 2 ¾"
Issued: 2000 • Current
Market Value: $____

8

Snowball Sweetie
60523 • N/A
Issued: 2000 • Current
Market Value: $____

9

Snowball Toss
60616 • 4 ¼"
Issued: 2000 • Current
Market Value: $____

10

Snowflake Rider
60079 • 6 ¼"
Issued: 2000 • Current
Market Value: $____

11

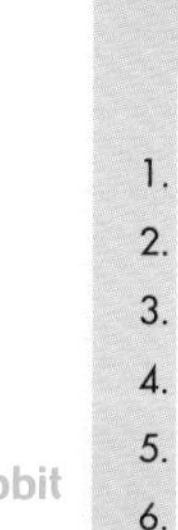

Snowshoe Rabbit
60764 • 7 ¾"
Issued: 2000 • Current
Market Value: $____

12

Soft Landing
60015 • 3 ⅛"
Issued: 1999 • Current
Market Value: $____

13

Something's Fishy
60613 • 3 ½"
Issued: 2000 • Current
Market Value: $____

14

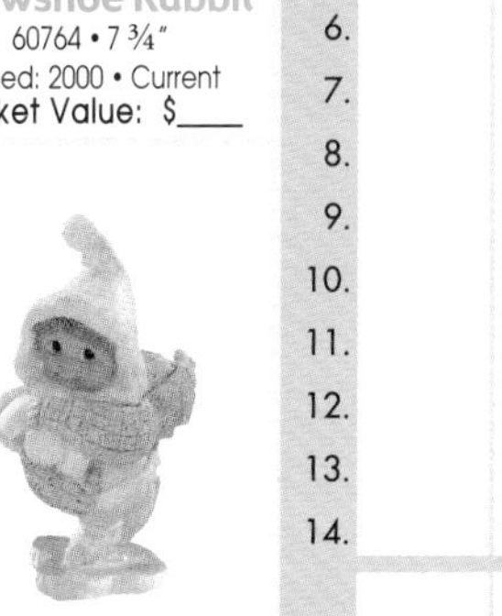

Speed Skater
60001 • 3 ¾"
Issued: 1999 • Current
Market Value: $____

Northern Lights™

	Price Paid	Value
1.		
2.		
3.		
4.		
5.		
6.		
7.		
8.		
9.		
10.		
11.		
12.		
13.		
14.		
Totals		

1

Stretch
60617 • 7 ¼″
Issued: 2000 • Current
Market Value: $____

2

Sweet Treat
60123 • 3 ½″
Issued: 2000 • Susp.: 2000
Market Value: N/E

3

Taking A Break
60262 • 3 ¼″
Issued: 2000 • Current
Market Value: $____

4

Tall, Cool One
60509 • 7 ¼″
Issued: 1999 • Current
Market Value: $____

5

Tall Wise One
60767 • 7 ¼″
Issued: 2000 • Current
Market Value: $____

6

Teeter Totter Fun
60125 • 6″ (wide)
Issued: 2000 • Current
Market Value: $____

7

Thrills And Chills
60614 • 4 ¾″
Issued: 2000 • Current
Market Value: $____

8

Top Of The Mornin'
60522 • 4 ½″
Issued: 2000 • Current
Market Value: $____

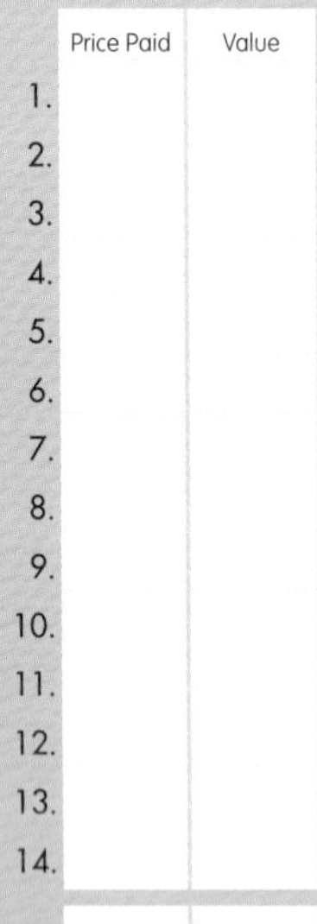
Northern Lights™

	Price Paid	Value
1.		
2.		
3.		
4.		
5.		
6.		
7.		
8.		
9.		
10.		
11.		
12.		
13.		
14.		
Totals		

9

Topaz (November)
Birthstone Collection
60047 • 3″
Issued: 2000 • Current
Market Value: $____

10

Tree Trimmers
60093 • 6″
Issued: 2000 • Current
Market Value: $____

11

True North
60511 • 5 ¾″
Issued: 1999 • Current
Market Value: $____

12
Turquoise (December)
Birthstone Collection
60048 • 3″
Issued: 2000 • Current
Market Value: $____

13

Two Cute
60055 • 3 ½″
Issued: 2000 • Current
Market Value: $____

14

Warm In His Arms
60254 • 7 ½″
Issued: 1999 • Current
Market Value: $____

1

Warm Welcome
60143 • 2 ¼″
Issued: 2000 • Current
Market Value: $____

2

Whale Of A Friend
60127 • 3 ¾″
Issued: 2000 • Current
Market Value: $____

3

What A Great Year
60758 • 7 ¼″
Issued: 2000 • Current
Market Value: $____

4

What A Kick!
60304 • 3 ½″
Issued: 2000 • Current
Market Value: $____

5

Winter Chore
60505 • 4 ⅝″
Issued: 1999 • Current
Market Value: $____

6

Winter's Rose
60064 • 13″
Issued: 2000 • Current
Market Value: $____

7

Work Of Ice
60300 • 4 ⅜″
Issued: 2000 • Current
Market Value: $____

8

Wrap It Up
60308 • 3 ¾″
Issued: 2000 • Current
Market Value: $____

9

You Melt My Heart
60031 • 3 ⅝″
Issued: 2000 • Current
Market Value: $____

10

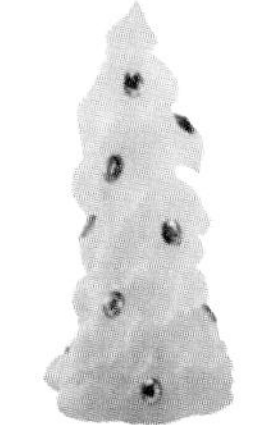

Crystal Forest (large)
60909 • 4 ½″
Issued: 2000 • Current
Market Value: $____

11

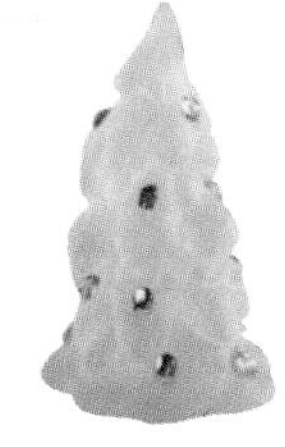

Crystal Forest (small)
60910 • 3 ½″
Issued: 2000 • Current
Market Value: $____

12

Extra Large Tree
60900 • 7″
Issued: 1999 • Current
Market Value: $____

13

Ice Castle (lighted)
60135 • 8 ¾″
Issued: 2000 • Current
Market Value: $____

14

The Ice Works (lighted)
60134 • 8 ½″
Issued: 2000 • Current
Market Value: $____

Northern Lights™

	Price Paid	Value
1.		
2.		
3.		
4.		
5.		
6.		
7.		
8.		
9.		
Accessories		
10.		
11.		
12.		
13.		
14.		
Totals		

1

Large Tree
60901 • 5″
Issued: 1999 • Current
Market Value: $____

2

Medium Tree
60902 • 4″
Issued: 1999 • Current
Market Value: $____

3

Northern Lights Logo
60000 • 5″
Issued: 1999 • Current
Market Value: $____

4

"Northern Lights Village" Logo
60130 • 3 ⅛″
Issued: 2000 • Current
Market Value: $____

5

Rainbow Bridge
60147 • 6 ¾″ (wide)
Issued: 2000 • Current
Market Value: $____

6

Santa's Place (lighted)
60131 • 7 ⅛″
Issued: 2000 • Current
Market Value: $____

7

Ski Lodge (lighted)
60133 • 7 ½″
Issued: 2000 • Current
Market Value: $____

8

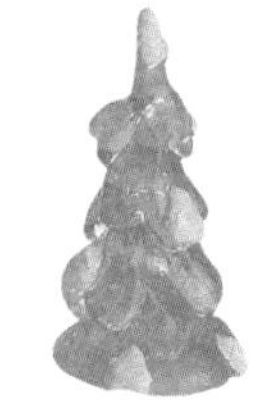

Small Tree
60903 • 2 ¾″
Issued: 1999 • Current
Market Value: $____

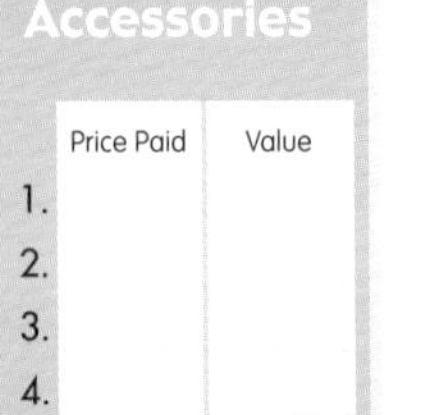

Accessories

	Price Paid	Value
1.		
2.		
3.		
4.		
5.		
6.		
7.		
8.		
9.		
10.		
Boxes		
11.		
12.		
Musicals & Waterglobes		
13.		
Totals		

9

Snowed Inn (lighted)
60132 • 6 ⅝″
Issued: 2000 • Current
Market Value: $____

10

Village Lamppost
60145 • 4 ¾″
Issued: 2000 • Current
Market Value: $____

11

Catch A Snowflake Hinged Box
60065 • 4 ¼″
Issued: 2000 • Current
Market Value: $____

12

Snowcone Surprise Hinged Box
60066 • 4 ½″
Issued: 2000 • Current
Market Value: $____

13

Downhill Racer
60072 • 3 ¼″
Issued: 2000 • Current
Market Value: $____

1

Everything's Rosy
60034 • 2 3/8"
Issued: 2000 • Current
Market Value: $____

2

Love Hearts
60033 • 2 3/8"
Issued: 2000 • Susp.: 2000
Market Value: N/E

3

Polar Pals
60075 • 3 1/4"
Issued: 2000 • Current
Market Value: $____

4

Rainbow Dreams
60035 • 2 3/8"
Issued: 2000 • Susp.: 2000
Market Value: N/E

5

Rockin' Reindeer
♪ *My Favorite Things*
60076 • 6"
Issued: 2000 • Current
Market Value: $____

6

Slip And Slide
60071 • 3 1/4"
Issued: 2000 • Current
Market Value: $____

7

Snowflake Rider
♪ *When You Wish Upon A Star*
60079 • 6 1/4"
Issued: 2000 • Current
Market Value: $____

8

Stargazing
60073 • 3 1/4"
Issued: 2000 • Current
Market Value: $____

9

Tribute To 2000
60074 • 3 1/4"
Issued: 2000 • Current
Market Value: $____

10

Candy Cane
60020 • 3 3/8"
Issued: 1999 • Current
Market Value: $____

11

Crystal Gift
60023 • 3 1/2"
Issued: 1999 • Current
Market Value: $____

12

Flocked Northern Lights Ornaments (sold separately)
11376 • Various
Issued: 2000 • Susp.: 2000
Market Value: N/E

13

Icicle Ornaments (sold separately)
60091 • Various
Issued: 2000 • Current
Market Value: $____

14

Icicle Princess
60012 • 3 1/2"
Issued: 2000 • Current
Market Value: $____

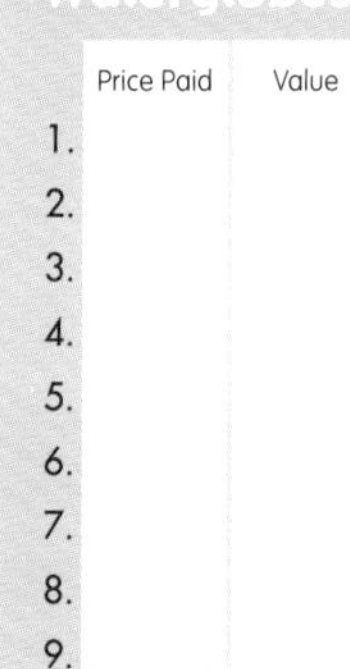

Musicals & Waterglobes

	Price Paid	Value
1.		
2.		
3.		
4.		
5.		
6.		
7.		
8.		
9.		
Ornaments		
10.		
11.		
12.		
13.		
14.		
Totals		

1

Icicle Princess (w/stand)
60006 • 6 ¼″
Issued: 1999 • Susp.: 1999
Market Value: N/E

2

Jingle Bell
60022 • 3 ½″
Issued: 1999 • Current
Market Value: $____

3

Penguin
60024 • 3 ½″
Issued: 1999 • Current
Market Value: $____

4

Pinecone
60021 • 3 ¼″
Issued: 1999 • Current
Market Value: $____

5

Seal Pup
60019 • 3 ¼″
Issued: 1999 • Current
Market Value: $____

6

Sleigh Bell
60018 • 3 ¼″
Issued: 1999 • Current
Market Value: $____

7

Loverboy
08051 • 9 ½″
Issued: 2000 • Current
Market Value: $____

8

Shivers
08050 • 6 ½″
Issued: 2000 • Current
Market Value: $____

9

Sparkle
08047 • 9 ½″
Issued: 2000 • Current
Market Value: $____

10

Squeak
08049 • 6 ½″
Issued: 2000 • Current
Market Value: $____

11

Sweetheart
08046 • 9 ½″
Issued: 2000 • Current
Market Value: $____

12

Twinkle
08048 • 9 ½″
Issued: 2000 • Current
Market Value: $____

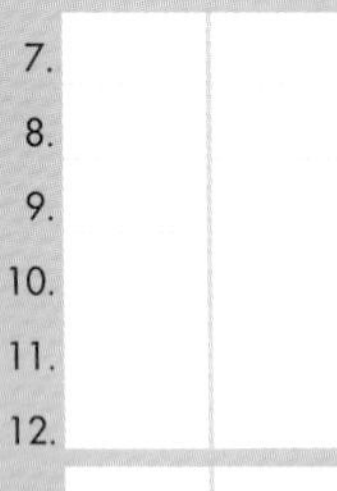

Ornaments

	Price Paid	Value
1.		
2.		
3.		
4.		
5.		
6.		
Plush		
7.		
8.		
9.		
10.		
11.		
12.		
Totals		

Other Collectibles

Dreamsicles come in many forms, including bells, bookends, boxes, frames, musicals, water-globes and much more.

1

The Finishing Touches
DS201 • 4 ½"
Issued: 1995 • Retired: 1995
Market Value: $22

2

Santa In Dreamsicle Land
DS216 • 4 ½"
Issued: 1996 • Retired: 1996
Market Value: $22

3
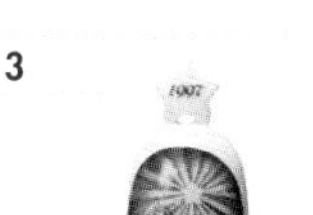
Star Of Wonder
10143 • 4"
Issued: 1997 • Retired: 1997
Market Value: $22

4

Bunny Bookends (pair)
DA122 (5022) • 5 ¼"
Issued: 1992 • Susp.: 1995
Market Value: $80

5

Bunny Bookends (pair)
5021 • 5 ¼"
Issued: 1992 • Susp.: 1992
Market Value: $114

6

Calling All Friends
11090 • 5 ½"
Issued: 2000 • Current
Market Value: $____

7

Cherub Bookends (pair)
10403 • 6 ½"
Issued: 1998 • Susp.: 1999
Market Value: N/E

8

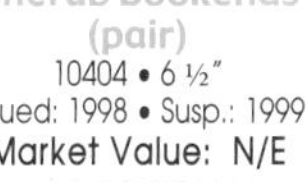
Cherub Bookends (pair)
10404 • 6 ½"
Issued: 1998 • Susp.: 1999
Market Value: N/E

9

Little Dickens
DC127 • 5 ½"
Issued: 1993 • Retired: 1995
Market Value: $40

10

Little Dickens
DX127 • 5 ½"
Issued: 1993 • Retired: 1995
Market Value: $40

11

Long Fellow
DC126 • 5 ½"
Issued: 1993 • Retired: 1995
Market Value: $37

12

Long Fellow
DX126 • 5 ½"
Issued: 1993 • Retired: 1995
Market Value: $40

13

Bee Hive Hinged Box
11486 • 4 ½"
Issued: 2000 • Current
Market Value: $____

14
Bible Hinged Box
11308 • 4"
Issued: 2000 • Current
Market Value: $____

15

Birdbath Box
10598 • 4 ⅜"
Issued: 1998 • Retired: 1999
Market Value: N/E

16

Bluebird On My Shoulder Box
10035 • 4"
Issued: 1997 • Current
Market Value: $___

17

Bouquet Hinged Box
11189 • 4 ¾"
Issued: 2000 • Current
Market Value: $____

18

Cherub In Manger Box
10456 • 4 ⅜"
Issued: 1998 • Susp.: 2000
Market Value: N/E

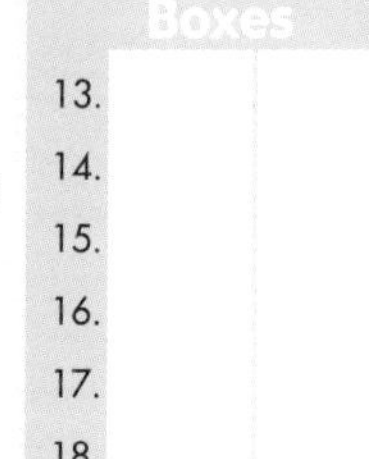

	Price Paid	Value
Bells		
1.		
2.		
3.		
Bookends		
4.		
5.		
6.		
7.		
8.		
9.		
10.		
11.		
12.		
Boxes		
13.		
14.		
15.		
16.		
17.		
18.		
Totals		

1

Christmas Ark Box
10457 • 4″
Issued: 1998 • Susp.: 1999
Market Value: N/E

2

Christmas Kiss Hinged Box
11309 • 4 ¾″
Issued: 2000 • Current
Market Value: ____

3

Christmas Quilt Box
10836 • 4 ¼″
Issued: 1999 • Current
Market Value: $____

4

Christmas Train Box
10192 • 4 ½″
Issued: 1997 • Susp.: 1999
Market Value: N/E

5

Cupcake Hinged Box
11487 • 4 ½″
Issued: 2000 • Current
Market Value: ____

6

Dear To My Heart Box
10629 • 4″
Issued: 1999 • Current
Market Value: $____

7

Decorative Egg Hinged Box – Flowers
11008 • 3 ¾″
Issued: 2000 • Current
Market Value: $____

8

Decorative Egg Hinged Box – Hearts
11007 • 3 ¼″
Issued: 2000 • Current
Market Value: $____

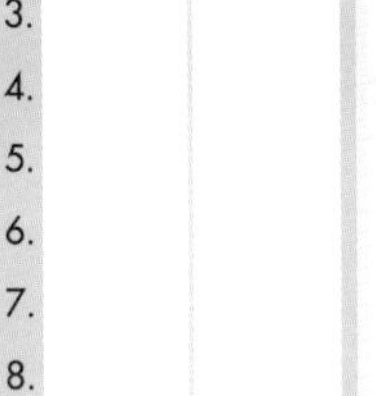

Boxes

	Price Paid	Value
1.		
2.		
3.		
4.		
5.		
6.		
7.		
8.		
9.		
10.		
11.		
12.		
13.		
14.		
15.		
16.		
17.		
18.		
19.		
20.		
Totals		

9

Decorative Egg Hinged Box – Stars
11009 • 3 ¼″
Issued: 2000 • Current
Market Value: $____

10

Dress-Up Hinged Box
11467 • 5 ⅛″
Issued: 2000 • Current
Market Value: ____

11

Dusty Rose Birdhouse Hinged Box
11465 • 4 ⅛″
Issued: 2000 • Current
Market Value: ____

12

Feathered Friends Box
10837 • 4 ¼″
Issued: 1999 • Current
Market Value: $____

13

First Christmas Box
10191 • 4 ½″
Issued: 1997 • Susp.: 1999
Market Value: N/E

14
New
First Kiss Trinket Box
11527 • 3 ⅞″
Issued: 2001 • Current
Market Value: ____

15

Flower Basket Box
10354 • 4″
Issued: 2000 • Current
Market Value: $____

16

Flower Cart Box
10353 • 4 ¼″
Issued: 1998 • Susp.: 2000
Market Value: N/E

17

Flower Pot Hinged Box
11188 • 4 ½″
Issued: 2000 • Current
Market Value: $____

18

Fountain Hinged Box
11191 • 4 ½″
Issued: 2000 • Current
Market Value: $____

19

Guardian Angel Box
10037 • 3 ½″
Issued: 1997 • Current
Market Value: $____

20

Heart Topiary Hinged Box
11186 • 3 ¾″
Issued: 2000 • Current
Market Value: $____

1

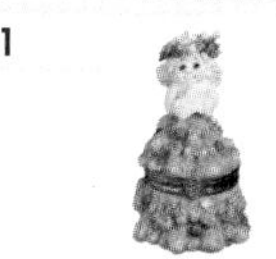

Here Comes Trouble Box
10190 • 4 ¾″
Issued: 1997 • Susp.: 1999
Market Value: N/E

2

Jolly Snowman Box
10839 • 3 ½″
Issued: 1999 • Current
Market Value: $____

3

King Heart "I Love You" Box
5850 • 7 ½″
Issued: 1991 • Susp.: 1992
Market Value: N/E

4

King Oval Cow Box
5860 • 10 ½″
Issued: 1991 • Susp.: 1992
Market Value: N/E

5

Kiss, Kiss Box
10034 • 4″
Issued: 1997 • Current
Market Value: $____

6

Let It Snow Box
10838 • 4 ¼″
Issued: 1999 • Current
Market Value: $____

7

Little Drummer Hinged Box
11306 • 4 ½″
Issued: 2000 • Current
Market Value: ____

8

Medium Heart Cherub Box
5751 • 4″
Issued: 1991 • Susp.: 1992
Market Value: $140

9

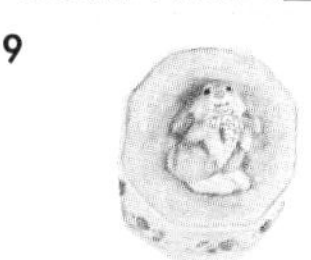

Medium Octagonal Bunny Box
5752 • 4″
Issued: 1991 • Susp.: 1992
Market Value: N/E

10

Medium Square "Speed Racer" Box
5750 • 4 ½″
Issued: 1991 • Susp.: 1992
Market Value: N/E

11

Mistletoe Kiss Box
10834 • 4 ½″
Issued: 1999 • Current
Market Value: $____

12

Morning Glory Birdhouse Box
10769 • 3 ½″
Issued: 1999 • Susp.: 2000
Market Value: N/E

13

Mother's Love Hinged Box
11466 • 4 ⅜″
Issued: 2000 • Current
Market Value: ____

14

Mushroom Hinged Box
11488 • 4 ½″
Issued: 2000 • Current
Market Value: ____

15

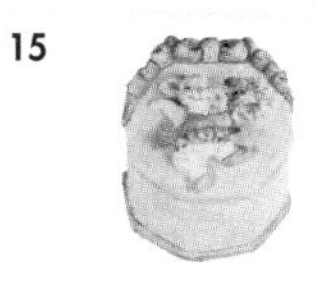

Octagonal Ballerina Box
5700 • 3″
Issued: 1991 • Susp.: 1992
Market Value: N/E

16

Pansies Birdhouse Box
10770 • 3 ¾″
Issued: 1999 • Current
Market Value: $____

17

Peace, Love, Joy, Noel Box
10835 • 4 ¼″
Issued: 1999 • Current
Market Value: $____

18

Pink Roses Birdhouse Box
10771 • 3 ⅜″
Issued: 1999 • Current
Market Value: $____

19

Queen Octagonal Cherub Box
5804 • 6 ½″
Issued: 1991 • Susp.: 1992
Market Value: $140

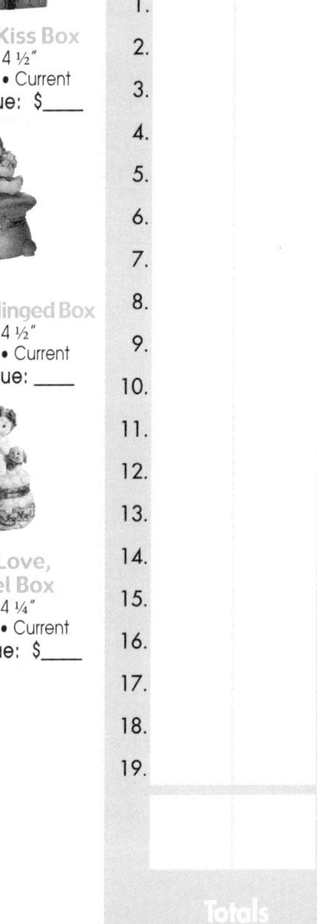

Boxes

	Price Paid	Value
1.		
2.		
3.		
4.		
5.		
6.		
7.		
8.		
9.		
10.		
11.		
12.		
13.		
14.		
15.		
16.		
17.		
18.		
19.		
Totals		

1

Queen Rectangle Cat Box
5800 • 6 ½″
Issued: 1991 • Susp.: 1992
Market Value: N/E

2

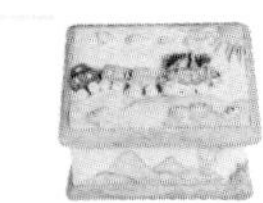

Queen Rectangle Train Box
5803 • 7″
Issued: 1991 • Susp.: 1992
Market Value: N/E

3

Queen Round Bears Box
5801 • 7″
Issued: 1991 • Susp.: 1992
Market Value: N/E

4

Queen Square "You're Special" Box
5802 • 6″
Issued: 1991 • Susp.: 1992
Market Value: N/E

5

Range Rider Hinged Box
11307 • 4 ½″
Issued: 2000 • Current
Market Value: $____

6

Red Apple Hinged Box
11485 • 4 ½″
Issued: 2000 • Current
Market Value: $____

7

Reindeer Rider Box
10455 • 5″
Issued: 1998 • Current
Market Value: $____

8

Rose Heart Box
10369 • 4 ⅜″
Issued: 2000 • Current
Market Value: $____

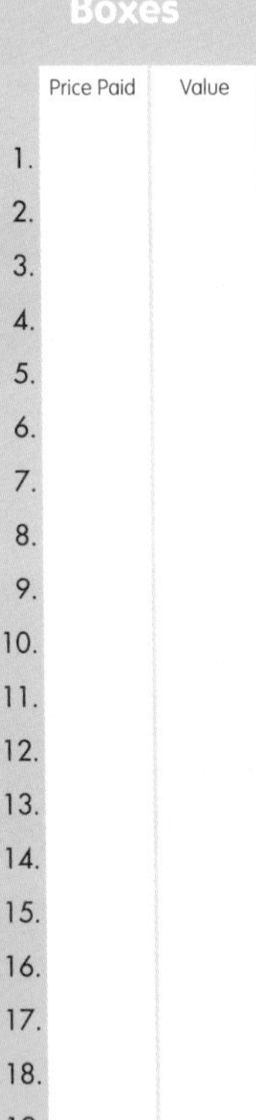

Boxes

	Price Paid	Value
1.		
2.		
3.		
4.		
5.		
6.		
7.		
8.		
9.		
10.		
11.		
12.		
13.		
14.		
15.		
16.		
17.		
18.		
19.		
20.		
Totals		

9

Round Topiary Hinged Box
11184 • 3 ¾″
Issued: 2000 • Current
Market Value: $____

10

Santa's Bag Hinged Box
11310 • 4 ¼″
Issued: 2000 • Current
Market Value: $____

11

Santa's Helper Box
10193 • 4 ¼″
Issued: 1997 • Susp.: 1999
Market Value: N/E

12

Secret Heart Box
10370 • 3 ¾″
Issued: 2000 • Current
Market Value: $____

13

Small Heart "I Love You" Box
5701 • 3 ¼″
Issued: 1991 • Susp.: 1992
Market Value: $95

14

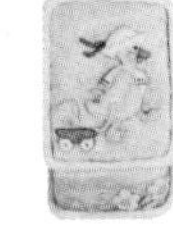

Small Rectangle "Dicky Duck" Box
5703 • 3 ½″
Issued: 1991 • Susp.: 1992
Market Value: $90

15

Small Square Dinosaur Box
5702 • 3″
Issued: 1991 • Susp.: 1992
Market Value: $140

16

Stolen Kiss Box
10630 • 4 ½″
Issued: 1999 • Current
Market Value: $____

17

Sunflower Birdhouse Box
10772 • 3 ⅝″
Issued: 1999 • Susp.: 2000
Market Value: N/E

18

Tea Party Hinged Box
11190 • 4 ½″
Issued: 2000 • Current
Market Value: $____

19

Tiny Dancer Box
10036 • 4 ¼″
Issued: 1997 • Susp.: 2000
Market Value: N/E

20

Tulip Birdhouse Hinged Box
11464 • 3 ⅝″
Issued: 2000 • Current
Market Value: $____

1

Watering Can Box
10597 • 4″
Issued: 1998 • Susp.: 1999
Market Value: N/E

2

Wedding Cake Box
10758 • 4″
Issued: 1999 • Current
Market Value: $____

3

Wishing Well Hinged Box
11187 • 3 ¾″
Issued: 2000 • Current
Market Value: $____

4

Flight School
DC340 • 4 ⅜″
Issued: 1996 • Susp.: 1997
Market Value: N/E

5

Star Factory
DC341 • 4 ⅜″
Issued: 1996 • Susp.: 1997
Market Value: N/E

6

Wreath Maker
10080 • 4″
Issued: 1997 • Susp.: 1997
Market Value: N/E

7

Cake Topper
10757 • 6 ⅜″
Issued: 1999 • Susp.: 2000
Market Value: N/E

8

All Aglow
10471 • 3 ¾″
Issued: 1998 • Susp.: 1999
Market Value: N/E

9

Bride & Groom Candlestick
10759 • 4 ¼″
Issued: 1999 • Susp.: 2000
Market Value: N/E

10

Cherub In Sleigh
10854 • 3 ¾″
Issued: 1999 • Current
Market Value: $____

11

Cherub Moon
10453 • 3″
Issued: 1998 • Current
Market Value: $____

12

Cherub On Train
10853 • 3 ¾″
Issued: 1999 • Current
Market Value: $____

13

Cherub Star
10454 • 3″
Issued: 1998 • Current
Market Value: $____

14

Chill Chaser
Early Release – Fall 1997
10117 • 4 ½″
Issued: TBA • Current
Market Value: $____

15

Dream Street
10118 • 5 ¼″
Issued: 1997 • Susp.: 1999
Market Value: N/E

16

Fireside Fun
DK041 • 3″
Issued: 1996 • Susp.: 1999
Market Value: N/E

17

Good Will To Men
10424 • 9 ¼″ (wide)
Issued: 1998 • Retired: 1999
Market Value: N/E

18

Large Candle Holder #1
DC138 • 6″
Issued: 1993 • Retired: 1994
Market Value: $66

19
Large Candle Holder #2
DC139 • 6″
Issued: 1993 • Retired: 1994
Market Value: $66

20

Light My Way
10122 • 3 ¾″
Issued: 1997 • Susp.: 1999
Market Value: N/E

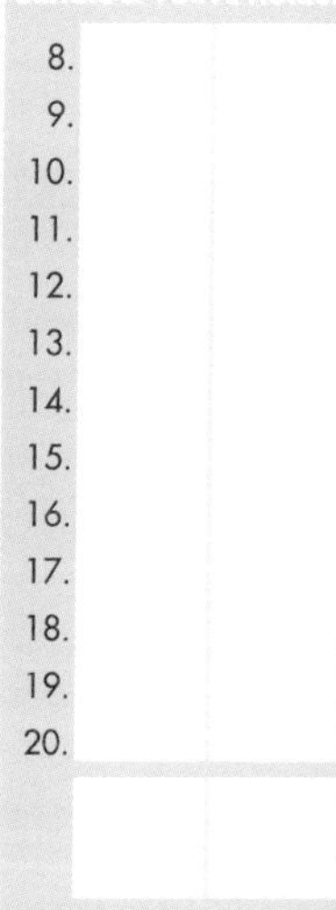

	Price Paid	Value
Boxes		
1.		
2.		
3.		
Buildings		
4.		
5.		
6.		
Cake Toppers		
7.		
Candle & Votive Holders		
8.		
9.		
10.		
11.		
12.		
13.		
14.		
15.		
16.		
17.		
18.		
19.		
20.		
Totals		

1

Pumpkin Capers
10201 • 3 ½"
Issued: 1997 • Current
Market Value: $____

2

Pumpkin Pretender
10202 • 3 ¼"
Issued: 1997 • Current
Market Value: $____

3

Small Candle Holder #1
DC136 • 2 ½"
Issued: 1993 • Susp.: 1996
Market Value: $30

4

Small Candle Holder #1
DX136 • 2 ½"
Issued: 1994 • Susp.: 1997
Market Value: $30

5

Small Candle Holder #2
DC137 • 2 ½"
Issued: 1993 • Susp.: 1996
Market Value: $20

6

Small Candle Holder #2
DX137 • 2 ½"
Issued: 1994 • Susp.: 1997
Market Value: $20

7

Star Of Wonder
10145 • 3 ½"
Issued: 1997 • Retired: 1997
Market Value: $20

8

Star Of Wonder
10148 • 3"
Issued: 1997 • Retired: 1997
Market Value: $23

Candle & Votive Holders

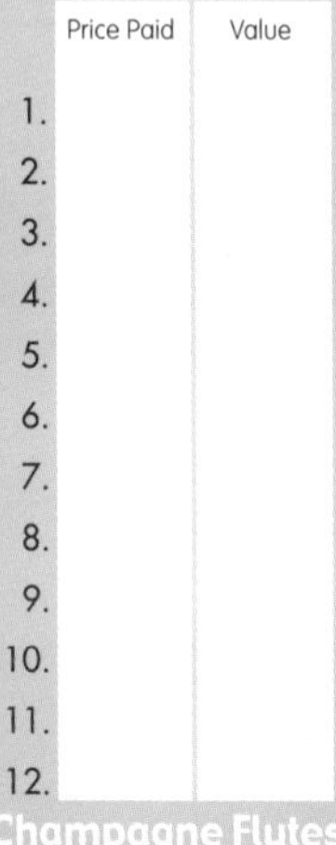

	Price Paid	Value
1.		
2.		
3.		
4.		
5.		
6.		
7.		
8.		
9.		
10.		
11.		
12.		

Champagne Flutes

	Price Paid	Value
13.		

Clocks

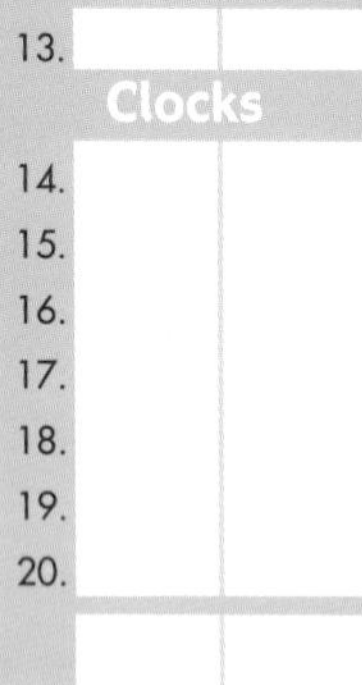

	Price Paid	Value
14.		
15.		
16.		
17.		
18.		
19.		
20.		
Totals		

9
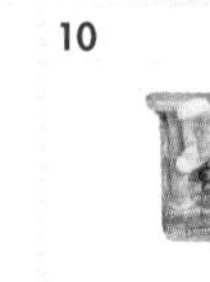
Strange Brew
10200 • 4 ¼"
Issued: 1997 • Current
Market Value: $____

10
Two Log Night
Early Release - Fall 1997
10119 • 4"
Issued: 1998 • Susp.: 2000
Market Value: N/E

11

Warm Wishes
DC359 • 4"
Issued: 1996 • Susp.: 1999
Market Value: N/E

12
You Light Up My Life
10640 • 3"
Issued: 1999 • Current
Market Value: $____

13
The Wedding Toast (set/2)
10218 • 8 ⅝"
Issued: 1997 • Current
Market Value: $____

14

Chatterbox Clock
10952 • 4 ¾"
Issued: 1999 • Current
Market Value: $____

15

Dress-Up Clock
11468 • 4 ⅞"
Issued: 2000 • Current
Market Value: $____

16

Flower Basket Clock
11469 • 4 ½"
Issued: 2000 • Current
Market Value: $____

17
Grandfather Clock
10209 • 5 ¾"
Issued: 1997 • Susp.: 1999
Market Value: N/E

18
Heart Clock
10211 • 3 ¼"
Issued: 1997 • Susp.: 1999
Market Value: N/E

19

Jack In The Box Clock
11470 • 3 ⅝"
Issued: 2000 • Current
Market Value: $____

20

Jukebox Clock
10951 • 4"
Issued: 1999 • Current
Market Value: $____

1

Kissing Clock
10530 • 3 ⅛"
Issued: 1998 • Susp.: 1999
Market Value: N/E

2

Mantle Clock
10210 • 3 ¾"
Issued: 1997 • Susp.: 1999
Market Value: N/E

3
New

Pocket Watch Clock
11471 • 3 ¾"
Issued: 2001 • Current
Market Value: $____

4

Wedding Clock
10529 • 3 ½"
Issued: 1998 • Susp.: 2000
Market Value: N/E

5

Business Card Easel
10901 • 2 ¼"
Issued: 1999 • Current
Market Value: $____

6

Cherub Business Card Holder
11136 • 4 ½"
Issued: 2000 • Susp.: 2000
Market Value: N/E

7

Cherub Envelope Holder
11137 • 3"
Issued: 2000 • Current
Market Value: $____

8

Letter Opener
10903 • 7 ¾"
Issued: 1999 • Susp.: 2000
Market Value: N/E

9

Note Pad Caddy
10902 • 3"
Issued: 1999 • Susp.: 2000
Market Value: N/E

10

Pencil & Notepad Holder
10076 • 3 ¾"
Issued: 1997 • Current
Market Value: $____

11

Pencil Holder
10900 • 4"
Issued: 1999 • Current
Market Value: $____

12

Cherub & Bear Egg
10459 • 4 ½"
Issued: 1998 • Susp.: 1999
Market Value: N/E

13

Cherub Nativity Egg
10458 • 4 ½"
Issued: 1998 • Susp.: 1999
Market Value: N/E

14

Heaven's Little Helper Egg
10390 • 4 ½"
Issued: 1998 • Susp.: 1999
Market Value: N/E

15

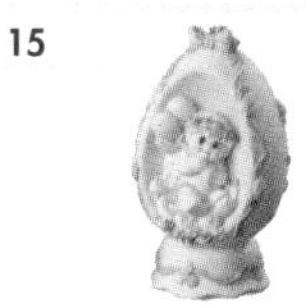

Join The Fun Egg
10394 • 4 ½"
Issued: 1998 • Current
Market Value: $____

16

Merry-Go-Round Egg
10391 • 4 ½"
Issued: 1998 • Susp.: 1999
Market Value: N/E

17

Snuggle Blanket Egg
10393 • 4 ½"
Issued: 1998 • Current
Market Value: $____

18

Sweethearts Egg
10392 • 4 ½"
Issued: 1998 • Susp.: 1999
Market Value: N/E

19

Christmas Prayer Flicker Light
11358 • 5 ½"
Issued: 2000 • Current
Market Value: $____

20

Santa And Me Flicker Light
11359 • 6"
Issued: 2000 • Current
Market Value: $____

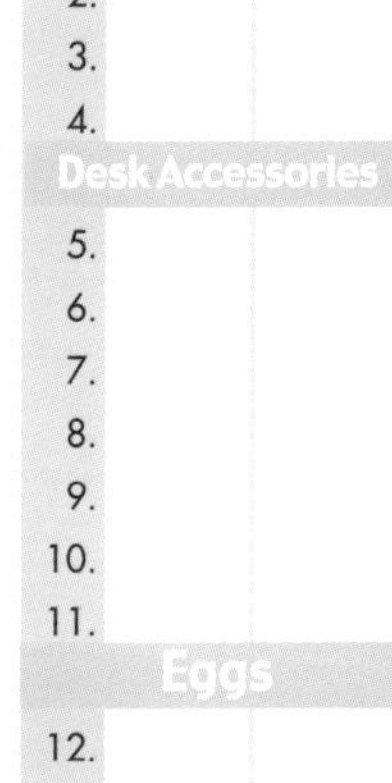

	Price Paid	Value
Clocks		
1.		
2.		
3.		
4.		
Desk Accessories		
5.		
6.		
7.		
8.		
9.		
10.		
11.		
Eggs		
12.		
13.		
14.		
15.		
16.		
17.		
18.		
Flicker Lights		
19.		
20.		
Totals		

1

Baby Buggy Frame
11463 • 4 ⅛"
Issued: 2000 • Current
Market Value: $____

2

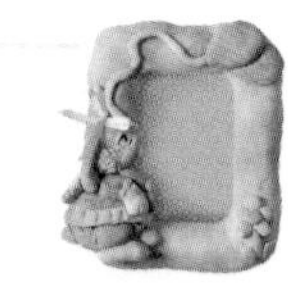

Balloons Frame
DF005 • 3 ½"
Issued: 1993 • Susp.: 1994
Market Value: N/E

3

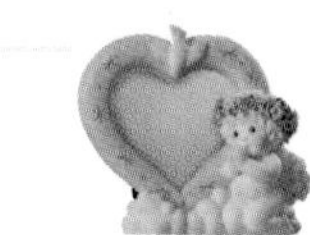

Bless This Day Frame
11104 • 3 ½"
Issued: 2000 • Current
Market Value: $____

4

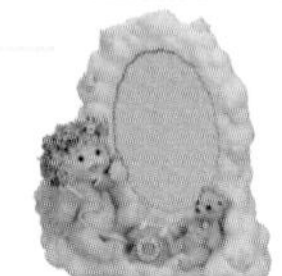

Calling You Frame
11462 • 4 ¼"
Issued: 2000 • Current
Market Value: $____

5

Cathedral Frame
11347 • 6"
Issued: 2000 • Current
Market Value: $____

6

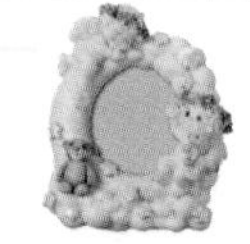

Cherub Crescent Moon Frame
10349 • 5 ⅜"
Issued: 1998 • Current
Market Value: $____

7

Cherub Heart Frame
10348 • 5 ½"
Issued: 2000 • Current
Market Value: $____

8

Cherub Rainbow Frame
10347 • 5"
Issued: 1998 • Susp.: 2000
Market Value: N/E

Frames & Photo Holders

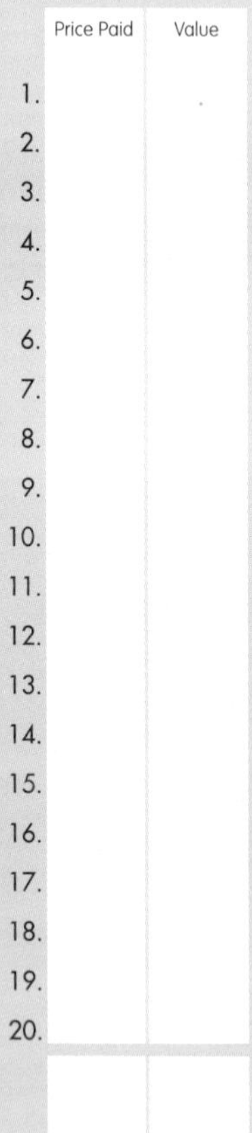

	Price Paid	Value
1.		
2.		
3.		
4.		
5.		
6.		
7.		
8.		
9.		
10.		
11.		
12.		
13.		
14.		
15.		
16.		
17.		
18.		
19.		
20.		
Totals		

9

Circus Buddies
10586 • 5 ½"
Issued: 1998 • Current
Market Value: $____

10

Column Picture Frame
10224 • 7"
Issued: 1997 • Susp.: 1999
Market Value: N/E

11

Count Your Blessings Frame
11103 • 3 ⅔"
Issued: 2000 • Current
Market Value: $____

12

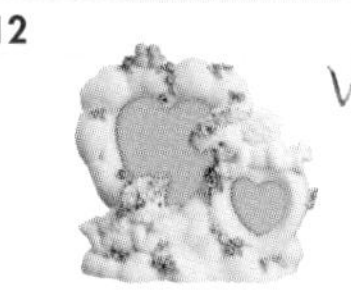

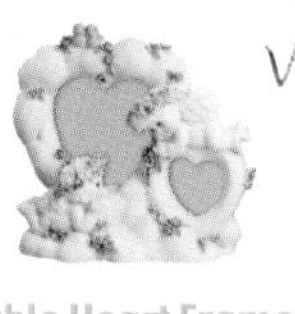

Double Heart Frame
10641 • 5"
Issued: 1999 • Current
Market Value: $____

13
New

First Kiss Frame
11526 • 4 ¼"
Issued: 2001 • Current
Market Value: $____

14

Friends Are The Sunshine Of Life Frame
11108 • 3 ½"
Issued: 2000 • Current
Market Value: $____

15
New

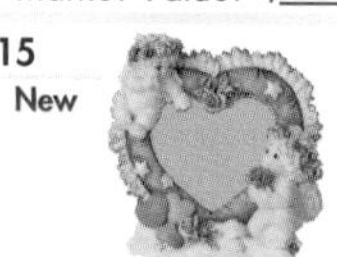

From The Heart Frame
11459 • 4 ⅜"
Issued: 2001 • Current
Market Value: $____

16

Heart Picture Frame
10225 • 4 ½"
Issued: 1997 • Susp.: 2000
Market Value: N/E

17

Kite Frame
DF006 • 3 ½"
Issued: 1993 • Susp.: 1994
Market Value: $15

18

Large Heart Frame
DF002 • 4"
Issued: 1993 • Susp.: 1994
Market Value: N/E

19
New

Mom's Little Angel Photo Holder
11581 • 7 ¼"
Issued: 2001 • Current
Market Value: $____

20

My Sweet Angel Frame
11461 • 4"
Issued: 2000 • Current
Market Value: $____

1

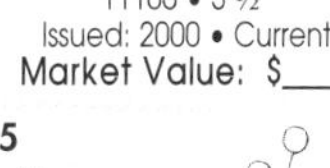

Our Love Grows Day By Day Frame
11106 • 3 ½"
Issued: 2000 • Current
Market Value: $____

2

Our Precious Gift Frame
11105 • 3 ¾"
Issued: 2000 • Current
Market Value: $____

3

Oval Frame
DF004 • 3 ⅞"
Issued: 1993 • Susp.: 1994
Market Value: $15

4

Small Heart Frame
DF001 • 3 ⅜"
Issued: 1993 • Susp.: 1994
Market Value: $15

5

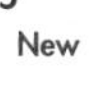

New

Special Friends Photo Holder
11460 • 7 ¼"
Issued: 2001 • Current
Market Value: $____

6

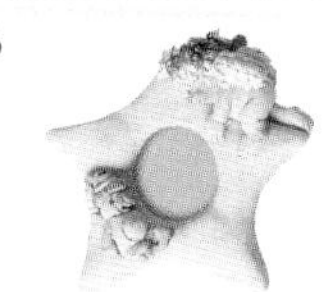

Star Frame
DF003 • 3 ⅛"
Issued: 1993 • Susp.: 1994
Market Value: $15

7

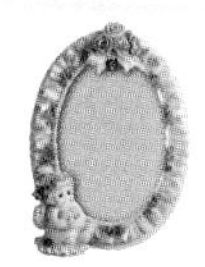

Surrounded By Love Frame
10222 • 6 ¼"
Issued: 1997 • Retired: 1999
Market Value: N/E

8

Wedding Bells Frame
10760 • 8 ¼"
Issued: 1999 • Susp.: 2000
Market Value: N/E

9

You're "Sew" Dear To My Heart Frame
11107 • 3 ⅛"
Issued: 2000 • Current
Market Value: $____

10

Above And Beyond
♪ *Wind Beneath My Wings*
11112 • 5 ¼"
Issued: 2000 • Current
Market Value: $____

11

New

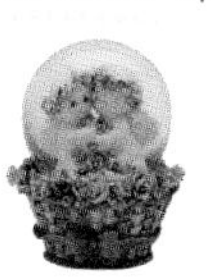

Basket Of Love
♪ *Love Me Tender*
11519 • 3 ½"
Issued: 2001 • Current
Market Value: $____

12

Bedtime Tales
♪ *Brahms' Lullaby*
11450 • 5 ⅝"
Issued: 2000 • Current
Market Value: $____

13

Bigtop Ballet
Early Release – Spring 1998
♪ *Music Box Dancer*
10207 • 5 ⅛"
Issued: 1998 • Current
Market Value: $____

14

Birthday Surprise
Early Release – Fall 1997
♪ *My Favorite Things*
10152 • 5 ⅛"
Issued: 1998 • Current
Market Value: $____

15

Carousel Ride
♪ *Carousel Waltz*
DS283 • 11 ¼"
Issued: 1996 • Retired: 1998
Market Value: $160

16

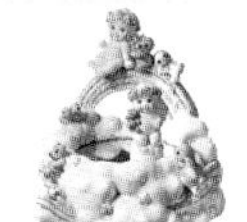

Cherub Twirler
♪ *Music Box Dancer*
10363 • 5 ¾"
Issued: 1998 • Susp.: 1999
Market Value: N/E

17

Christmas Chorus
♪ *Hark The Herald Angels Sing*
11274 • 5 ½"
Issued: 2000 • Susp.: 2000
Market Value: N/E

18

The Christmas Story
♪ *Hark The Herald Angels Sing*
10841 • 6 ⅜"
Issued: 1999 • Susp.: 1999
Market Value: $55

19

Coming To Town
♪ *Santa Claus Is Coming To Town*
10206 • 6"
Issued: 1997 • Susp.: 1999
Market Value: N/E

Frames & Photo Holders

	Price Paid	Value
1.		
2.		
3.		
4.		
5.		
6.		
7.		
8.		
9.		
Musicals & Waterglobes		
10.		
11.		
12.		
13.		
14.		
15.		
16.		
17.		
18.		
19.		
Totals		

1 New

Cupid's Touch
11523 • 2 ½"
Issued: 2001 • Current
Market Value: $____

2

Dance Ballerina Dance
♪ *Music Box Dancer*
DC140 • 8"
Issued: 1992 • Retired: 1995
Market Value: $82

3

Dance With Me
♪ *Dance Of The Sugarplum Fairy*
HC103 • 6"
Issued: 1996 • Susp.: 1997
Market Value: N/E

4

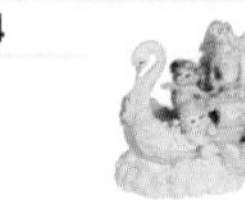

Dreamboat
Early Release – Fall 1997
♪ *Wind Beneath My Wings*
10154 • 6 ¼"
Issued: TBA • Current
Market Value: $____

5 New

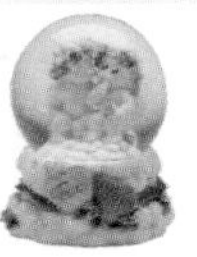

First Kiss
♪ *Endless Love*
11516 • 5 ¼"
Issued: 2001 • Current
Market Value: $____

6

Floral Carousel
♪ *Wind Beneath My Wings*
10596 • 11 ¼"
Issued: 1998 • Current
Market Value: $____

7

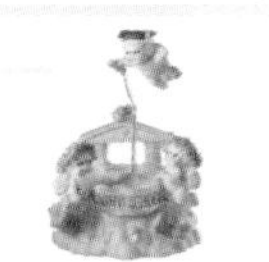

Flying High
♪ *Wind Beneath My Wings*
10302 • 7 ¼"
Issued: 1998 • Current
Market Value: $____

8

The Flying Lesson
♪ *We've Only Just Begun*
DS281 • 5"
Issued: 1996 • Susp.: 1997
Market Value: N/E

9 New

Gentle Heart
11524 • 2 ½"
Issued: 2001 • Current
Market Value: $____

10

God Bless The Child
HC107 • 5"
Issued: 1996 • Susp.: 1997
Market Value: N/E

11

Heart To Heart
♪ *Cherish*
HC100 • 6"
Issued: 1996 • Susp.: 1997
Market Value: $33

12

Holiday Dancer
♪ *Dance Of The Sugarplum Fairy*
11275 • 6 ¼"
Issued: 2000 • Current
Market Value: $____

13

Hush Little Baby
HC104 • 4 ½"
Issued: 1996 • Susp.: 1997
Market Value: N/E

14

Jumbo Ride
♪ *You Light Up My Life*
10049 • 6 ½"
Issued: 1997 • Susp.: 1997
Market Value: $50

15

Jump Over The Moon
♪ *Twinkle, Twinkle Little Star*
10377 • 6"
Issued: 1998 • Current
Market Value: $____

16

Life Is But A Dream
♪ *Raindrops Keep Falling On My Head*
11115 • 5 ¼"
Issued: 2000 • Current
Market Value: $____

17 New

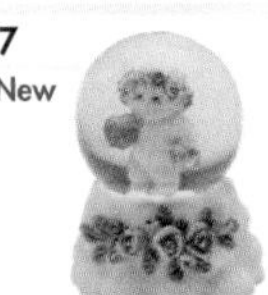

Love Note
11522 • 2 ½"
Issued: 2001 • Current
Market Value: $____

18

Lullaby And Goodnight
Early Release – Fall 1998
♪ *Brahms' Lullaby*
10613 • 6 ⅝"
Issued: 1999 • Susp.: 2000
Market Value: N/E

19

The May Pole
Early Release – Fall 1998
♪ *Carousel Waltz*
10614 • 6 ¼"
Issued: 1999 • Current
Market Value: $____

20

The Melody Makers
Early Release – Fall 1998
♪ *We've Only Just Begun*
10611 • 5"
Issued: 1999 • Susp.: 1999
Market Value: N/E

Musicals & Waterglobes

	Price Paid	Value
1.		
2.		
3.		
4.		
5.		
6.		
7.		
8.		
9.		
10.		
11.		
12.		
13.		
14.		
15.		
16.		
17.		
18.		
19.		
20.		
Totals		

1

Merry-Go-Round
♪ *Memories*
DS278 • 7"
Issued: 1995 • Susp.: 1997
Market Value: N/E

2
New

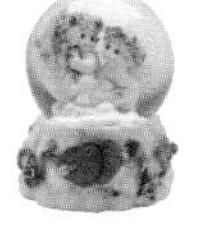

Moonlight Romance
♪ *Through The Eyes Of Love*
11515 • 5 ¼"
Issued: 2001 • Current
Market Value: $____

3

Moonstruck
♪ *You've Got A Friend*
DS277 • 7"
Issued: 1995 • Susp.: 1997
Market Value: N/E

4

Music Lesson
♪ *Memories*
HC102 • 6"
Issued: 1996 • Susp.: 1997
Market Value: $60

5

My Special Angel
♪ *Impossible Dream*
HC101 • 5 ½"
Issued: 1996 • Susp.: 1997
Market Value: N/E

6

Oh Christmas Tree
♪ *O Tannenbaum*
DS276 • 7 ⅛"
Issued: 1995 • Susp.: 1997
Market Value: N/E

7

On Wings Of Love
HC106 • 5"
Issued: 1996 • Susp.: 1997
Market Value: N/E

8

Our Father
HC105 • 4 ½"
Issued: 1996 • Susp.: 1997
Market Value: N/E

9

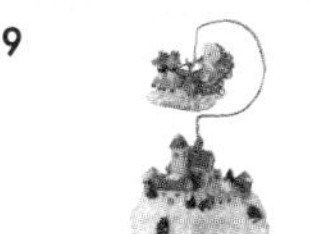

Over The Rooftops
♪ *Sleigh Ride*
11276 • 6 ½"
Issued: 2000 • Current
Market Value: $____

10

Pirouette
♪ *Music Box Dancer*
DS279 • 6 ½"
Issued: 1995 • Susp.: 1997
Market Value: N/E

11

Playtime
♪ *Rock-A-Bye-Baby*
11451 • 6 ½"
Issued: 2000 • Current
Market Value: $____

12

Rise And Shine
Early Release – Fall 1998
♪ *Over The Rainbow*
10612 • 5 ⅛"
Issued: 1999 • Current
Market Value: $____

13

'Round And 'Round
♪ *Frosty The Snowman*
10840 • 6 ¼"
Issued: 1999 • Susp.: 1999
Market Value: N/E

14

Santa's Goodies
♪ *Jingle Bells*
10842 • 5 ¼"
Issued: 1999 • Susp.: 1999
Market Value: N/E

15

Shooting Star
♪ *Twinkle, Twinkle Little Star*
DS275 • 6 ⅛"
Issued: 1995 • Susp.: 1997
Market Value: N/E

16

Sleep Tight
Early Release – Fall 1997
♪ *Rock-A-Bye Baby*
10153 • 4 ¼"
Issued: 1998 • Current
Market Value: $____

17
New

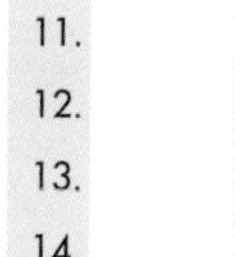

A Special Gift
♪ *Theme From Love Story*
11518 • 3 ½"
Issued: 2001 • Current
Market Value: $____

18

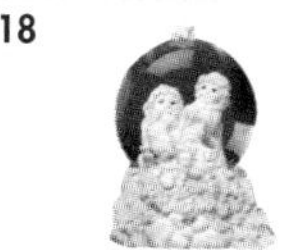

Star Of Wonder
♪ *Silent Night*
10149 • 5 ½"
Issued: 1997 • Current
Market Value: $____

19

Star Seekers (revolving)
♪ *Somewhere Out There*
HC109 • 6"
Issued: 1996 • Susp.: 1997
Market Value: N/E

20

Starry Starry Night
HC108 • 5"
Issued: 1996 • Susp.: 1997
Market Value: N/E

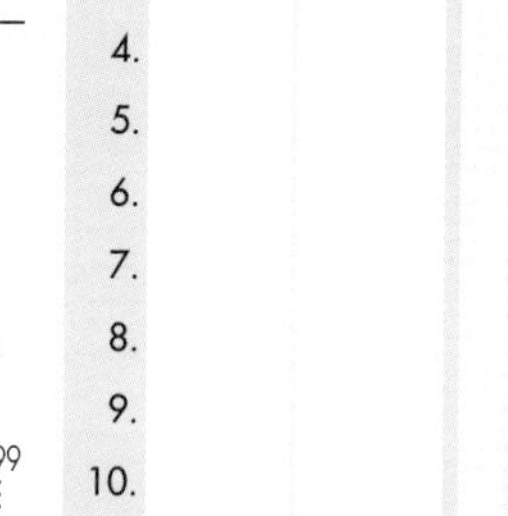

Musicals & Waterglobes

	Price Paid	Value
1.		
2.		
3.		
4.		
5.		
6.		
7.		
8.		
9.		
10.		
11.		
12.		
13.		
14.		
15.		
16.		
17.		
18.		
19.		
20.		
Totals		

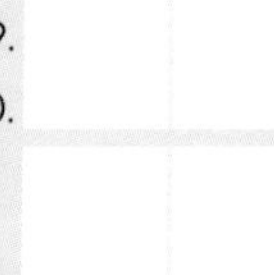

1

Stolen Kiss
♪ *Theme From Love Story*
DS282 • 5 ¾"
Issued: 1996 • Susp.: 1997
Market Value: $55

2

Swanderful
♪ *Memories*
10048 • 6 ½"
Issued: 1997 • Susp.: 1997
Market Value: $58

3

Teddy Bear Waltz
♪ *Music Box Dancer*
11110 • 6"
Issued: 2000 • Current
Market Value: $____

4

Teeter Tots
♪ *Over The Rainbow*
DS280 • 6"
Issued: 1996 • Susp.: 1997
Market Value: N/E

5

Together Forever
♪ *Endless Love*
10303 • 7"
Issued: 1998 • Susp.: 1999
Market Value: N/E

6

Top Of The World
Early Release – Spring 1998
♪ *I'm Sitting On Top Of The World*
10208 • 6"
Issued: TBA • Current
Market Value: $____

7

Two By Two
Early Release – Spring 1998
♪ *Over The Rainbow*
10304 • 6"
Issued: 1998 • Current
Market Value: $____

8

Wedding Vows
♪ *The Wedding March*
10223 • 6"
Issued: 1997 • Susp.: 1999
Market Value: N/E

Musicals & Waterglobes

	Price Paid	Value
1.		
2.		
3.		
4.		
5.		
6.		
7.		
8.		
9.		
10.		
Ornaments		
11.		
12.		
13.		
14.		
15.		
16.		
17.		
18.		
19.		
20.		
Totals		

9

Whale Of A Time
♪ *You've Got A Friend*
10047 • 6 ¼"
Issued: 1997 • Susp.: 1997
Market Value: N/E

10
New

Won't You Be Mine?
♪ *I Will Always Love You*
11517 • 5 ¼"
Issued: 2001 • Current
Market Value: ____

11

Baby's First
10136 • 3"
Issued: 1997 • Current
Market Value: $____

12

Bear
DX274 • 2 ½"
Issued: 1991 • Susp.: 1993
Market Value: $30

13

Bunny
DX270 • 2 ½"
Issued: 1991 • Susp.: 1993
Market Value: $30

14

Cherub Facing Bunny
DX283 • 2"
Issued: 1994 • Susp.: 1999
Market Value: $10

15

Cherub Hands On Cheeks
10442 • 5"
Issued: 1998 • Susp.: 1999
Market Value: N/E

16

Cherub Hands Under Chin
10440 • 5"
Issued: 1998 • Susp.: 1999
Market Value: N/E

17

Cherub On Cloud
DX263 • 2 ½"
Issued: 1991 • Susp.: 1993
Market Value: $30

18

Cherub On Skis
10446 • 2 ¾"
Issued: 1998 • Current
Market Value: $____

19

Cherub On Sled
10449 • 2"
Issued: 1998 • Current
Market Value: $____

20

Cherub On Train
10447 • 3"
Issued: 1998 • Current
Market Value: $____

1

Cherub With Baby
DX286 • 2"
Issued: 1994 • Susp.: 1999
Market Value: N/E

2

Cherub With Bear
DX282 • 2"
Issued: 1994 • Susp.: 1999
Market Value: $10

3

Cherub With Bell
10448 • 2 ¾"
Issued: 1998 • Current
Market Value: $____

4

Cherub With Bird
DX287 • 2"
Issued: 1994 • Susp.: 1999
Market Value: N/E

5

Cherub With Book
DX280 • 2"
Issued: 1994 • Susp.: 1999
Market Value: N/E

6

Cherub With Bunny
DX288 • 2"
Issued: 1994 • Susp.: 1999
Market Value: N/E

7

Cherub With Drum
DX281 • 2"
Issued: 1994 • Susp.: 1999
Market Value: N/E

8

Cherub With Flute
DX285 • 2"
Issued: 1994 • Susp.: 1999
Market Value: N/E

9

Cherub With Horn
DX289 • 2"
Issued: 1994 • Susp.: 1999
Market Value: N/E

10

Cherub With Lamb
10450 • 2 ⅜"
Issued: 1998 • Current
Market Value: $____

11

Cherub With Lute
10444 • 5"
Issued: 1998 • Susp.: 1999
Market Value: N/E

12

Cherub With Moon
DX260 • 2 ½"
Issued: 1991 • Susp.: 1993
Market Value: $30

13
Cherub With Reindeer
10451 • 3"
Issued: 1998 • Current
Market Value: $____

14

Cherub With Star
DX262 • 2 ½"
Issued: 1991 • Retired: 1993
Market Value: $30

15

Cherub With Star
10445 • 5"
Issued: 1998 • Susp.: 1999
Market Value: N/E

16
Eager To Please
DX295 • 2 ⅛"
Issued: 1995 • Susp.: 1999
Market Value: N/E

17
The Finishing Touches
DS202 • 3 ½"
Issued: 1995 • Retired: 1995
Market Value: $20

18

Flocked Cherub Ornaments (sold separately)
11378 • Various
Issued: 2000 • Current
Market Value: $____

19

Flocked Christmas Ornaments (sold separately)
11377 • Various
Issued: 2000 • Current
Market Value: $____

20

Flying High
10137 • 2 ⅝"
Issued: 1997 • Current
Market Value: $____

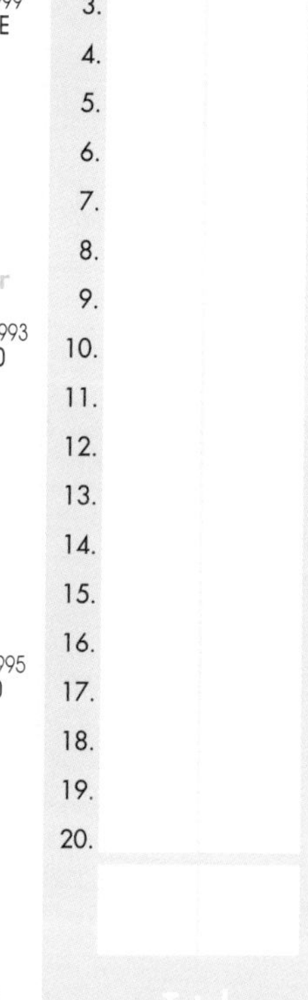

Ornaments

	Price Paid	Value
1.		
2.		
3.		
4.		
5.		
6.		
7.		
8.		
9.		
10.		
11.		
12.		
13.		
14.		
15.		
16.		
17.		
18.		
19.		
20.		
Totals		

1

Golden Bell
10195 • 3 ½"
Issued: 1997 • Current
Market Value: $____

2

Golden Candle
10198 • 4 ⅛"
Issued: 1997 • Current
Market Value: $____

3

Golden Cross
10197 • 3 ⅜"
Issued: 1997 • Current
Market Value: $____

4

Golden Heart
10194 • 3 ¼"
Issued: 1997 • Current
Market Value: $____

5
Golden Snowflake
10196 • 4 ¼"
Issued: 1997 • Current
Market Value: $____

6

Golden Wreath
10199 • 4"
Issued: 1997 • Current
Market Value: $____

7
Hang My Stocking
DX291 • 2 ⅜"
Issued: 1995 • Susp.: 1999
Market Value: $10

8

Holiday Cherub Ornaments (sold separately)
10831 • Various
Issued: 2000 • Current
Market Value: $____

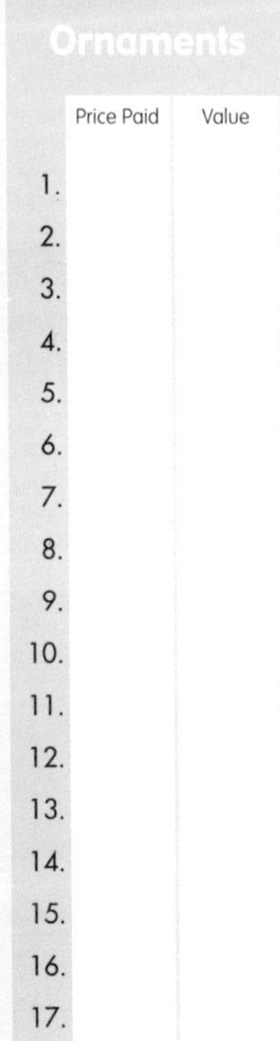

Ornaments

	Price Paid	Value
1.		
2.		
3.		
4.		
5.		
6.		
7.		
8.		
9.		
10.		
11.		
12.		
13.		
14.		
15.		
16.		
17.		
18.		
19.		
20.		
Totals		

9
Holiday Express
10132 • 3"
Issued: 1997 • Current
Market Value: $____

10

Holiday Hugs
10134 • 2 ¼"
Issued: 1997 • Current
Market Value: $____

11

I Can Read
DX297 • 1 ¾"
Issued: 1995 • Current
Market Value: $____

12
Just For You
10135 • 2 ⅝"
Issued: 1997 • Current
Market Value: $____

13

Kiss, Kiss
DX298 • 1 ⅞"
Issued: 1995 • Susp.: 1999
Market Value: $10

14
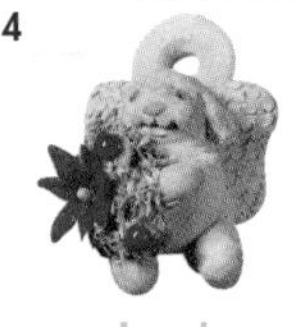
Lamb
DX275 • 2 ½"
Issued: 1991 • Susp.: 1993
Market Value: $28

15

Mini Ornaments (sold separately)
11295 • Various
Issued: 2000 • Current
Market Value: $____

16

Nativity Ornament Set (set/6)
DX466 • Various
Issued: 1996 • Susp.: 1999
Market Value: N/E

17

Piggy
DX271 • 2 ½"
Issued: 1991 • Susp.: 1993
Market Value: $26

18

Piggy Back Kitty
DX284 • 2"
Issued: 1994 • Susp.: 1999
Market Value: N/E

19

Poinsettia
DX292 • 1 ¾"
Issued: 1995 • Susp.: 1999
Market Value: N/E

20

Praying Cherub
DX261 • 2 ½"
Issued: 1991 • Susp.: 1993
Market Value: $30

1

Praying Cherub
10443 • 5"
Issued: 1998 • Susp.: 1999
Market Value: N/E

2

Raccoon
DX272 • 2 ½"
Issued: 1991 • Susp.: 1993
Market Value: $28

3
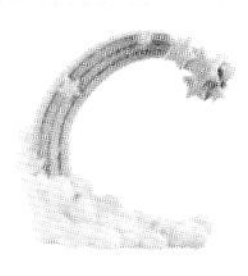
Rainbow Ornament Stand
10089 • 6"
Issued: 1997 • Susp.: 1999
Market Value: N/E

4

Santa In Dreamsicle Land
DS217 • 4 ½"
Issued: 1996 • Retired: 1996
Market Value: $16

5

Sculpted Ornaments (sold separately)
11303 • Various
Issued: 2000 • Current
Market Value: $____

6

Sleeping Cherub
10441 • 5"
Issued: 1998 • Susp.: 1999
Market Value: N/E

7

Squirrel
DX273 • 2 ½"
Issued: 1991 • Susp.: 1993
Market Value: $28

8

Star Of Wonder
10142 • 3 ½"
Issued: 1997 • Retired: 1997
Market Value: $16

9

Sucking My Thumb
DX293 • 2"
Issued: 1995 • Susp.: 1999
Market Value: N/E

10

Surprise Gift
DX296 • 1 ¾"
Issued: 1995 • Susp.: 1999
Market Value: $15

11

Sweet Treat
10133 • 3 ⅛"
Issued: 1997 • Current
Market Value: $____

12
Under The Tree (ornament stand)
11277 • N/A
Issued: 2000 • Current
Market Value: $____

13

Up All Night
DX294 • 1 ⅞"
Issued: 1995 • Susp.: 1999
Market Value: N/E

14

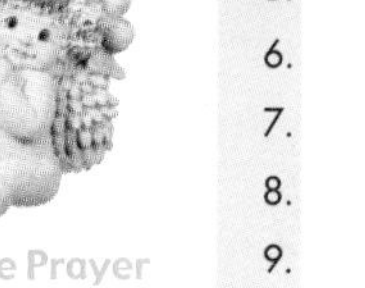
Bedtime Prayer
10214 • 9 ¼"
Issued: 1997 • Susp.: 1999
Market Value: N/E

15
Bless This House
DC177 • 5"
Issued: 1994 • Susp.: 1999
Market Value: N/E

16
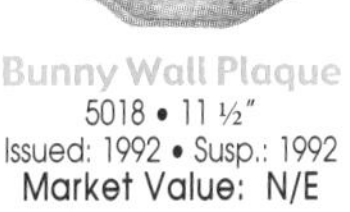
Bunny Wall Plaque
5018 • 11 ½"
Issued: 1992 • Susp.: 1992
Market Value: N/E

17

Bunny Wall Plaque
5019 • 12 ½"
Issued: 1992 • Susp.: 1992
Market Value: N/E

18
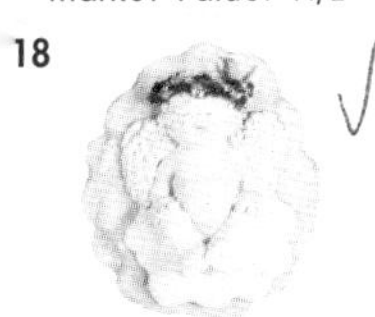
Cherub Wall Plaque
5130 • 7"
Issued: 1992 • Susp.: 1992
Market Value: N/E

19
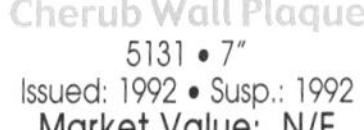
Cherub Wall Plaque
5131 • 7"
Issued: 1992 • Susp.: 1992
Market Value: N/E

20

Heavenly Harp
10215 • 8 ¼"
Issued: 1997 • Susp.: 1999
Market Value: N/E

Ornaments	Price Paid	Value
1.		
2.		
3.		
4.		
5.		
6.		
7.		
8.		
9.		
10.		
11.		
12.		
13.		
Plaques		
14.		
15.		
16.		
17.		
18.		
19.		
20.		
Totals		

1

Join The Fun
10212 • 10 ½"
Issued: 1997 • Susp.: 1999
Market Value: N/E

2

Moonbeams
10213 • 11"
Issued: 1997 • Susp.: 1999
Market Value: N/E

3

Snuggle Blanket
10216 • 9"
Issued: 1997 • Susp.: 1999
Market Value: N/E

4

Starburst
10217 • 10"
Issued: 1997 • Susp.: 1999
Market Value: N/E

5

Watching Over You
DC176 • 5"
Issued: 1994 • Susp.: 1999
Market Value: N/E

6

25th Anniversary Plate
10762 • 6 ¾"
Issued: 1999 • Susp.: 2000
Market Value: N/E

7

50th Anniversary Plate
10763 • 6 ¾"
Issued: 1999 • Current
Market Value: $____

8

Anniversary Plate
10761 • 6 ¾"
Issued: 1999 • Current
Market Value: $____

	Price Paid	Value
Plaques		
1.		
2.		
3.		
4.		
5.		
Plates		
6.		
7.		
8.		
9.		
10.		
11.		
Plush		
12.		
13.		
14.		
15.		
16.		
17.		
18.		
19.		
20.		
Totals		

9

The Finishing Touches
DS200 • 8 ¼"
Issued: 1995 • Retired: 1995
Market Value: $45

10

Santa In Dreamsicle Land
DS215 • 8 ¼"
Issued: 1996 • Retired: 1996
Market Value: $40

11

Star Of Wonder
10144 • 8"
Issued: 1997 • Retired: 1997
Market Value: $30

12

An Angel's Watching Over You
08087 • 8"
Issued: 2000 • Current
Market Value: $____

13
New

Be Mine
08126 • 8"
Issued: 2001 • Current
Market Value: $____

14
New

Best Friends
08123 • 8"
Issued: 2001 • Current
Market Value: $____

15

Birthday Hugs
08090 • 8"
Issued: 2000 • Current
Market Value: $____

16

Bluebeary
08002 • 7 ½"
Issued: 1999 • Retired: 1999
Market Value: N/E

17

Bride
08077 • 8"
Issued: 2000 • Current
Market Value: $____

18

Bubbles
08013 • 8"
Issued: 1999 • Current
Market Value: $____

19

Candy
08021 • 8"
Issued: 1999 • Retired: 1999
Market Value: N/E

20

Collectible Plush Nativity Set (set/5)
08108 • N/A
Issued: 2000 • Current
Market Value: $____

1

Creampuff
08001 • 8 ½″
Issued: 1999 • Retired: 1999
Market Value: N/E

2

Crystal
08025 • 8″
Issued: 1999 • Retired: 1999
Market Value: N/E

3

Cupcake
08003 • 8 ½″
Issued: 1999 • Retired: 1999
Market Value: N/E

4

Daisy
08004 • 5 ½″
Issued: 1999 • Retired: 1999
Market Value: N/E

5

Dawn
08029 • 8″
Issued: 1999 • Current
Market Value: $____

6

Evergreen
08026 • 8″
Issued: 1999 • Retired: 1999
Market Value: N/E

7

Faith
08012 • 8″
Issued: 1999 • Current
Market Value: $____

8

Gingerbread
08097 • 8″
Issued: 2000 • Current
Market Value: $____

9

Girlfriends For Life
08086 • 8″
Issued: 2000 • Current
Market Value: $____

10

Graduate
08079 • 8″
Issued: 2000 • Current
Market Value: $____

11

Groom
08078 • 8″
Issued: 2000 • Current
Market Value: $____

12

Holly
08023 • 8″
Issued: 1999 • Retired: 1999
Market Value: N/E

13

Honey Bunny
08041 • 10 ½″
Issued: 2000 • Current
Market Value: $____

14
New

Hug Me
08127 • 8″
Issued: 2001 • Current
Market Value: $____

15
New

I Love Grandma
08122 • 8″
Issued: 2001 • Current
Market Value: $____

16
New

I Love Mom
08121 • 8″
Issued: 2001 • Current
Market Value: $____

17

I Love You
08089 • 8″
Issued: 2000 • Current
Market Value: $____

18
New

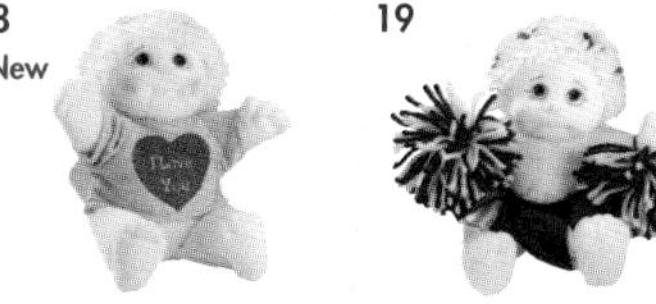

I Love You
08125 • 8″
Issued: 2001 • Current
Market Value: $____

19

Joy
08014 • 8″
Issued: 1999 • Current
Market Value: $____

20

Mittens
08022 • 8″
Issued: 1999 • Retired: 1999
Market Value: N/E

Plush

	Price Paid	Value
1.		
2.		
3.		
4.		
5.		
6.		
7.		
8.		
9.		
10.		
11.		
12.		
13.		
14.		
15.		
16.		
17.		
18.		
19.		
20.		
Totals		

1

Moms Are Angels
08085 • 8″
Issued: 2000 • Current
Market Value: $____

2

Moose L. Toe
08024 • 8″
Issued: 1999 • Retired: 1999
Market Value: N/E

3

Mrs. Claus
08095 • 8″
Issued: 2000 • Current
Market Value: $____

4

A New Baby Boy
08076 • 8″
Issued: 2000 • Current
Market Value: $____

5

A New Baby Girl
08075 • 8″
Issued: 2000 • Current
Market Value: $____

6

Peaches
08005 • 8 ½″
Issued: 1999 • Retired: 1999
Market Value: $15

7

Peanut
08006 • 5″
Issued: 1999 • Retired: 1999
Market Value: $15

8

Peg
08017 • 8″
Issued: 1999 • Current
Market Value: $____

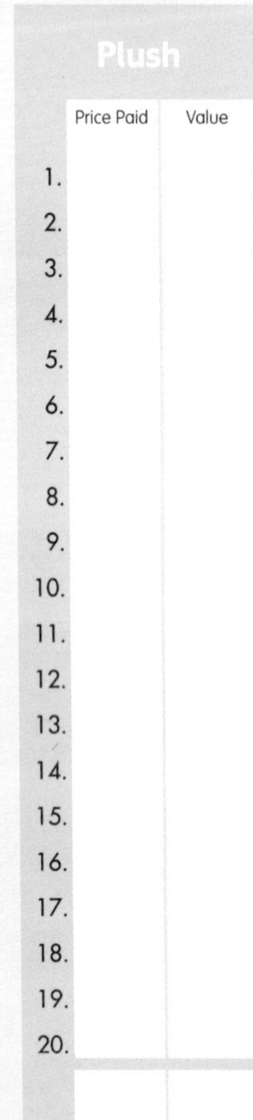

Plush

	Price Paid	Value
1.		
2.		
3.		
4.		
5.		
6.		
7.		
8.		
9.		
10.		
11.		
12.		
13.		
14.		
15.		
16.		
17.		
18.		
19.		
20.		
Totals		

9

Peppermint
08099 • 8″
Issued: 2000 • Current
Market Value: $____

10

Rosebud
08016 • 8″
Issued: 1999 • Current
Market Value: $____

11
New

Roses For Mom
08129 • 8″
Issued: 2001 • Current
Market Value: $____

12

Rosie (I.C.E. Exclusive)
08030 • 8″
Issued: 1999 • Retired: 1999
Market Value: N/E

13

Santa
08094 • 8″
Issued: 2000 • Current
Market Value: $____

14

Sisters Forever
08088 • 8″
Issued: 2000 • Current
Market Value: $____

15

Smooches
08039 • 8″
Issued: 2000 • Current
Market Value: $____

16

Snowball
08096 • 8″
Issued: 2000 • Current
Market Value: $____

17

Splash
08015 • 8″
Issued: 1999 • Current
Market Value: $____

18

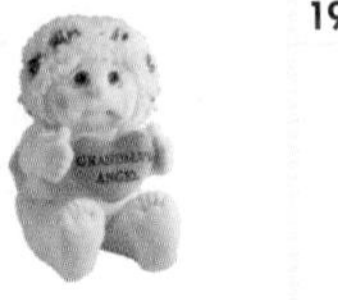

Sugar
08038 • 8″
Issued: 2000 • Current
Market Value: $____

19

Sunshine
08040 • 8″
Issued: 2000 • Current
Market Value: $____

20

Sweetie
08037 • 8″
Issued: 2000 • Current
Market Value: $____

1

Toasty
08098 • 8"
Issued: 2000 • Current
Market Value: $____

2

Tooth Fairy
08042 • 8"
Issued: 2000 • Current
Market Value: $____

3

Cherub Bowl – Hearts
DC160 • 4"
Issued: 1994 • Susp.: 1997
Market Value: N/E

4

Cherub Bowl – Stars
DC161 • 4"
Issued: 1994 • Susp.: 1996
Market Value: $50

5

Fresh As Spring
11006 • 4 ½"
Issued: 2000 • Susp.: 2000
Market Value: N/E

6

Heaven Scent
10994 • 4 ⅞"
Issued: 2000 • Current
Market Value: $____

7

Potpourri Bunnies
DA117 • 4 ½"
Issued: 1994 • Susp.: 1996
Market Value: $22

8

Potpourri/Candy Dish
10639 • 4 ⅜"
Issued: 1999 • Current
Market Value: $____

9

Potpourri Pals
DA118 • 3 ½"
Issued: 1994 • Susp.: 1996
Market Value: $22

10

Boxful Of Stars
DX224 • 3 ¾"
Issued: 1994 • Susp.: 1997
Market Value: N/E

11

Cherub With Moon
10460 • 3 ⅞"
Issued: 1998 • Current
Market Value: $____

12

Cherub With Train
10461 • 4 ⅛"
Issued: 1998 • Current
Market Value: $____

13

Cherub With Tree
10462 • 3 ½"
Issued: 1998 • Current
Market Value: $____

14

Sock Hop
DX222 • 3 ¾"
Issued: 1994 • Susp.: 1997
Market Value: N/E

15

Stocking Holder Christmas Tree
DX221 • 5"
Issued: 1993 • Susp.: 1995
Market Value: $31

16

Stocking Holder Snowman
DX219 • 5"
Issued: 1993 • Susp.: 1995
Market Value: $31

17

Stocking Holder Toboggan
DX220 • 5"
Issued: 1993 • Susp.: 1995
Market Value: $31

18

Sweet Gingerbread
DX223 • 3 ¾"
Issued: 1994 • Susp.: 1997
Market Value: N/E

19

Christmas Wreath
11316 • 9 ½"
Issued: 2000 • Susp.: 2000
Market Value: N/E

20

Poinsettia Wreath
11315 • 9 ½"
Issued: 2000 • Current
Market Value: $____

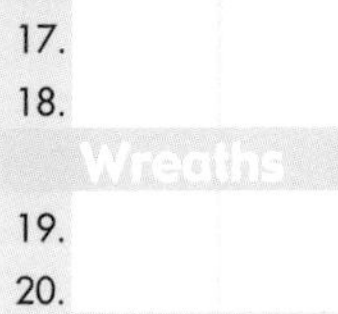

Plush	Price Paid	Value
1.		
2.		
Potpourri Holders		
3.		
4.		
5.		
6.		
7.		
8.		
9.		
Stocking Holders		
10.		
11.		
12.		
13.		
14.		
15.		
16.		
17.		
18.		
Wreaths		
19.		
20.		
Totals		

Future Releases

Check our web site, ***CollectorsQuest.com***, for new product releases and record the information here.

Dreamsicles®	Original Price	Price Paid	Market Value

Page Totals:	Price Paid	Market Value

Total Value Of My Collection

Record your collection here by adding the totals from the bottom of each Value Guide page.

Dreamsicles®			Dreamsicles®, con't.		
Page Number	Price Paid	Market Value	Page Number	Price Paid	Market Value
Page 41			Page 66		
Page 42			Page 67		
Page 43			Page 68		
Page 44			Page 69		
Page 45			Page 70		
Page 46			Page 71		
Page 47			Page 72		
Page 48			Page 73		
Page 49			Page 74		
Page 50			Page 75		
Page 51			Page 76		
Page 52			Page 77		
Page 53			Page 78		
Page 54			Page 79		
Page 55			Page 80		
Page 56			Page 81		
Page 57			Page 82		
Page 58			Page 83		
Page 59			Page 84		
Page 60			Page 85		
Page 61			Page 86		
Page 62			Page 87		
Page 63			Page 88		
Page 64			Page 89		
Page 65			Page 90		
Subtotals			**Subtotals**		

Page Totals:	Price Paid	Market Value

Total Value Of My Collection

Record your collection here by adding the totals from the bottom of each Value Guide page.

Dreamsicles®, con't.			Dreamsicles®, con't.		
Page Number	Price Paid	Market Value	Page Number	Price Paid	Market Value
Page 91			Page 116		
Page 92			Page 117		
Page 93			Page 118		
Page 94			Page 119		
Page 95			Page 120		
Page 96			Page 121		
Page 97			Page 122		
Page 98			Page 123		
Page 99			Page 124		
Page 100			Page 125		
Page 101			Page 126		
Page 102			Page 127		
Page 103			Page 128		
Page 104			Page 129		
Page 105			Page 130		
Page 106			Page 131		
Page 107			Page 132		
Page 108			Page 133		
Page 109			Page 134		
Page 110			Page 135		
Page 111			Page 136		
Page 112			Page 137		
Page 113			Page 138		
Page 114			Page 139		
Page 115			Page 140		
Subtotals			**Subtotals**		

	Price Paid	Market Value
Page Totals:		

Total Value Of My Collection

Record your collection here by adding the totals from the bottom of each Value Guide page.

Dreamsicles®			Dreamsicles®, con't.		
Page Number	Price Paid	Market Value	Page Number	Price Paid	Market Value
Page 141			Page 166		
Page 142			Page 167		
Page 143			Page 168		
Page 144			Page 169		
Page 145			Page 170		
Page 146			Page 171		
Page 147			Page 172		
Page 148			Page 173		
Page 149			Page 174		
Page 150			Page 175		
Page 151			Page 176		
Page 152			Page 177		
Page 153			Page 178		
Page 154			Page 179		
Page 155			Page 180		
Page 156			Page 181		
Page 157			Page 182		
Page 158			Page 183		
Page 159			Page 184		
Page 160			Page 185		
Page 161			Page 186		
Page 162			Page 187		
Page 163			Page 188		
Page 164			Page 189		
Page 165					
Subtotals			**Subtotals**		

Grand Totals:	Price Paid	Market Value

Secondary Market Overview

Thanks to new advances in technology, collectors now have a wide variety of ways to track down the elusive pieces they are missing from their collections. Before the advent of the Internet, collectors were often limited to searching their local area to find those hard to locate retired, suspended or limited edition pieces which had eluded them in retail stores.

Shopping On-Line

These days, collectors are no longer limited by geography. The Internet can put you in touch with Dreamsicles fans throughout the country and around the globe. By simply typing the word "Dreamsicles" into an Internet search engine, collectors are provided with lists of retail sites, individual fan sites and on-line auctions pertaining to Dreamsicles.

Dreamsicles fans are so devoted to their cherubs that several have created personal web sites about their angelic heirlooms. While these fan sites do not always list pieces for sale, sometimes the collectors who run them are willing to sell their cherubs or trade them for a piece they desire. Even if they aren't willing to give up a priceless piece, the long-term friendships that can be formed between like-minded collectors are equally as priceless.

Many Dreamsicles retailers have set up storefronts in cyberspace. In these cases, you no longer have to drive all the way to your local gift store, only to discover that it has sold out of the piece you desire. You can now log onto the store's web site and check out its stock without even leaving your home.

Remember to exercise caution and common sense when dealing with strangers over the Internet. To ensure that you do not run into any problems, talk with other reputable collectors and dealers to get an idea of who is to be trusted on-line. This holds especially true when giving credit card numbers or personal information out over the web. Make sure that the site you are using is secure so that no unwanted parties can access your personal information.

Internet auctions offer the potential for a great deal of excitement, as well as some fantastic bargains! Before bidding in an auction, however, remember to establish a limit as to what you are comfortable spending. On-line auctions are as intense and exciting as regular auctions, and it's easy to get caught up in the heat of the moment and overbid as a result! If you play it cool, you stand a good chance of nabbing your desired piece at a price lower than you thought possible.

Before buying anything over the Internet, always request to see a picture of what you are purchasing. Sight-unseen purchases can lead to heartbreak if the figurine you receive is not in the condition that you expected. Any flaws in a piece should be accurately described by the seller. While there is nothing wrong with buying a cherub that has been cracked, chipped or comes without its box, these imperfections should lower the secondary market value accordingly. Sellers can usually be contacted through E-mail and should always be willing to provide you with any information they can regarding the figurine's condition. If they do not, the buyer should beware.

Where Else Can I Look?

While new collectors may have a tough time remembering what collecting was like before the Internet, there are many rewards to be had for savvy collectors who utilize other secondary market sources such as local retailers. It is unlikely that these retailers are actively involved in the secondary market, but they often know of individuals who are and can put you in contact with them.

If you have exhausted the supply of Dreamsicles at your local gift shop, attending a collectibles show will put you in the same room as hundreds of dealers and thousands of Dreamsicles enthusiasts. You could never visit 100 stores in a single day, but a collectibles show brings these shops and dealers directly to you. In fact, some of the larger shows even attract dealers from all over the country!

Another source for finding Dreamsicles may arrive on your doorstep every morning. The classified section of your daily newspaper might have listings of collectibles that are for sale. This can be a hit-or-miss proposition, but it is worth exploring. There might be a Dreamsicles collector that you never knew about right in your own town! Secondary market exchanges are another tried-and-true source for buying and selling your cherubs. An exchange publishes a list of collectors with pieces for sale. The exchange acts as a middleman between the two interested parties and usually charges a fee of 10% to 20% for brokering the sale. While this method may seem less favorable now that the Internet has limited the need for a middleman, these exchanges reach a wide range of collectors (including those who may not have access to the Internet), so you may find a piece here that you cannot find elsewhere. In addition, the dealers who run these exchanges often possess excellent knowledge of the collectibles market.

Variations

Variations often end up for sale on the secondary market. These are differences that occur among otherwise identical pieces and most commonly include color changes, production changes and spelling errors. Variations are the result of either intentional changes by the Dreamsicles manufacturer, Cast Art, or unintentional errors that occur during the manufacturing process.

No two Dreamsicles are exactly alike as each piece is individually painted by hand. This can cause slight differences in color between two pieces of the mold. Sometimes, however, color changes are carefully planned. For example, in 1997, 40 figurines underwent a significant color change. These Dreamsicles, which included "Burning Love," "The Graduate" and "Joyful Noise," had their vibrant colors changed to muted, pastel tones.

Misspellings are another form of variation that have been known to appear on figurines. "Poetry In Motion" originally had the misspelled word "Potery" engraved on its nameplate rather than the correctly spelled "Poetry." Fewer than 100 pieces were released to the public before the error was caught and corrected. Also, nearly 5,000 "Rainbow's End" cherubs were released with the misspelling "Ranibow" on the bottom label of the figurine. So, you see, some variations are produced in sizable numbers,while others can be extremely rare.

Most importantly, remember to enjoy the time you spend searching the Dreamsicles secondary market, whether it be for a hard-to-find limited edition, a particular variation or, perhaps, even a new friend. You never know what you may find on the secondary market, which makes it a great place to shop!

Behind The Scenes At Cast Art

Production

Before each piece from the Dreamsicles collection is packaged and sent to stores, it undergoes a rigorous production process. In fact, from the initial prototype to the final product, your favorite cherubs will endure being poked and prodded, all to ensure that they are the best that they can be.

1. At her home studio in rural Washington, artist Kristin Haynes creates prototypes of the Dreamsicles sculptures which are then sent to Cast Art to be reproduced into molds. Skilled artisans at Cast Art's facilities in California and Mexico are responsible for the production of each of the Dreamsicles molds. After the molds have been cast, they are injected with a special formulation of natural gypsum material.

2. Once the material has completely dried, the figurine is removed from the mold and finished by hand to remove any imperfections caused by the molding process.

3. Next, the piece is painted and is given its signature stamp. The hand-painting process is used to achieve the delicate pastel shading and expressive eyes characteristic of the Dreamsicles figurines.

4. In the last step of the production process, a dried floral wreath is applied to the figurine's head. After a final inspection to ensure consistent high quality, the piece is packaged into a recycled foam liner and boxed.

Packaging

There are several varieties of Dreamsicles boxes that feature unique designs for holiday, limited edition, Northern Lights and Dreamsicles Club pieces. As collectibles generally command a higher price on the secondary market if they are accompanied by their original boxes, you should be sure to keep all original packaging in the event that you later decide to sell the piece. (Also, the packaging provides a great way to store your pieces when they are not on display.) Treat your boxes with as much care as you would your pieces. Be sure to keep them in a safe, dry place where they will not be ruined by moisture or other elements, as well as curious children or pets.

The stickers on the bottoms of the Dreamsicles pieces come in several styles. White labels identify the pieces in the general line; gold stickers indicate limited editions, early releases and exclusives; and blue/green metallic stickers can be found on pieces made exclusively for the Dreamsicles Club.

Pricing

The cost of Dreamsicles collectibles can vary depending on the size and availability of the piece. Dreamsicles pieces usually range in retail price from $7 to $30 for smaller pieces, from $30 to $100 for the larger figurines and from $100 to $150 for limited edition pieces. Prices for the other collectibles, such as ornaments, clocks, Angel Hugs plush pieces and candle holders vary, though they usually can be found for about $10 to $20.

Caring For Your Collection

For any Dreamsicles fan, one of the best parts of collecting is displaying your pieces for all to see. However, once you remove the pieces from their packaging, care must be taken to ensure that they remain in "mint" condition.

Dusting

Use a small, soft-bristled paintbrush to gently remove dust from the body of your figurine. Be sure to avoid contact with the delicate wreath.

Cleaning

To absorb oil and dust, apply a light coat of baking soda to the piece. Let it set for about five minutes before wiping off the residue with a dry, soft cloth.

Refreshing Or Replacing A Damaged Wreath

If you find that the dried-flower wreaths on your Dreamsicles' pieces are starting to show their age, you have the option of either "refreshing" or replacing the headpiece. The "Dreamsicles T.L.C. Kit," which is available through the Dreamsicles Club, contains all the materials necessary to refresh about 20 floral wreaths. You may find that adding just a few new flowers in areas that have become damaged is enough to do the trick, or, if the entire wreath is damaged, you can gently remove the old wreath and construct a new one by following the instructions in the kit.

Protecting Your Investment

In addition to the proper cleaning and maintenance of your Dreamsicles collection, you should also make sure that your collection is adequately insured in the event of theft, flood, fire or other unforeseen circumstances. Insuring your collection is a wise move, and it doesn't have to be costly or difficult.

1. Assess the value of your collection. If your collection is extensive, you may want to have it professionally appraised. However, you can determine the value of your collection yourself by consulting a reputable price guide such as the Collector's Value Guide.

2. Determine the amount of coverage you need. Collectibles are often covered under a homeowner's or renter's insurance, but ask your agent if your policy covers all possibilities, including damage due to routine handling. Also, find out if your policy covers claims at "current replacement value" – the amount it would cost to replace items if they were damaged, lost or stolen. You may want to consider adding a Personal Articles Floater or a Fine Arts Floater ("rider") to your policy if your insurance does not cover your collection.

3. Keep documentation of your collectibles and their values. Save all your receipts and photograph each item, taking special care to show variations, artist signatures and other special features. Keep your documentation in a safe place, such as a safe deposit box, or make two copies and give one to a friend or relative.

A Look At "Love, Kristin™" The Heartland Collection

In April of 1999, Cast Art introduced a new collection designed by Kristin Haynes called "Love, Kristin™" The Heartland Collection. These new figurines feature chubby-cheeked children and their animal friends and share many of the common themes from the beloved Dreamsicles collection.

This collection, however, utilizes the style of Americana folk art. Pieces are detailed to simulate a wood carving and whimsical touches like ribbons in yarn hair, strings on balloons and feathers on hats add individuality to each piece. The colors that are chosen for these figurines are hearty, vibrant "country" colors – including shades of russet red, gingham blue and eggshell white. Polka dots, stripes, checks and hand painted flowers add to the homespun, warmhearted look of this collection of loveable country characters.

The first 20 figurines that were released by Cast Art in 1999 included 10 young ladies, all accompanied by a tiny animal friend. "Allison" carries a pot of flowers as a yellow bunny takes a ride in her pocket. With her eyes checking the skies, "Katie" is watching for the sun to reappear as she clutches her kitty. "Madeline" is the studious one, as she reads to her bear buddies and "Hannah" seems to be taking a long time to make her wish – so long in fact, that her cat has fallen asleep at her side!

"Diana" is standing on her tiptoes as she offers seeds to her feathered friends at the local birdhouse. Counting chickens is a chore for "Emily" – there are little ones coming to join the fun! It's nap time for "Rachel" and her floppy friend and "Ashley" seems to have the "dropsies" – but someone is there to help her out! "Madison" holds her bag and doll tightly as she waits for her ride to town, while "Sarah Jessica" is ready to hang a garland of stars for the holidays.

Also included in the line are figurines of four young men who are engaged in a variety of outdoor activities. "Zachary" drags a bat along the ground as he heads for the dugout after the game has been rained out. "Jordan" is keeping a close eye on his balloon and "William" is headed for the pond to launch his sailboat. He might catch a glimpse of "Nicholas and Tyler," two fishing buddies hanging out along the shore.

The remainder of the collection consists of furry and feathered friends such as "Betsy & Ross," a cow (who carries a chick on its back), "Brianna" the bunny and a large grizzly bear with some pals named "Theodore & Friends." Completing the collection are a trio of Christmas pieces: "Papa Claus," "Snowflake & Friends" and "Lewis & Clark."

New for 2000 were eight more adorable figurines including four animal figurines alive with ducks, pigs and bunnies. The additional four new pieces depict girls spreading hugs and lots of love and are sure to be a hit with collectors. As the "Love, Kristin" collection continues to grow, so do the number of fans who appreciate Kristin Haynes' artistic touch in every character she designs.

For a closer look at this collection, visit our web site at ***CollectorsQuest.com***.

More Dreamsicles® Products

Through the years, Cast Art has licensed a number of additional companies to manufacture products featuring the images of the beloved Dreamsicles cherubs. Currently, there are 15 licensees which provide Dreamsicles collectors with everything from wedding cake toppers to musical water fountains. Here is a brief overview of what is available for Dreamsicles fans.

Crafting With Dreamsicles

Are you in the mood to start a new project? Or are you looking to create the perfect gift for another Dreamsicles enthusiast? If so, then stop by your local craft, hobby or fabric store where you will find a wide variety of Dreamsicles cross-stitch design books from Leisure Arts, perfect for baby and sweetheart. And that's not all! Leisure Arts also produces design books containing a collection of designs for each month of the year!

Also from Leisure Arts are plastic canvas and ribbon embroidery kits, scrapbooking supplies and line art transfer books for the Dreamsicles collector who is handy with a needle and thread. Embroidery memory cards are also available from Great Notions.

Does your own little angel have blonde hair and love sunflowers and ballet? If so, you can create a personalized Angel Hugs stuffed doll for her by using the Dreamsicles craft pattern made by The McCall Pattern Company. Choose yellow tulle for the doll's skirt and cheerful yellow flowers to decorate her yellow yarn hair. Your little one will love it, and the different design possibilities are endless!

Decorating With Dreamsicles

If your display of Dreamsicles cherubs isn't enough to let everyone know of your love for the precious angels, then consider some of these home decor ideas. Come home from work and relax to the soothing sounds of trickling water and melodious tunes with a tabletop water fountain from Berkeley Designs. Dreamsicles cherubs are featured on these fountains which play assorted love songs, while on others, Northern Lights Snow Angels and their frosty friends frolic in the snow to the accompaniment of assorted Christmas tunes. Non-musical water fountains are also available in wishing well and water wheel designs, for those who feel that just the gentle sound of trickling water is relaxation enough.

It's easy to start a holiday tradition and showcase your love of Dreamsicles at the same time by displaying The Dreamsicles Christmas Tree from The Danbury Mint. This eye-catching piece shines with over 60 sparkling lights, including a shining star atop the tree and features our favorite little cherubs and their animal friends joyfully decorating each bough of the tree. As they carefully string the garland and hang the ornaments, these Dreamsicles cherubs are preparing the tree for the big day – and for the appreciative Dreamsicles collector.

There's plenty of other delightful and decorative Dreamsicles products available in all kinds of specialty shops, including an anniversary clock, suncatchers and collectible plates from The Hamilton Collection, which is famous for its high-quality plates and other fine collectibles.

Dreamsicles, Take Me Away

Make your bath a fragrant respite from the rigors of the outside world with the help of Dreamsicles products such as scented lotions, candles, relaxing bath salts and shower gels from Mostly Memories. These aromatherapy products come in three different scents and are perfect both for yourself or as a gift for a well-deserving friend or loved one.

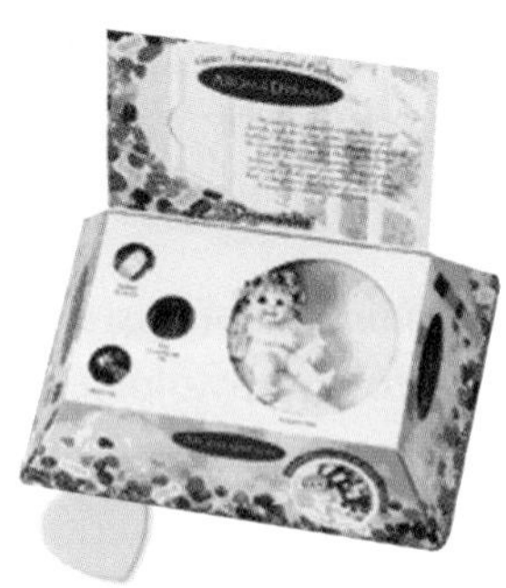

And if you're a fan of aromatherapy, you surely won't want to miss Retail Products Corporation's offering of fragrant oils that are specially created for their AromaDreams bowls (which come complete with a beautiful Dreamsicles cherub tucked inside). Additionally, Dreamsicles incense burners and scented incense are available and are sure to inspire heavenly musings.

Giftware

Looking for the perfect "little something" for a Dreamsicles collector on your gift list? Desired Confections offers chocolate-filled tins sure to satisfy any sweet tooth, in addition to mug gift sets.

Giftco, Inc. provides a selection of Dreamsicles gift items perfect for school fundraising efforts. So the next time a child appears at your doorstep with a catalog in hand, don't be surprised to find your favorite cherubs featured on the products! Attach one of Betallic's mylar Dreamsicles balloons to your purchase and you have the ideal gift for any celebration. Betallic's balloons are also the perfect way to celebrate Valentine's Day (along with a dozen roses and several Dreamsicles cherubs, of course).

Stationery/Party Supplies

Make that chore of paying bills a bit more cheerful by using Dreamsicles checks from The Check Gallery, which sells personalized checks, checkbook covers and address labels printed with pictures of the delightful Dreamsicles.

More Dreamsicles labels are available through the Colorful Images catalog from Concepts Direct. Colorful Images also sells other Dreamsicles products including a cameo T-shirt and personalized calling cards featuring an assortment of Dreamsicles designs. The company also makes other wonderful items such as the Dreamsicles Crescent Moon lamp, which features a sleeping cherub snuggled in a crescent moon.

If you are planning your wedding and are looking to add a special touch, consider the Dreamsicles wedding accessories available from Jamie Lynn, who is the first licensee of Dreamsicles wedding supplies. You can even have a Dreamsicles-themed wedding and celebrate your big day with an assortment of cherubs, perfect for watching over you and your new mate as your start your new life together.

Aside from the specific wedding-themed designs, Jamie Lynn also offers Dreamsicles-designed glassware and decorations, memory and guest books, plumed pens, cake knives, cake servers and cake toppers; all of which will add a wonderful element to your next party. In fact, all of the Dreamsicles products are so cute, you just may find any excuse to celebrate!

Fun With Dreamsicles®

In this hectic world of juggling car pools, PTA meetings, school concerts and soccer games with busy work schedules, not much time is left for enjoying hobbies. Since the adorable cherubs in the Dreamsicles collection have a special way of warming hearts and bringing smiles to faces, they are a perfect form of "stress relief." So why not incorporate your favorite cherubs into your favorite leisure activities for some extra added fun? Here are some rather "unconventional" ways to enjoy your Dreamsicles collection.

Getting Together With Friends

Whether you prefer quilting, cross-stitching or knitting, there is a Dreamsicles project out there that is perfect for you! With a needle and some pink, blue and white thread, some creativity and a few embroidery kits or cross-stitch design books, you can settle in for hours of crafting entertainment and create a wall display or heirloom that you can enjoy for years to come.

For those who would rather make something cuddly to hug rather than a quilted or embroidered wall hanging, why not create your own Dreamsicles doll for yourself or a loved one? The McCall Pattern Company has created a specific Angel Hugs pattern, but you can also use any angel pattern found in stores. Use your imagination to personalize the cherub and don't forget to add the trademark Dreamsicles blue eyes and halo!

For those who would rather work without needle and thread, scrapbooking kits are the perfect solution. Why not create a memory book for a special person or "guardian angel" who has touched your life? Dreamsicles stickers and stamps are available to help decorate the album. You may even want to draw halos around some of the close-up pictures of your special "angel!"

A crafting get-together is the perfect excuse to decorate with Dreamsicles-designed mylar balloons. Give favors (Dreamsicles Angel Hugs key rings or clip-ons are the perfect present) and offer prizes of Dreamsicles pieces that coordinate with your theme of the day. For example, the Dreamsicles Day event piece from 2000, "With All My Heart," would be a perfect raffle or door prize since the cherub is assembling a quilt. The "Christmas Quilt Box" is perfect for storing pins, thread or whatever else you might need to complete your sewing adventures. And the "You're 'Sew' Dear Frame" is also an appropriate reminder of a fun day with friends – and it's perfect for keeping a picture taken at the get-together!

Sweet Treats

Baking cookies is enjoyable, relaxing and the result usually tastes good, too! Since the cherubs in the Dreamsicles collection are as "sweet as sugar," here's a recipe for Dreamsicles-designed sugar cookies:

Ingredients

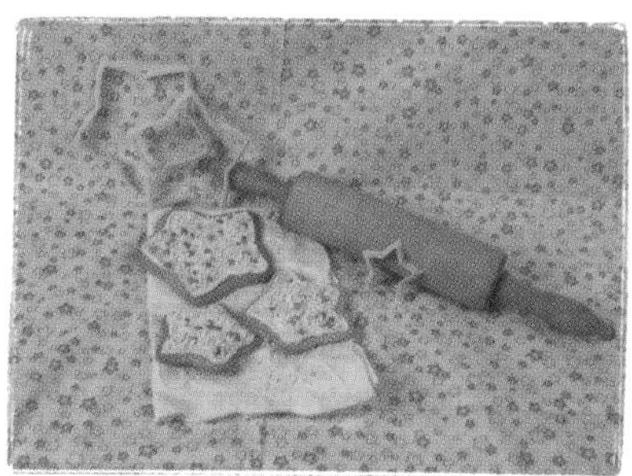

- 2/3 cup shortening
- 2/3 cup margarine
- 2 1/2 cup all-purpose flour

- 1 1/2 cup sugar
- 2 eggs
- 1 teaspoon baking powder
- 1 teaspoon vanilla extract

Directions

Preheat oven to 375°F.

Use an electric mixer to beat the shortening and margarine together for about 30 seconds or until softened. Gradually add the sugar, followed by the egg and vanilla. Beat well.

Combine flour and baking powder in a separate bowl, then add to the shortening and butter mixture. Continue to beat until the dough is soft.

On lightly floured surface, roll dough out and then cut with an angel-shaped cookie cutter. Place cookies on a well-greased cookie sheet and bake for approximately 10 minutes, until the edges are golden.

When the cookies are cool, the fun begins! Decorate your angels with white and pastel colored frosting. Use silver balls and candy flowers to create a halo for each cookie. Experiment with different frosting colors and candies to give each cherub cookie its own unique look. You're sure to have as much fun making the cookies as eating them! Enjoy!

Party Planning And Gift Giving

Hosting an upcoming party? Why not invite your favorite Dreamsicles cherubs to join in on the fun? Choose invitations in soft pastel colors and, after addressing the envelopes, attach your Dreamsicles-designed address labels in the upper left-hand corner. A visit to your favorite Dreamsicles retailer can fire your imagination and provide ideas to use at your celebration. Here are just a few to get you started.

Arrange bunches of Dreamsicles balloons festooned with the angelic designs at every table – or tied to each chair! The colors and shapes found in Dreamsicles figurines – soft pastel hues of blues, greens, pink hearts and yellow stars – can be repeated in table floral arrangements, napkins and other decorations. Using different sized heart and star-shaped cookie cutters, several tasty treats can be made to complement your Dreamsicles-themed party. Also, you can plan a variety of fun party games – from a scavenger hunt to bingo – and be sure to present special Dreamsicles pieces as prizes.

And don't forget that Dreamsicles make perfect gifts as well! With over 1,000 pieces in the line, there is a perfect piece for everyone and every occasion. In addition to the traditional reasons to give gifts such as birthdays, holidays and graduations, why not surprise a loved one with a special Dreamsicles angel "just because?"

Gift baskets are a great idea for those away from home for the holidays. Have a friend or relative in the Armed Forces? Why not sneak "A Few Good Men" in with a handwritten letter, some homemade baked goods (maybe the Dreamsicles cookies discussed earlier), some photographs and a few nostalgic reminders of home to really brighten up his or her day?

Seasonal Celebrations

On nearly every holiday celebration you can find easy ways to incorporate the festive cherubs from the Dreamsicles collection. One easy way to include the angels is to add them to table centerpieces (such as the Thanksgiving display we picture here).

Angels play a particularly special role in the Christmas holiday, so why not include your Dreamsicles angels in the decorating festivities? Start off by spreading a few well-placed holiday-themed cherubs around the house to get you in the holiday spirit. These cherubs wear wreaths made from seasonal berries and flowers and will add life to your Christmas displays. And when you put up your tree, don't forget to add some Dreamsicles ornaments. You can even make your own Dreamsicles ornaments to give your tree a personal touch. Here's how:

Go to any craft or hobby shop and purchase a few clear ball ornaments and Leisure Arts' Dreamsicles Line Art Transfer Book. Gently use a pencil to trace one of the cherubs from the line art book onto the ornament. Then, carefully use a thin paintbrush to trace the pencil marks with colored paint. Finally, fill in the design with the colors of your choice. Another option is to use glue to trace the pattern rather than paint. Coat the glued areas with colored glitter for an eye-catching design. This activity is great fun, not only for the Dreamsicles fan, but for the whole family!

Once your tree is decorated, it's time to think about giving gifts. Have some friends who enjoy Dreamsicles just as much as you do?

Why not wrap their gifts in your own homemade Dreamsicles wrapping paper? Buy some plain colored wrapping paper (we recommend white or gold for Christmas, but pastels work well too) and stamp the paper repeatedly with a Dreamsicles rubber stamp design. Or, for more Dreamsicles fun, you can adhere Dreamsicles stickers to your unadorned gift wrap. Either way, it's sure to be as treasured as the gift you give!

Chilly Cherubs

To chase away the winter blues, why not put on your winter woolies and head out into the yard to build your very own "snow cherub?" Use the designs found in the Dreamsicles and Northern Lights collections for inspiration. Form sticks and dried grass in the shape of a halo and place on the head of your Dreamsicles cherub, or put a fluffy winter hat and coat to make your own Northern Lights character. Make sure to use extra snow to form the fluffy trim around the clothing on these pieces! Berries, pinecones, fruits and vegetables make great eyes and accessories and are also a great way to add color to your snow creatures. Use your imagination! You would be surprised what else you can find around the house or the yard to help give your "snow angel" personality! Whether trying to replicate a design that already exists, or designing your own brand-new Dreamsicles cherub, you're sure to have a ball!

We hope that you have found these ideas exciting and easy to use! And to share your ideas on how you enjoy displaying and gift-giving with other collectors, make sure to add a posting to the bulletin board at ***www.CollectorsQuest.com.***

Glossary

bas-relief – the sculptural process that leaves a raised design on the product, causing it to appear as if it were three-dimensional.

collectible – anything that is "able to be collected." Generally, it is thought that a true collectible should be something that will increase in value over a period of time.

current – a piece that is in production and, subsequently, available in retail stores.

Dreamsicles Day – an "in-store" event that allows collectors to participate in Dreamsicles-related activities and to purchase special event figurines.

early release – a piece released as a "special preview" to selected stores before its introduction into the general Dreamsicles collection.

exchange – a secondary market service that lists pieces collectors wish to buy or are looking to sell. The exchange works as a middleman and usually requires a commission for a transaction.

exclusive – a figurine made especially for, and available through, a specific store, catalog or buying group.

Gift Creations Concepts (GCC) – a syndicated catalog group for stores nationwide. Exclusive pieces and early releases are commonly available through these retailers.

Hydrastone – a specially formulated gypsum material from which most Dreamsicles pieces are made.

International Collectible Exposition (I.C.E.) – a national collectibles show which is held twice a year. For 2001, the show will be in Anaheim, California, in April and Rosemont, Illinois, in June.

issue year – for Dreamsicles, the year that a piece becomes available in stores as a part of the general collection.

limited edition (LE) – a piece whose production will cease after a certain period of time or after a specific quantity of pieces has been produced.

Members-Only piece – a special Dreamsicles item which is only available for purchase by people who belong to the Dreamsicles Club.

mid-year introductions – Dreamsicles pieces that are released to the line in June as follow-ups to the major introductions which take place each January.

mint condition – a term used for a piece offered on the secondary market that is in very good or "like-new" condition.

Miralite™ – the high-gloss metallic finish that is used on certain Dreamsicles holiday ornaments and figurines.

new introductions – new pieces that are announced to the public each January.

open edition – a Dreamsicles piece that has no predetermined limit on the time it will be produced or the size of its production run.

Parade Of Gifts – a syndicated catalog group for retail stores nationwide. Exclusive pieces and early releases are commonly available through these retailers.

primary market – the conventional collectibles purchasing process in which collectors buy pieces directly from retailers at issue price.

resin – the thick liquid that is used to bind together different materials for the production of a Dreamsicles collectible.

retired – a piece taken out of production, never to be made again.

secondary market – the source for buying and selling retired and hard-to-find collectibles. It can include exchanges, auctions and "swap & sells."

suspended – a piece that has been removed from production but has the potential to return to the line in the future.

Symbol Of Membership piece – a special gift given to collectors who join or renew their memberships to the Dreamsicles Club.

variations – items with color, design or text changes from the "original" piece.

Numerical Index

All Dreamsicles pieces are listed here in numerical order by stock number, followed by the page and picture box in which the piece is located.

Numerical Index

Alphabetical Index

All Dreamsicles pieces are listed here in alphabetical order, followed by the page and picture box in which the piece is located.